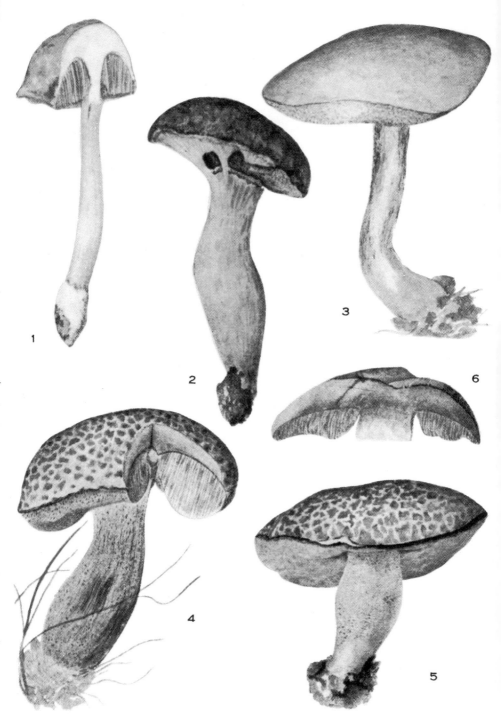

FIG. 1. BOLETUS CURTISII. No. 10023.
FIG. 2. B. RAVENELII. No. 4521.
FIG. 3. B. CHROMAPES. No. 3334.
FIGS. 4-6. B. RIMOSELLUS. Nos. 10666 and 4615. The stem is usually nearly
equal and often relatively longer.

This illustration is also reproduced in full color following page 22.

THE
BOLETI
OF
NORTH
CAROLINA

BY

WILLIAM CHAMBERS COKER, Ph.D., LL.D.

Kenan Professor of Botany and Director of the Arboretum
in the University of North Carolina

AND

ALMA HOLLAND BEERS, A.B.

Research Assistant in Botany
in the University of North Carolina

DOVER PUBLICATIONS, INC.
NEW YORK

International Standard Book Number: 0-486-20377-8
Library of Congress Catalog Card Number: 73-90299

Manufactured in the United States of America
Dover Publications, Inc.
180 Varick Street
New York, N.Y. 10014

TABLE OF CONTENTS

PLATES

The Frontispiece and Plates 1 through 5, which are in full color, follow page 22. Plates 6 through 65 are at the end of this volume.

PREFACE

While there has been some excellent mycological work on the fungi of eastern America, there have been too few mycologists to cover the vast field with any degree of thoroughness. With a view to making some contribution to an understanding of the difficult group Boletaceae, the senior author began about forty years ago to take notes and photographs of the species found by him. For a good many years both authors have worked on the group and have made many collections. We have tried to describe the plants exactly as they are found by us, and it will be seen that the species, as we are interpreting them, often vary in some details from the usual published descriptions. We have been conservative in our treatment, not giving new names because of small variations, as will be seen from the very limited number of new species or varieties described herein.

Most of our work has been done in Orange County, North Carolina, and in the Blue Ridge and Alleghany Mountains of this state. We are also including such South Carolina and northern Georgia species as we have met with, but since the number is small we are not including these regions in our title. All the species collected by us in those states have also been found in North Carolina. Unless otherwise stated, all numbered collections entered are now in the herbarium of the University of North Carolina. We have also numerous collections not listed in the text.

Our grateful acknowledgements for many favors are due to: Dr. William A. Murrill, former assistant director of the New York Botanical Garden; Dr. Homer D. House, state botanist of New York and curator of the Peck Herbarium; Dr. Walter H. Snell of Brown University.

We are greatly indebted to the artists who have furnished the colored illustrations for this book. They are Mrs. Lucia P. Johnson, Mrs. Maude Wilson, Mrs. Dorothy Coker Rowland, Miss Nell Henry, Miss Cornelia Love, and Mrs. Mary Motz Wills. A number of our students have assisted in the photographic work. Our thanks are also due to Dr. F. A. Wolf of Duke University for his careful reading of our manuscript.

INTRODUCTION

The first comprehensive systematic work on the Boletaceae was done by C. H. Persoon, a Dutch mycologist, who in his *Synopsis Methodica Fungorum* (1801) treated under the genus name *Boletus* ninety-three species, over half of which were disposed in other genera by Persoon himself in his *Mycologia Europaea* (1825). The next important European treatment was by Elias Fries of Sweden, who laid the foundations for the modern understanding of this group. In his *Systema Mycologicum* (1821) he treated twenty species; in *Epicrisis* (1836–38), sixty species; and in *Hymenomycetes Europaei* (1874), one hundred in all, including five under the subgenus *Gyrodon*, one under *Boletinus*, and ten doubtful species.

The first species of *Boletus* described from the United States were by L. D. von Schweinitz. In his *Synopsis Fungorum Carolinae Superioris* (1822) he listed seventeen species that we now include in this family and described three of them, *B. Betula*, *B. floccosus* (= *Strobilomyces strobilaceus*), and *B. alboater*, as new. Later (1832) in his *Synopsis Fungorum in America Boreali* he also listed, with some duplication, seventeen species and described *B. Pocono* from Pennsylvania as new.

Miles J. Berkeley of England and M. A. Curtis of the Carolinas described a number of species from the eastern United States, most of them from our territory.

Henry W. Ravenel, the well known South Carolina mycologist, collected many Boleti, among them *B. Ravenelii*, which was named for him by Berkeley and Curtis. Ravenel himself described *B. conicus* (Ann. Mag. Nat. Hist., 1853, p. 14) from damp pine woods in South Carolina, but it has not been found in our state.

The first important step in an understanding of the Boletaceae of the United States was taken by Charles H. Peck, state botanist of New York. Peck was an excellent mycologist and his work has been of fundamental importance in any further study of these fungi. He used Fries's works assiduously, and also described many new species of his own, most of which have been permanently established as valid. His herbarium, now in the Education Building in Albany, is frequently consulted by all serious students of the family.

Charles C. Frost of Vermont, a correspondent of Peck, collected extensively in the New England States and published a number of new species in the Bulletin of the Buffalo Society of Natural Sciences in 1874.

George F. Atkinson and Herman Schrenk (1892) listed nineteen members of the Boletaceae from Blowing Rock, North Carolina.

Charles McIlvaine of Pennsylvania, in his large general work, *American Fungi* (1900, 1902) reported many species and, consulting Peck for his identifications, tested most of them for edibility.

William A. Murrill, formerly of the New York Botanical Garden, reviewed the Boletaceae of North America first in Mycologia (**1**: 4, 140, 1909), then in *North*

American Flora, vol. **9** (1910). He published in these works many new species and in later publications has described numerous others, mostly from Florida.

Henry C. Beardslee, long a resident of Asheville, N. C., was much interested in this group and described as new one species, *B. carolinensis*, from western North Carolina.

Some of the most accurate and beautiful illustrations of our Boleti are to be found in *Icones Farlowianae*, published in 1929, where twenty-three species, including three in the genus *Boletinus*, are shown in full color.

Walter H. Snell of Brown University, Providence, Rhode Island, has for a number of years been working on the Boletaceae and has published a good many new species.

The plants here treated under *Boletus* have been subdivided into several genera by some authors. In Murrill's treatment in *North American Flora*, nine genera are recognized besides *Strobilomyces* and *Boletinus*, which we are also recognizing.

Throughout this work we have tried to use the simplest language that would clearly express our meaning and have used as few technical terms as possible. Some of our friends have suggested that we use "sporophore," "fructification," or "fruiting body" in most places where we have used the word "plant," but while we recognize the strict technical accuracy of the above terms we do not feel that anyone will be misled by our use of the word "plant" for the above-ground part of the fungus, commonly known as a mushroom or toadstool. We feel that it would be an affectation to use over and over again a long Latin word or cumbersome phrase where a simple English word will not be misunderstood. Moreover, in such usage we are joined by such students as Peck, Atkinson, Murrill, Snell, and others.

THE GENUS BOLETUS

Fleshy fungi with a cap and central (rarely excentric) stem. Hymenium inferior, made up of a distinct layer of narrow tubes that are separable from each other and from the flesh of the cap (not easily so in the *granulatus* group). Spore color very variable (pale yellow, rosy, olivaceous, brown, etc.), spore surface smooth in most species, but in a few it is warted, lined or ridged.

The species of *Boletus* grow in various habitats, usually on the ground, rarely on rotten wood; one species (*B. parasiticus*) is a parasite on *Scleroderma*, and another, *B. Ananas*, may be a parasite on pine.

This is a large genus with many conspicuous species, often highly colored. The flesh of many plants changes to blue or greenish when cut or wounded, and in not a few to other colors, such as pinkish, brick red, or brown. This color change is variable in its intensity and even in its presence in plants of the same species at times and should not be made a major basis for specific distinction.

Furthermore, we do not feel that the so-called "stuffing" of the tube mouths in youth can be used accurately or to much advantage in defining groups or species of *Boletus* except in a few cases. The term "stuffing" is relative, and may mean anything from a delicate fringe of threads growing inwardly from the mouth edges, but by no means closing the mouth, to the condition seen in the *edulis* group where the overgrowth of threads is so complete as to appear like a white membrane covering the tubes. Moreover, individuals of the same species vary to some extent in the degree of stuffing, as, for example, *B. bicolor*. This appearance of being stuffed is further complicated by the fact that often in youth the mouths are so tightly folded together as to obscure the openings and appear stuffed. In other cases of optical illusion, the hymenial layer lying just inside the minute tube opening is nearly white, while the tube flesh is of a darker color, so that the naked eye does not notice the small opening in the center of the white hymenial disk surrounding it. A section under the microscope shows that the opening is as large at the surface as it is farther down. For illustrations of several of the above conditions, see text figures 1–7.

So far as is known at present, this is one of the safest groups of all the cap fungi for the beginner to experiment with for food, as only a few species are now thought to be poisonous. One of these, *miniato-olivaceus*, belongs to a small group of very closely related species which are not easily distinguished from each other, so that all this complex of species should be avoided by the beginner. While *miniato-olivaceus* does not seem to have killed anyone, it is really dangerous (see Rhodora **1:** 21. 1899). Another species said to be poisonous is *B. Satanas*, which belongs to the *luridus* group, all the members of which are under suspicion and should be avoided.

The genus *Boletus* is of considerable importance in its symbiotic relation with the roots of higher plants with which it forms mycorrhizae. Not enough is known about mycorrhizae at present, but it is certain that the mycelium of a number of species of *Boletus* is regularly associated with the rootlets of certain

1

trees.   The mycelial filaments encircle the rootlets with a coat of closely woven
tissue and send filaments more or less deeply into the cortical cells of the rootlets, extending from the rootlets into the soil at some seasons and producing

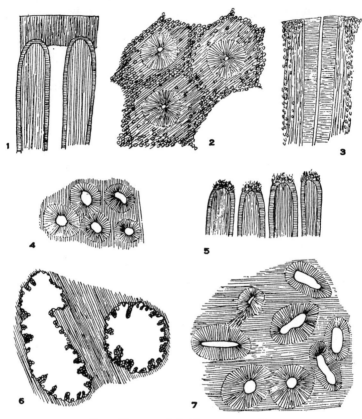

TEXT FIGURES 1–7. DIAGRAMS × 100

Fig. 1. *Boletus separans.*   Longitudinal section view of two young tubes showing blanket
of hyphae (about 125–150µ thick) covering the opening.

Figs. 2 and 3. *B. eximius.*   Surface and section views of tubes of young plant (only 3.5 cm.
wide) showing minute openings surrounded by disk of hymenial tissue; many
granules in tube context, more densely grouped in the boundary regions of the
individual tubes.   Mouths apparently completely closed to naked eye.

Fig. 4. *B. luridus.*   Surface view of tubes which were apparently closed.

Fig. 5. *B. granulatus.*   Longitudinal section view of tubes of very young plant (3.2 cm.
wide) showing fimbriate dissepiments with secretions of gluten.   The openings were
invisible to the eye.

Fig. 6. *B. subaureus* var. *siccipes.*   Surface view of two tubes showing granular tissue
around the mouths.

Fig. 7. *B. bicolor.*   Surface view of tubes of very young plant.

above ground the fruit-bodies that we know as the sporophores or mushrooms.
For good papers on the mycorrhizal relationship between fungi and higher plants,
see Rayner and Melin, as cited in the literature list.   The latter author has

shown, for example, that the following species of *Boletus* are definitely connected as mycorrhizae with the European *Pinus sylvestris* and *P. montana: B. badius, B. granulatus, B. luteus,* and *B. variegatus;* with European larch: *B. elegans, B. luteus,* and *B. variegatus;* with *Populus tremula: B. rufus* and *B. scaber;* with *Betula verrucosa: B. edulis, B. rufus,* and *B. scaber.**

As seen from this list, a fungus forming mycorrhizae need not be confined to any one species of flowering plant, but it will be noted that none of the Boleti mentioned above were found on both coniferous and deciduous trees. In one of the earlier papers on mycorrhiza which prove the actual connection between a basidiomycete fruit-body and a higher plant, Kauffman (1906) has shown that *Cortinarius rubipes* has mycorrhizal association with three species, "red oak," sugar maple, and *Celastrus scandens.* Previously Noack (1889) had shown that *Geaster fimbriatus* and *fornicatus* were associated with roots of spruce and pine. Even earlier Reess (1880) had proved conclusively that *Elaphomyces,* a truffle, grew in connection with pine roots. In addition to the fungi mentioned above as shown to be associated with higher plants as mycorrhizae, a considerable number of others of the higher basidiomycetes, among them some of the common gill mushrooms, have been shown to be likewise associated. See also the list given by Peyronel, as cited in the literature list.

This association with certain trees is reflected in the occurrence of the fruiting bodies of some species only under or near these trees. In our entries of numbers under the various species, it will be seen, for instance, that some occur only under pines or other conifers, while others are found only in deciduous woods. Still other species are found in both coniferous and deciduous woods.

* For our own observations showing probable mycorrhizal connection of *B. subtomentosus* with sassafras, see notes under that species.

KEY TO THE SPECIES OF BOLETUS*

A. Parasitic on *Scleroderma*; plant yellowish..............................*B. parasiticus*
A. Not parasitic on *Scleroderma*
  B. Cap and stem covered with a yellow powder
    C. Veil present; flesh turning bluish when cut..........................*B. Ravenelii*
    C. Veil lacking
      D. Growing on roots and stumps of pine; stem smooth..............*B. hemichrysus*
      D. Growing on the ground; stem reticulated
        E. Tube mouths becoming scarlet at least in patches by maturity; plants yellow
                    B. auriflammeus
        E. Tube mouths not becoming scarlet; cap yellow to brown or gray-drab..*B. retipes*
  B. Cap and stem not covered with yellow powder
    C. Cap with conspicuous scales
      D. Plants small; scales purple..............................*B. Vanderbiltianus*
      D. Plants larger; scales fleshy buff to paler
        E. Spore striate..*B. Ananas*
        E. Spores smooth..*B. cyanescens*
    C. Cap without conspicuous scales
      D. Stem with conspicuous viscid annulus, dotted........................ *B. luteus*
      D. Stem without an annulus (slight veil in *B. americanus* but no annulus)
        E. Stem shaggy and lacerated with reticulating plates
          F. Tube mouths red; cap smooth and viscid........................*B. Frostii*
          F. Tube mouths not red
            G. Spores smooth; cap dry.......................................*B. retipes*
            G. Spores strongly warted; cap viscid............................*B. Betula*
            G. Spores longitudinally ridged................................*B. Russellii*
        E. Stem not lacerated but often strongly reticulated
          F. Stem and tubes with glandular viscid dots that turn reddish brown to black-
            ish; cap glutinous (see also *rubropunctus*)
            G. Cap pure white or nearly so................................*B. placidus*
            G. Cap not pure white
              H. Hymenium *brownish* from the first; stem nearly rhubarb color from dense
                droplets..*B. punctipes*
              H. Hymenium creamy white to yellowish when young
                I. Cap bay red to dull tan, becoming more yellow, especially on the margin
                  J. Stem stout, white or whitish........................*B. granulatus*
                  J. Stem slender, pallid, with a veil in youth.................*B. luteus*
                I. Cap reddish chestnut to purplish with blackish or olive stains; stem
                  very short; plant occurring late in fall.................*B. brevipes*
                I. Cap yellow
                  J. Tube mouths large; stem slender...................*B. americanus*
                  J. Tube mouths small to medium
                    K. Cap dotted with tufts of brownish fibrils; spores olive brown
                        B. hirtellus
                  K. Cap when mature nearly glabrous; stem somewhat larger than
                    above; spores rusty ochraceous....................*B. subaureus*
           F. Stem with dots as in *subaureus* but these not viscid; otherwise as in that
            species..*B. subaureus* var. *siccipes*

---

*It will be noted that in this key there are often *several coordinate headings*. Since in some cases these are on different pages, the reader is urged to be sure he has considered *all* the choices.

4

F. Stem and tubes dotted in youth with viscid dots that, on the stem, do not darken but run together to form a continuous layer resembling lacquer; stem base with a white, volva-like boot......................*B. Curtisii*

F. Stem without glandular dots (noticeable dots may be present but these not viscid)

  G. Stem distinctly hollow (or with very soft stuffing)

    H. Flesh and tubes turning intensely indigo blue when cut.....*B. cyanescens*

    H. Flesh not becoming blue when cut

      I. Cap yellow, viscid..*B. Curtisii*

      I. Cap buffy to chestnut or vinaceous, dry.................*B. castaneus*

  G. Stem not distinctly hollow

    H. Tube mouths (mature) and spores flesh colored to dull salmon (very pale in *indecisus* and *felleus* var. *minor*; see also a form of *scaber*)

      I. Cap smooth, buffy brown to leather color (often with a purplish tint in *felleus*)

        J. Taste bitter

          K. Cap medium to large; tubes strongly rosy.............*B. felleus*

          K. Cap small; tubes paler....................*B. felleus* var. *minor*

        J. Taste mild...*B. indecisus*

      I. Cap more or less tomentose or with a bloom

        J. Cap smoky or vinaceous brown, gray, or blackish, over 7 cm. broad
            B. alboater

        J. Cap tan to red-brown, usually less than 7 cm............*B. gracilis*

        J. Cap rosy; base of stem bright yellow.................*B. chromapes*

    H. Tube mouths dark brown or purple-brown to nearly black even in youth

      I. Tube flesh same color as mouths; stem grayish or lilac flecked with small purplish scales..*B. eximius*

      I. Tube flesh not same color as mouths; stem bright or dull yellow, often with darker lines..................................*B. vermiculosus*

    H. Tube mouths fawn color in youth to near maturity, later dull pink
           B. felleus, a form

    H. Tube mouths distinctly red in youth or maturity or both

      I. Tube flesh yellowish or dull whitish

        J. Plants small, cap 4–6 cm...............................*B. parvus*

        J. Plants medium to large

          K. Cap very pale, whitish.............*B. Satanas* var. *americanus*

          K. Cap darker, reddish or brownish

            L. Stem strongly reticulated above, red except at base; cap blood red..*B. Frostii*

            L. Stem not strongly reticulated, usually yellow above and darkening to cap color below, rarely red or yellow all over; cap red or brownish, variable.....................*B. luridus*

      I. Tube *flesh red throughout*, at least at maturity

        J. Tube flesh and mouths red in youth and maturity

          K. Taste peppery; tubes adnate to decurrent; stem yellow below or all over......................................*B. piperatus*

          K. Taste mild; tubes adnate to depressed; stem reddish all over
            B. rubinellus

        J. Tube flesh and mouths yellow in youth, red at maturity
            B. subfraternus

    H. Tubes mouths becoming scarlet at least in patches before maturity; cap and stem chrome yellow or cap duller orange in youth; stem strongly reticulated..*B. auriflammeus*

    H. Tubes not as above

I. Tubes brilliant chrome yellow at all ages; cap and stem base brown

                                                            B. auriporus

I. Tubes whitish in youth and remaining pale flesh or tan at maturity, brown when rubbed

    J. Taste bitter; plants small.....................*B. felleus* var. *minor*

    J. Taste mild; plants larger..............................*B. indecisus*

I. Tubes light flesh color when young, yellow-buff at maturity; spores bright rust color...*B. affinis*

I. Tubes white or whitish when young, becoming buffy or olivaceous yellow or brownish (in *scaber* and *indecisus* the tubes may be more flesh tinted than brown)

    J. Flesh turning blue

        K. Cap and stem brown or brownish at all ages

            L. Taste mild...*B. sordidus*

            L. Taste bitter.............................*B. subclavatosporus*

        K. Cap rosy in youth, fading to brownish; stem rosy to deeper red; stem reticulated.....................................*B. Peckii*

    J. Flesh not turning blue (faintly so in *pallidus*) but tubes may do so

        K. Stem not reticulated but scabrous or longitudinally lined

            L. Stem strongly marked with dark fibrous dots over a pale surface; tubes small and deeply depressed..................*B. scaber*

            L. Stem white and thickly covered with fine granular or fibrous dots and lines of same color; cap white or nearly so, often strongly pitted..*B. niveus*

            L. Stem scabrous-granular, rosy at top, bright *chrome yellow at base*..*B. chromapes*

            L. Stem more or less streaked with darker lines, also minutely dotted in *badius* (see also *affinis, Roxanae,* and *variipes*)

                M. Cap bay brown or darker, viscid in youth and when wet

                                    B. badius

                M. Cap pale gray in youth, later buffy gray to brownish, dry

                                  B. pallidus

        K. Stem reticulated (may be only delicately so in *indecisus* and *edulis*)

            L. Tubes typically adnate

                M. Cap gray; tubes not stuffed.......................*B. griseus*

                M. Cap yellowish brown or light grayish brown, minutely tomentose to squamulose-warted; tubes distinctly stuffed in youth

                                    B. variipes

            L. Tubes free or deeply depressed (may be adnate in youth in *separans*)

                M. Tubes not stuffed in youth.....................*B. indecisus*

                M.· Tubes distinctly stuffed in youth

                    N. Cap glabrous

                        O. Stem white or pallid to brownish..............*B. edulis*

                        O. Stem dull lilac to rhubarb...................*B. separans*

                  N. Cap tomentose to squamulose..................*B. variipes*

         K. Stem not reticulated or scabrous

            L. Cap bright apricot-orange to bittersweet; tubes passing through pale straw or flesh color to brownish, quickly brown when bruised.....................................*B. subsanguineus*

            L. Cap pale gray in youth, buffy gray in age; tubes passing through pale gray to bright olivaceous, dull blue when bruised

                                    B. pallidus

            L. Cap not as above

M. Stem quite short; cap glutinous..................*B. brevipes*
M. Stem of moderate length
  N. Cap dry
    O. Cap subtomentose to smooth; stem buffy to brownish
        B. affinis and var. *maculosus* (see also *edulis*)
    O. Cap with fasciculate reddish brown tomentum; stem
        yellow.....................................*B. Roxanae*
  N. Cap quite viscid when damp, glabrous; tubes small; stem
    smooth, cartilaginous..................*B. Atkinsonianus*
I. Tubes a peculiar grayish white with flesh tint, becoming brownish
  straw; stem usually with blue-green ring at top; flesh staining paper
  blue-green..*B. sordidus*
I. Tubes yellow or yellowish from the first, darker with age
  J. Growing on roots and stumps of pine; cap bright yellow
                               B. hemichrysus
  J. Not as above
    K. Mouths of tubes "stuffed" when young (truly so only in *auripes*,
      see page 1), sometimes becoming reddish at maturity
      L. Cap some shade of red or rose; dry
        M. Stem reticulated
          N. Stem bright yellow all over or nearly so; flesh yellow, turning
            intensely blue, mild in taste.................*B. speciosus*
          N. Stem red nearly all over; flesh whitish, bitter......*B. Peckii*
        M. Stem not reticulated (rarely faintly so in *bicolor*)
          N. Stem yellow above, red-velvety below; flesh unchanging or
            slowly to blue................................*B. bicolor*
          N. Stem yellow nearly all over (may be stained with red at
            base); flesh turning quickly blue.....*B. miniato-olivaceus*
      L. Cap yellow-brown to red-brown or olivaceous; dry
        M. Stem bright golden yellow all over, lightly reticulated above
                           B. auripes
        M. Stem olive gold, distinctly dotted with reddish squamules
                           B. Morrisii
        M. Stem dull yellow or tawny, closely set with brownish scabrous
          dots; cap becoming rimose all over...........*B. rimosellus*
    K. Mouths of tubes not stuffed when young
      L. Cap viscid when damp (glutinous in *brevipes* and at times in
      rubropunctus)
        M. Sterile margin distinct, inrolled in youth (see also *rubro-*
        punctus)
          N. Tube mouths very small (2 or 3 to a mm.)
            O. Cap alutaceous to fulvous; stem moderately long and
              quite g'abrous.....................*B. Atkinsonianus*
            O. Cap chestnut to purplish with blackish or olive stains, very
              glutinous; stem very short, rarely dotted above
                               B. brevipes
          N. Tube mouths medium sized
            O. Cap reddish brown, tomentose; spores 20–26μ long
                           B. projectellus
            O. Cap olive gold or alutaceous with olive tints, glabrous at
              maturity; spores 11–15μ long.............*B. viridiflavus*
        M. No distinct sterile margin (see also *viridiflavus*)
          N. Tube mouths small, yellow; stem dotted with dry, rosy or
            pale flecks over yellowish...............*B. rubropunctus*

  N. Tube mouths medium sized, brilliant golden yellow at all
    ages; cap and stem base brown..............*B. auriporus*
  N. Tube mouths medium to large, pale, then olive yellow,
    usually blue-green when wounded.............*B. badius*
L. Cap not viscid; smooth or tomentose
 M. Stem reticulated
  N. Cap chocolate red, velvety; flesh white, unchanging; stem
    yellow above, brownish below.................*B. Housei*
  N. Cap red-brown; flesh rose colored in cap and upper part
    of stem; spores very large, 20-26μ long
                B. projectellus
  N. Cap not red
   O. Stem white; cap quite glabrous, "avellaneous-isabelline"
                B. subpallidus
   O. Stem whitish to pale yellow, with darker reticulations,
    pointed below; cap yellow-brown, felted-tomentose;
    flesh white.................................*B. illudens*
   O. Stem dull yellow to golden brown; cap dull yellow to drab;
    flesh yellow................................*B. retipes*
   O. Stem a beautiful deep chrome yellow throughout; cap
    yellow..................................*B. auriflammeus*
 M. Stem not reticulated
  N. Stem strongly reddish scabrous over olive gold; cap glabrous,
    golden olive with brownish or reddish areas..*B. Morrisii*
  N. Stem minutely scurfy-tomentose to smooth, sometimes
    slightly ridged above
   O. Cap glabrous; tubes small
    P. Stem yellow..........................*B. subglabripes*
    P. Stem red except above......................*B. bicolor*
   O. Cap subtomentose to distinctly fibrous
    P. Spores longitudinally striate........*B. chrysenteroides*
    P. Spores smooth
     Q. Cap usually areolated when mature (see also *communis*)
      R. Cracks appearing reddish...........*B. chrysenteron*
      R. Cracks yellowish
       S. Tubes brilliant chrome yellow at all ages
                B. auriporus
       S. Tubes yellow but not remaining so in age
        T. Flesh changing to blue
         U. Plants very small, 1.9-2.3 cm.....*B. parvulus*
         U. Plants larger, about 4-9 cm......*B. fraternus*
        T. Flesh not changing to blue... *B. subtomentosus*
     Q. Cap usually not areolated
      R. Flesh usually changing to blue; cap red or reddish
       S. Plants small; flesh not rosy under cuticle; tube
        mouths and flesh becoming red at maturity
                B. subfraternus
       S. Plants medium to large; flesh rosy under cuticle;
        tube mouths not becoming red....*B. communis*
      R. Flesh not changing to blue, whitish throughout;
       cap not red....................*B. subtomentosus*

SUPPLEMENTARY KEY TO THE SPECIES OF BOLETUS

A. Cap white to dull buffy yellow or light tan
 B. Cap glutinous..*B. placidus*
 B. Cap dry to somewhat viscid when wet
  C. Cap set with fibrous-squamulose or floccose scales
   D. Spores pale canary yellow, smooth.............................*B. cyanescens*
   D. Spores brown, large, striate.......................................*B. Ananas*
  C. Cap smooth to tomentose, not scaly
   D. Tube surface white in youth, then pallid yellowish or fleshy
    E. Stem conspicuously marked with dark or nearly white scabrous dots over a whitish ground..*B. niveus*
    E. Stem only minutely scabrous, whitish to rosy above, bright chrome yellow below...*B. chromapes*
    E. Stem nearly smooth, white in youth, later streaked with grayish brown, especially downward.......................................*B. pallidus*
   D. Tube surface bright red in youth and maturity, finally brownish
     B. Satanas var. *americanus*
A. Cap pale gray in youth, later buffy gray to rosy buff or darker; stem nearly smooth, white in youth, then streaked with gray-brown.........................*B. pallidus*
A. Cap distinctly yellow to orange
 B. Cap distinctly viscid to glutinous
  C. Tube surface light or dull yellow in youth, darker at maturity
   D. Stem with a distinct annulus near top (rarely disappearing in age)....*B. luteus*
   D. Stem without an annulus
    E. Stem covered with prominent yellow reticulated lacerations.........*B. Betula*
    E. Stem not lacerated but reticulated with soft surface tissue which is *not* viscid
     B. americanus var. *reticulipes*
    E. Stem not lacerated or reticulated
     F. Stem set with glandular dots that turn reddish brown to blackish
      G. Cap dotted all over with tufts of brownish fibrils.............*B. hirtellus*
      G. Cap not as above (scattered fibrils or small squamules may be present)
       H. Tube mouths large; stem slender......................*B. americanus*
       H. Tube mouths small to medium; stem larger..............*B. subaureus*
     F. Stem dotted with *dry* fibrous warts and flecks
      G. Stem dots prevailingly rosy; cap orange-red, darker at maturity
       B. rubropunctus
      G. Stem dots not rosy; cap yellow.................*B. subaureus* var. *siccipes*
     F. Stem dotted in youth with viscid particles that do not darken but run together to form a continuous layer resembling lacquer; stem base covered with a white, volva-like boot..*B. Curtisii*
  C. Tube surface muddy yellow-brown at all ages.......................*B. punctipes*
 B. Cap dry or somewhat viscid when wet
  C. Veil present..*B. Ravenelii*
  C. Veil lacking
   D. Stem reticulated
    E. Tube mouths scarlet at least in patches before maturity; cap and stem chrome yellow...*B. auriflammeus*
    E. Tube mouths not becoming scarlet; cap duller yellow or gray.........*B. retipes*
   D. Stem not reticulated
    E. Cap bright yellow, floccose-squamulose, covered with a yellow powder; plants found on roots and stumps of pine.........................*B. hemichrysus*
    E. Cap apricot orange to bittersweet, glabrous and without powder
     B. subsanguineus

9

A. Cap some shade of yellowish brown, olive brown, or olive gold
  B. Cap distinctly viscid to glutinous
    C. Tube surface yellowish or straw-colored in youth, darker at maturity
      D. Stem with a distinct annulus near top (rarely disappearing in age)....*B. luteus*
      D. Stem without an annulus
        E. Stem distinctly viscid
          F. Stem very short, not dotted or with a few granules near top; occurring late in fall..*B. brevipes*
          F. Stem longer in proportion, dotted nearly all over with reddish brown glutinous droplets...*B. granulatus*
        E. Stem not viscid, quite glabrous and cartilaginous...........*B. Atkinsonianus*
    C. Tube surface bright greenish yellow at all ages and retaining this color if properly dried...*B. viridiflavus*
    C. Tube surface muddy yellow-brown at all ages......................*B. punctipes*
  B. Cap dry or somewhat viscid when wet
    C. Tube surface white in youth, later yellow to buff or olivaceous
      D. Stem distinctly hollow...*B. castaneus*
      D. Stem not hollow
        E. Stem covered with wide lacerated plates which gelatinize and swell when wet
                B. Russellii
        E. Stem not lacerated but distinctly reticulated, at least above
          F. Tube mouths distinctly stuffed in youth
            G. Cap glabrous...*B. edulis*
            G. Cap tomentose to squamulose-warted......................*B. variipes*
          F. Tubes mouths not stuffed when young; stem white...........*B. subpallidus*
        E. Stem not lacerated or distinctly reticulated
          F. Stem conspicuously marked with dark scabrous dots over a whitish or dingy yellowish ground...*B. scaber*
          F. Stem not scabrous
            G. Tubes distinctly stuffed in youth........................*B. edulis*, form
            G. Tubes not distinctly stuffed in youth
              H. Cap distinctly fasciculate-tomentose; spores olivaceous.....*B. Roxanae*
              H. Cap nearly glabrous; spores rusty ochraceous
                  B. affinis and var. *maculosus*
    C. Tube surface white, then rosy to brownish flesh......................*B. gracilis*
    C. Tube surface yellow even in youth, later greenish yellow
      D. Stem distinctly reticulated, at least above
        E. Tube mouths stuffed in youth; stem bright golden yellow, reticulated above
                B. auripes
        E. Tube mouths not stuffed in youth; stem reticulated all over
          F. Tubes medium sized, adnate-depressed; stem dull yellow throughout
                B. retipes
          F. Tubes large, adnate-decurrent; stem with long dark reticulations over a much paler ground..*B. illudens*
      D. Stem not reticulated but dotted with conspicuous red squamules over a greenish yellow surface..*B. Morrisii*
      D. Stem neither reticulated nor strongly dotted
        E. Cap distinctly felted-tomentose; tubes adnate-depressed.....*B. subtomentosus*
        E. Cap glabrous
          F. Plants parasitic on *Scleroderma*; tubes more or less decurrent
                B. parasiticus
          F. Plants not parasitic; tubes adnate-depressed...............*B. subglabripes*
    C. Tube surface red in youth and age or yellowish or brownish in age
      D. Plants large and heavy...*B. luridus*

D. Plants quite small; tube flesh red throughout........*B. piperatus* and *rubinellus*
C. Tube surface dark brown to blackish brown in youth, becoming brownish yellow; plants of medium size......................................*B. vermiculosus*
A. Cap rosy or blood red or purplish red
  B. Cap distinctly viscid to glutinous; tube mouths deep red................*B. Frostii*
  B. Cap dry or slightly viscid when wet
    C. Cap with dense, dark purple scales in center; plants small.....*B. Vanderbiltianus*
    C. Cap without purple scales
      D. Tube surface white or nearly so in youth, later yellowish or fleshy
        E. Stem not reticulated
          F. Spores rosy brown or dull salmon, about 9–12.5μ long.........*B. chromapes*
          F. Spores yellow-ochre, about 7–8.5μ long...................*B. subsanguineus*
        E. Stem reticulated at least above
          F. Cap finely tomentose and with a bloom like a peach; taste bitter.*B. Peckii*
          F. Cap glabrous and without a bloom; taste mild.................*B. separans*
      D. Tube surface yellow even in youth, later dull yellow to olivaceous
        E. Plants quite small, usually less than 4 cm. broad
          F. Stem reticulated above; tubes decurrent.......................*B. Housei*
          F. Stem not reticulated; tubes depressed.......................*B. parvulus*
        E. Plants larger (some small in *B. fraternus*)
          F. Tubes large and relatively long for size of plant...............*B. fraternus*
          F. Tubes small and relatively quite short
            G. Stem reticulated nearly all over, yellow.....................*B. speciosus*
            G. Stem not reticulated
              H. Stem red-velvety nearly all over or only below..............*B. bicolor*
              H. Stem yellow nearly all over and smooth or nearly so
                B. miniato-olivaceus
      D. Tube surface and tube flesh yellow in youth, red-brown at maturity; plants small
                B. subfraternus
      D. Tube surface red in youth and age or dull olivaceous in age
        E. Tube flesh also reddish.....................................*B. rubinellus*
        E. Tube flesh olivaceous yellow...................................*B. parvus*
A. Cap some shade of red-brown, vinaceous brown, dull red, or orange red
  B. Cap distinctly viscid to glutinous
    C. Tube surface bright chrome yellow at all ages and when dry........*B. auriporus*
    C. Tube surface creamy white to pale yellow when young, later more yellow to brownish and with or without olive tints
      D. Stem distinctly viscid
        E. Stem very short, not dotted or with a few granules near top; occurring late in fall...*B. brevipes*
        E. Stem longer in proportion, dotted nearly all over with reddish brown, glutinous droplets...*B. granulatus*
      D. Stem not viscid
        E. Cap and stem (except at base) quite glabrous; stem cartilaginous
                B. Atkinsonianus
        E. Cap and stem both tomentose-dotted; stem pale brownish, often abruptly yellow at top, streaked with darker lines..........................*B. badius*
        E. Cap glabrous; stem creamy yellowish, dotted with dry rosy or pale flecks and squamules...*B. rubropunctus*
  B. Cap dry to somewhat viscid when wet
    C. Tube surface bright chrome yellow at all ages and when dry........*B. auriporus*
    C. Tube surface white in youth, later yellow to buff or olivaceous
      D. Stem distinctly hollow.......................................*B. castaneus*
      D. Stem not hollow

E. Stem covered with wide lacerated plates which gelatinize and swell when wet
.... *B. Russellii*
E. Stem not lacerated but distinctly reticulated, at least above
  F. Tube mouths distinctly stuffed in youth, as if covered by a white membrane
    G. Cap glabrous
      H. Stem white to brownish..*B. edulis*
      H. Stem rhubarb or strongly lilac colored...................*B. separans*
    G. Cap tomentose to squamulose.............................*B. variipes*
  F. Tube mouths not stuffed in youth
    G. Stem white..*B. subpallidus*
    G. Stem rosy brown.......................................*B. projectellus*
E. Stem not lacerated or distinctly reticulated
  F. Tubes strongly stuffed in youth...........................*B. edulis*, form
  F. Tubes not strongly stuffed in youth (lightly so in *affinis*)
    G. Cap fasciculate-tomentose; spores olivaceous................*B. Roxanae*
    G. Cap glabrous or nearly so; spores rusty ochraceous...........*B. affinis*
C. Tube surface white or nearly so in youth, later flesh colored or rosy to fleshy brown
  D. Taste quite bitter.................................*B. felleus* and var. *minor*
  D. Taste mild
    E. Stem long and slender, pruinose brown-velvety; tubes and stem not turning
    brown when rubbed...*B. gracilis*
    E. Stem much shorter in proportion to cap width, distinctly reticulated at least
    above; tubes and stem quickly brown when rubbed.............*B. indecisus*
C. Tube surface fawn colored in youth to near maturity, later dull pink
                                            B. felleus, form
C. Tube surface yellow even in youth, later more or less olivaceous
  D. Plants quite small, not over 4 cm. wide
    E. Flesh white, unchanging; tubes decurrent......................*B. Housei*
    E. Flesh pale yellow, turning blue; tubes nearly free.............*B. parvulus*
  D. Plants larger
    E. Stem with long brownish reticulations; spores very large, up to 26μ long
                                        B. projectellus
    E. Stem not reticulated but conspicuously dotted with squamules
      F. Cap rimose; squamules on stem brown over dull yellow or brownish surface
                                        B. rimosellus
      F. Cap not rimose; squamules red over greenish gold surface......*B. Morrisii*
    E. Stem neither reticulated nor strongly squamulose
      F. Spores distinctly *longitudinally striate*.................*B. chrysenteroides*
      F. Spores smooth
        G. Cap quite glabrous; flesh pale yellow, not changing to blue..*B. subglabripes*
        G. Cap subtomentose to velvety; flesh usually changing to blue
          H. Cap usually areolated
            I. Cracks appearing reddish........................*B. chrysenteron*
            I. Cracks yellowish....................................*B. fraternus*
         H. Cap usually not areolated...........................*B. communis*
C. Tube surface and tube flesh yellow in youth, red-brown at maturity; plants small
                                          B. subfraternus
C. Tube surface dark brown or purple-brown even in youth
  D. Tube flesh same color as mouths; stem grayish or lilac flecked with small purplish
  scales..*B. eximius*
  D. Tube flesh not same color as mouths; stem bright or dull yellow, often with
  darker lines..*B. vermiculosus*
C. Tube surface red to dark red in youth and age or olivaceous yellow or brownish
  in age

   D. Plants large and heavy..*B. luridus*
   D. Plants small
      E. Flesh of tubes red or reddish throughout
         F. Taste very peppery; tubes adnate to decurrent...............*B. piperatus*
         F. Taste mild; tubes adnate to depressed.......................*B. rubinellus*
      E. Flesh of tubes olivaceous yellow.................................*B. parvus*
A. Cap purplish brown
   B. Plants small, not over 4 cm. broad; cap set with dark purple scales. .*B. Vanderbiltianus*
   B. Plants larger; cap smooth
      C. Tube surface white (rarely fawn colored), then deep flesh to rosy......*B. felleus*
      C. Tube surface dark brownish purple at all ages......................*B. eximius*
A. Cap medium to dark gray or gray-brown
   B. Tube surface white, then rosy.....................................*B. alboater*
   B. Tube surface white, then gray-clay or pale drab
      C. Stem distinctly reticulated..*B. griseus*
      C. Stem not reticulated but marked with dark scabrous dots over a whitish or yel-
         lowish ground..*B. scaber*
   B. Tube surface deep yellow in youth, then duller yellow.........*B. retipes* (dark forms)
A. Cap dark brown (with or without chestnut tint) to blackish
   B. Cap distinctly viscid
      C. Stem pale brownish, often abruptly yellow at top; streaked with darker lines and
         minutely dotted...*B. badius*
      C. Stem creamy yellow or brownish yellow, conspicuously dotted with dry, reddish
         or pale flecks and squamules.................................*B. rubropunctus*
   B. Cap dry or faintly viscid when wet
      C. Tube surface white, then flesh colored to rosy
         D. Taste quite bitter...*B. felleus*
         D. Taste mild
            E. Plants very dark; cap, tubes, and stem turning black when injured; spores
             deep rosy salmon...*B. alboater*
            E. Plants medium dark; tubes and stem turning brown when injured; spores
             fleshy brown...*B. indecisus*
      C. Tube surface whitish, then brownish straw with a reddish sheen; plants staining
         paper blue-green...*B. sordidus*
      C. Tube surface yellow in youth, then darker to olivaceous or brownish
         D. Spores longitudinally striate.................................*B. chrysenteroides*
         D. Spores smooth, not striate...................................*B. auripes*

Boletus cyanescens Bull. Herb. Fr., pl. 369. 1787.

B. constrictus Pers. Syn. Fung., p. 508. 1801.

B. lacteus Lév. Ann. Sci. Nat., 3rd ser., **9**: 124. 1848.

Plate 6 and pl. 61, fig. 2

Cap 4.5–10 cm. broad, plane, convex or irregular, creamy tan or light straw color, the margin pale, when young pale all over, surface harshly fibrous-squamulose or floccose, pitted very much as in *Hydnum*; margin strongly incurved. Flesh moderately soft, up to 12 mm. thick, pallid but turning instantly when cut to an indigo blue which finally darkens to almost blackish blue; nearly tasteless and odorless. Young buttons covered all over with a cortina of woven threads which may leave pendent wisps on the cap edge.

Tubes small, 3–7 mm. long, roundish, depressed at stem, pallid white, then light olive yellow, turning deep indigo when cut or rubbed.

Stem about 5.5–8 cm. long and 1.5 cm. thick above unless swollen there, irregularly swollen at any point, not reticulated or squamulose but with a fibrous appearance under the lens, very hollow with soft stuffing here and there or the stuffing may remain intact even when mature, concolorous with cap, intense indigo when cut.

Spores (of No. 9520) pale canary yellow, subelliptic, flattened on one side, smooth, 4–5 x 7.4–10(–11)μ.

The cap and stem of this species assume a much brighter olivaceous yellow color when dry. The species is fairly common in our mountains, and is easily recognized by the pale color, fibrous-squamulose surface, and instant change of all parts to indigo blue when cut or bruised. The spores are relatively short and thick, more so than in most Boleti.

Form with unchanging flesh. On a gravelly roadside bank in Jackson County, N. C., near the Chattooga River, we found (No. 12924, Aug. 7, 1942) a strange aberrant form of this species in which no part of the plant showed any change to blue whatever. It occurred in two places about one hundred yards apart. One lot was fully mature but in perfectly fresh condition, the other younger but approaching maturity. The plants were otherwise perfect examples of the species in every respect, including the pale yellow spores. There had been plenty of rain and the lack of change was certainly not due to aridity.

ILLUSTRATIONS: Bresadola. Icon. Mycol. **19**: pl. 939. 1931.
  Bulliard. Herb. Fr., pl. 369.
  Farlow. Icones Farlowianae, pl. 88. 1929.
  Fries. Sveriges Svampar, pl. 80. 1861.
  Gillet. Champ. Fr., Hymén., pl. 54.
  Kallenbach. Die Pilze Mitteleuropas **1**: pl. 53.
  Léveillé. As above, pl. 9, figs. 1, 2.
  Michael. Führer f. Pilzfreunde **2**: fig. 126.
  Richon and Roze. Atl. Champ., pl. 59, figs. 10–14.
  Rolland. Atl. Champ. Fr., pl. 88, fig. 195. 1910.

NORTH CAROLINA. Highlands. No. 8825. In sandy soil, mixed woods, July 22, 1931. No. 9520. Occurring in a scattered colony under hemlock, rhododendron, etc., Aug. 21, 1932. No. 9766. On a bank by road, Aug. 12, 1934. No. 10536. By road up Whiteside Mt., Aug. 17, 1937. Spores pale lemon yellow, oblong-elliptic, 4.2–5.5 x 7.2–9.8μ. No. 12567. By Rhododendron Trail, Aug. 13, 1941. No. 12877. By trail up Fodderstack Mt., July 28, 1942. Also numerous other collections from Highlands.
Macon County. Standing Indian. No. 10965. Road bank in deciduous woods, Aug. 20, 1938.
Asheville. Beardslee.
Pink Bed Valley, Pisgah Forest. Murrill.

SOUTH CAROLINA. Hartsville. No. 11032. In low mixed woods, Sept. 14, 1938. Spores yellow, 4.2–5.5 x 7.5–10μ.

Boletus castaneus Bull. Herb. Fr., pl. 328. 1786.

Plate 4, figs. 1, 2; pl. 6; pl. 61, fig. 1

Cap 3–6 cm. broad, convex or nearly flat, dry, minutely tomentose with granular-looking squamules, chestnut brown to biscuit color or vinaceous red, the margin usually paler and becoming uplifted. Flesh up to 10 mm. thick, firm, white, not changing at all or becoming sordid ochraceous when bruised; taste mild and pleasant, odor none.
Tubes small, 1–2 to a mm., up to 7 mm. long, depressed at stem, white in youth, passing through cream to a distinct light yellow, slightly brownish when bruised.
Stem up to 7 cm. long and 2 cm. thick toward the base, tapering upward and often pinched at the very base, surface like that of cap but usually paler above and irregularly channelled and grooved; flesh consisting of a thin ochraceous rind, enclosing a large cavity which is more or less lined and chambered with soft pure white cottony fibers, finally hollow.
Spores (of No. 10191) clear light yellow in a good print, oblong-elliptic, smooth, 4.2–5.5 x 7.5–10(–11)μ.

This well known species is fairly common in our mountains, less so at Chapel Hill, and occurs in deciduous or mixed woods. It is easily determined by its hollow stem, yellow, short, blunt spores, dry, brownish to vinaceous, granular-tomentose cap, and flesh not changing to blue. The form with purplish color has been given the form name *purpurinus* by Snell (Mycologia **28**: 465. 1936).

ILLUSTRATIONS: Barla. Champ. Nice, pl. 32, figs. 11–15. 1859.
Bulliard. Herb. Fr., pl. 328.
Farlow. Icones Farlowianae, pl. 89.
Gillet. Champ. Fr., Hymén., pl. 51.
McIlvaine. Amer. Fungi, pl. 114, fig. 3. Stem too long.
Murrill. Mycologia **5**: pl. 80, fig. 1. 1913.
Peck. Rept. N. Y. St. Mus. **48**: pl. 36, figs. 1–7. 1895.

NORTH CAROLINA. Chapel Hill. No. 2306. In cool woods under oaks, June 29, 1916. Spores 5–6.5 x 8–10.5(–11.8)μ. No. 3311. Same spot as above, June 7, 1919. No. 4389. Woods near Meeting of Waters, July 13, 1920. No. 11606. In rich earth under shrubs, Aug. 30, 1940. Purple form. Asheville. Beardslee, No. 16115 (U. N. C. Herb.).

Blowing Rock. No. 5688. Under rhododendron, Aug. 22, 1922. Also reported from Blowing Rock by Atkinson.

Haywood County. No. 8099. Rich low ground, Aug. 8, 1926. Spores clear yellow, 4.5–5.5 x 7.4–10μ.

Highlands. No. 8966. Mixed mountain woods, July 29, 1931. No. 9639. On bank by road, Aug. 21, 1933. No. 10883. On roadside by Mirror Lake, Aug. 7, 1938. No. 12679. At base of a rock wall, Aug. 24, 1941.

Jackson County. No. 10191. On bank by road back of Big Yellow Mountain, Aug. 20, 1936.

Polk County. No. 11929. In Pearson's Falls gorge near Tryon, Aug. 24, 1940. Purple form.

Also numerous other collections in our herbarium from Chapel Hill and Macon County.

SOUTH CAROLINA. Hartsville. No. 39. In humus-filled earth near bottom of a ditch, Aug. 6, 1917. Spores clear yellow, 4–5.5 x 7.4–9.3μ.

Oconee County. No. 11805. On clay bank near Whitewater River, Aug. 3, 1940.

Boletus felleus Bull. Herb. Fr., pl. 379. 1787.

Plate 5, fig. 1; pl. 7; pl. 61, fig. 3

Plants usually large and heavy, up to 23.5 cm. broad and 22 cm. high, but the broadest ones with relatively short stems; cap convex, smooth, glabrous, dry (rarely slimy in very wet weather), wood brown to buffy brown or paler leather color, often with a distinct vinaceous tint and sometimes, especially in youth, a beautiful vinaceous purple with a bloom. Flesh thick, soft, white, changing here and there to pinkish, grub channels strongly so; taste distinctly to intensely *bitter*, odor oily.

Tubes medium small, 1–2 to a mm., 1–2 cm. long, "stuffed" when very young, depressed around the stem or squarely attached, white when young or in some plants a pretty "ashes of roses" color, about fawn (Ridg.), turning brownish flesh color when bruised, deep flesh or rose color at maturity.

Stem 4–10 cm. long, rarely up to 20 cm., not usually very stout but sometimes bulbous and up to 5 cm. thick near base, concolorous with cap or darker downward or varying to a beautiful lilac purple, especially in youth, rarely with a dull greenish tint above, smooth all over or reticulated at top or nearly to base, sometimes lined longitudinally with the brown or purple color; solid, white-mycelioid at base.

Spores (of No. 10554) deep rose in a heavy print, narrowly elliptic, smooth, 3.4–3.8 x 10–12.5μ. Basidia long-clavate, 4-spored, about 7–8μ thick.

This is a common and well known species, distinguished by its brownish or violaceous colors, rather large size, white, *bitter* flesh, and rosy tubes and spores.

The form with violaceous colors has been given the form name *plumbeoviolaceus* by Snell (Mycologia **28**: 465. 1936), who also lists forms *rubrobrunneus* Snell and *albiceps* Kauffman.

ILLUSTRATIONS: Atkinson. Mushrooms, pl. 49, fig. 1. 1900 (pl. 55 of the 2nd ed., 1901).

Bresadola. Icon. Mycol. **19**: pl. 938. 1931.

Bulliard. Herb. Fr., pl. 379.

Dufour. Atlas Champ., pl. 54, fig. 125. 1891.

Fries. Sveriges Svampar, pl. 52. 1861 (t.p. date).

Gibson. Our Edible Toadstools and Mushrooms, pl. 24 (below).

Kallenbach. Die Pilze Mitteleuropas **1**: pl. 42.

Krieger. Mushroom Handbook, pl. 8. 1936.

McIlvaine. Amer. Fungi, pl. 122, figs. 2–4. 1900.

Palmer. Mushrooms of America, pl. 11, fig. 1. 1885.

Peck. Rept. N. Y. St. Mus. **48**: pl. 43. 1895.

Richon and Roze. Atlas Champ., pl. 57, figs. 1–3.

Taylor. Food Products II, pl. 2, fig. 11. 1893.

NORTH CAROLINA. Chapel Hill. No. 229. In mixed woods near a cedar, Sept. 14, 1910. Spores elliptic, 3.5–4 x 9–11μ. No. 716. On a lawn, Sept. 8, 1913. No. 9870. On mossy lawn under willow oak, Sept. 29, 1934. No. 10664. On mossy lawn, Sept. 14, 1937. Spores long-elliptic, 3.4–3.8 x 9–11.2μ.

Highlands. No. 9017. In a yard, Aug. 2, 1931. Spores clear rose color, narrow, 3.2–3.7 x 8.5–12.5μ. No. 9626. On a clay bank under roots, Aug. 17, 1935. Entire plant was a beautiful grayish lilac. No. 10554. On bank near foot of Bear Pen Mountain, Aug. 19, 1937. No. 12495. Mixed mountain woods by Ravenel Lake, Aug. 4, 1941.

Also many other collections from Chapel Hill and Highlands.

Haywood County. No. 8122.

Jackson County. No. 10925.

Pink Bed Valley, Pisgah Forest. Murrill. Also our No. 10975.

Polk County. No. 11931.

Asheville. Beardslee.

Blowing Rock. Atkinson and Schrenk.

Middle and low districts. Schweinitz and Curtis.

Boletus felleus var. **minor** n. var.

Plate 8 and pl. 61, fig. 4

Cap 1.7–5.2 cm., rarely up to 8.5 cm. broad, convex to nearly plane in center but frequently with the margin upturned, exposing the tubes, surface minutely felted-tomentose, at times areolated with flat appressed scales, medium brown in center, fading to clay color on margin, or buffy brown or dark brown all over without any purplish tint; narrow sterile margin often obvious. Flesh firm, at

first pale apple meat color, turning pale brown on standing; usually quite bitter and often also sweetish, odor mildly of rancid oil.
Tubes small to medium, 2–3 to a mm. except near stem where the mouths are more elongated radially, distinctly depressed, creamy white at first, becoming pale flesh color at maturity and turning brown when bruised.
Stem often excentric, up to 6 cm. long and 1.5 cm. thick, usually larger above and tapering below, minutely tomentose and sometimes reticulated, concolorous with cap or paler, especially near the top.
Spores (of No. 10550) a fine rose color in a heavy print (about vinaceous pink of Ridg.), narrowly elliptic, smooth, 2.8–3.5 x 9–12.2µ. Basidia 4-spored, long-clavate, 7–8µ thick.

This variety, which is frequent on exposed roadside banks at Highlands, differs from typical *felleus* in much smaller size (average about 4 cm.), much paler tubes at maturity, more tomentose cap, and stem often flattened above and pinched below instead of enlarged below as is frequent in *felleus*. This variety is found in the same habitat as *B. castaneus* and has a strong superficial resemblance to that species, but *castaneus* of course, with its yellow spores and hollow stem, belongs to a different group. The present variety differs from *B. indecisus* in smaller size, bitter and often also sweetish taste, and more rosy spores.

NORTH CAROLINA. Highlands. No. 9653. On clay bank by a road, Aug. 22, 1933. Spores rosy, 3.2–3.6 x 9.3–12µ. No. 9750. On bank near Lake Ravenel, Aug. 11, 1934. Spores bright rose, 3.2–3.7 x 8–11µ. No. 10550. On bank by road around Bear Pen Mountain, Aug. 19, 1937. No. 10824. On bank at foot of Bear Pen, July 28, 1938. No. 10845. By road near the school house, Aug. 3, 1938. No. 11009. On bank by Dillard road, Aug. 28, 1938. Spores 2.6–3.5 x 10–13µ, longer than usual. No. 12033. By road to Sewell place, July 23, 1939. No. 12460. From mossy base of a stump in Primeval Forest, July 30, 1941. Stem reticulated. Also many other collections from Highlands.
Jackson County. No. 10924. Near Tuckaseigee Falls, Aug. 14, 1938.

GEORGIA. Rabun County. No. 12472. On bank in deciduous woods by Big Creek, Aug. 1, 1941.

Boletus indecisus Peck. Rept. N. Y. St. Mus. **41**: 76–77. 1888.
? *B. tabacinus* Peck. Bull. Torr. Bot. Club **23**: 418. 1896.

Plate 3, fig. 4; pl. 9; pl. 61, figs. 5, 6

Single or cespitose; cap 5–15 cm. broad, convex or slightly irregular, dry, minutely tomentose-felted, hazel brown or deep dull brown with tint of chocolate or lighter sayal brown (Ridg.), the colors being rather well retained on drying.
Flesh up to 2 cm. thick, pure white or about as in apple meat, with or without a tint of flesh above the tubes, soft, in some specimens almost like marshmallow, changing to brownish or fleshy brown when bruised; taste mild, odor none.
Tubes 4.5–17 mm. long, small to medium, about 2–3 to a mm., unequal in size,

adnate and usually strongly depressed around the stem, tightly folded together but not stuffed when young, nearly white when young, passing through sordid straw or pallid flesh to fleshy brown, turning deep brown when rubbed.

Stem 4–7.5 cm. long, 2–3.5 cm. thick, or if enlarged above or below up to 5 cm. thick, sometimes irregular, flattened and grooved, color of cap below, paler above, distinctly reticulated above or nearly to base, turning brown when rubbed; flesh firm and solid, but often attacked by grubs.

Spores (of No. 12142) fleshy brown in a good print, subelliptic, often slightly broader toward the proximal end but many with broadest part near middle, 3.4–3.8 x 7.4–11.2μ.

This is a common species on banks and in open places around Highlands, N. C., and less common at Chapel Hill. It has a strong superficial resemblance to B. *felleus*, but differs in absence of bitter taste, color of tubes which turn from whitish through a pallid flesh or straw to fleshy brown instead of rose, and in the color of the spores which are much less rose. Peck placed the species in the tribe Hyporhodii, but in his treatment of this group (Boleti of the United States, p. 151) he says that he has admitted species in which the spores incline to ferruginous and under the species *indecisus* emphasizes the *brownish* flesh color of the spores. We find that the spores vary not only in color but somewhat in size and shape, even on the same spore print. We have examined the spores of two of Peck's own collections and find that one (Port Jefferson, N. Y.) has spores rather evenly elliptic, 3.5–4.2 x 8.5–11.2μ, while another (Menands, N. Y.) has spores elliptic to subventricose, 3.8–5 x 10–13μ.

In drying the tubes frequently shrink away from the stem, giving the appearance of being distantly free.

The type of B. *tabacinus* looks very much like this species and it grew in a similar location, but the flesh is quite brown and the spores average larger. The species was at least in part described from the dried condition and the color of the flesh may not be typical for fresh plants.

Small specimens of this species are, in general appearance, almost indistinguishable from larger forms of B. *felleus* var. *minor*, but in the latter the flesh is bitter in taste and the spores are distinctly more rosy.

From B. *affinis*, which specimens of *indecisus* with practically no flesh color in tubes and spores may closely resemble, it may be distinguished as follows: B. *affinis* has tubes stuffed when young, the flesh does not change when cut, the stem is smooth, sometimes with the darker color more or less in longitudinal lines, and the spores are a brighter rusty ochre.

ILLUSTRATIONS: McIlvaine. Amer. Fungi, pl. 122, fig. 1.

NORTH CAROLINA. Chapel Hill. No. 1673. Under oaks, July 30, 1915. No. 9869. In rich deciduous woods, Sept. 27, 1934. Spores rather narrowly elliptic, some slightly broader toward proximal end, 3.4–3.7 x 8.5–11.2μ. No. 11095. In deciduous woods, July 15, 1939. Spores medium brown, elliptic to subventricose, 3.6–4 x 10–13μ.

Highlands. No. 8935. On bank by roadside, July 28, 1931. Spores 3–3.8 x 7.5–9.5(–11)μ. No. 9014. By trail up Mt. Satulah, July 31, 1931. No. 9774. On bank by road, Aug. 12, 1934. Spores brownish, elliptic or slightly broader toward proximal end, 3.2–3.7 x 8–10μ. No. 12142. By road near entrance to Ravenel Lake, Aug. 11, 1939. No. 12227. On a roadside bank, Aug. 25, 1939.

Also many other collections in our herbarium from Macon County.

Haywood County. No. 8097. In open place by Pigeon River, Aug. 8, 1926. Spores rosy brown, elliptic-ventricose, 3.8–4.8 x 10–13μ.

Pisgah Forest. No. 10997. Near Gunstand Gap, Aug. 23, 1938.

GEORGIA. Rabun County. No. 11914. In rich ravine by Big Creek, Aug. 22, 1940.

Boletus alboater Schw.   Syn. Fung. Car., No. 864.   1822.
B. nigrellus Peck.   Rept. N. Y. St. Mus. **29**: 44.   1878.

Plate 10 and pl. 61, fig. 7

Cap about 7–11 cm. (rarely 28 cm.) broad, convex to nearly flat or irregular, dry, distinctly velvety-tomentose, color very dark, from nearly black with a grayish bloom through dark smoky drab with a fleshy tint to brownish gray, turning black when bruised; margin free, inturned in youth and often at maturity. Flesh thick near center, white or creamy gray, turning pinkish or purplish brown when bruised, then blackish; taste mild or none, odor none.

Tubes short for size of cap, about 5–7 mm. long (up to 12 mm. in a plant 23 cm. broad), small, variable, 1–3 to a mm., adnate to depressed with decurrent lines, white at first, later flesh colored, turning brown then black when cut; not stuffed in youth but so crowded and folded together as to obscure the openings.

Stem 6–10.5 cm. long, usually heavy and irregular, largest below or rarely above, color of cap but paler at apex at least when young, usually reticulated above, the longitudinal lines much stronger than the cross veins, pruinose, black when rubbed; flesh solid and firm like that of cap.

Spores (of No. 9592) deep rosy salmon, ovate-elliptic, broader near proximal end, thick-walled, 3.7–4.5 x 8.5–11μ.

A handsome plant which is rather rare with us. The species is characterized by very dark color of cap and stem, small white tubes which later become rosy, change of all parts to black when bruised, and rosy spores. The plant is quite firm and durable, and herbarium specimens are often entirely black. Peck at first described the flesh of *nigrellus* as white and unchanging, but later agreed with Beardslee that the flesh did blacken throughout (Torreya **1**: 38. 1901).

ILLUSTRATIONS: Hard. Mushrooms, fig. 303. 1908. (As *B. nigrellus* and not in color.)
Murrill. Mycologia **12**: pl. 2, fig. 2. 1920.

NORTH CAROLINA. Chapel Hill. No. 74. In a low place with smilax, Sept. 25, 1911. No. 1220. In a cane brake in a swamp, July 27, 1914. Spores 3.6–4.2 x 8.5μ. No. 4538. Damp rich soil in mixed woods, July 26, 1920. No. 4583. Mixed woods by Bowlin Creek, July 28, 1920. Spores 4–5 x 9.3–12μ, a few apparently abnormal ones larger.

Highlands. No. 9550. On bank by road in oak-chestnut woods, Aug. 25, 1932. Cap 9 inches wide. Spores rosy brown, subelliptic, usually broad at proximal end, thick-walled, 3.7–4.2 x 8–10.2μ. No. 9592. In mixed mountain woods, Sept. 1, 1932. No. 12028. In old wagon road near Shortoff Mt., July 18, 1939. No. 12447. In open ground in a cow pasture, July 27, 1941.

Clay County. No. 10964. On road bank about 6 miles from top of Standing Indian, Aug. 20, 1938. Spores 3.7–4 x 9.3–11μ.

Boletus gracilis Peck. Rept. N. Y. St. Mus. **24**: 78. 1872.

Plate 11 and pl. 61, fig. 8

Cap 4–7, rarely up to 10 cm. broad, convex to hemispheric, margin free and often elevated, dry, delicately felted to tomentose and finely areolated, sometimes subglabrous, uniformly chestnut brown or somewhat paler and more yellowish brown. Flesh up to 1 cm. thick near stem, white or palely concolorous, sometimes with faint tint of pink above, unchanging, slimy to the touch; taste mild, subacid, odor slight.

Tubes rather small, 0.8–1.8 cm. long, of unequal lengths, making the hymenial surface somewhat pitted, deeply depressed at stem, when young almost pure white or silvery vinaceous with the mouths frosted, then deeper flesh color or brownish flesh, unchanging.

Stem very characteristic, slender, small above, increasing to large or quite bulbous at base, 5–9 mm. thick above to 1.5–3 cm. thick at base, 6–15 cm. long, often bent, color of cap or paler, sometimes yellow below, surface finely pruinose velvety, granular in appearance and often conspicuously lined, the lines sometimes anastomosing, base usually whitened with mycelium; flesh white, firm, solid.

Spores (of No. 9635) rosy brown (hazel of Ridg.), fusiform-elliptic, smooth, 4.8–6.5 x 11–13(–14)μ.

This species is common in humus in our mountain woods, but so far we have never found it at Chapel Hill. The slender form, reddish brown cap and stem, the latter granular in appearance, and the flesh colored tubes deeply depressed around the stem are characteristic features.

ILLUSTRATIONS: McIlvaine. Amer. Fungi, pl. 114, fig. 1. The stem should be more brown. His fig. 3 on the same plate, labelled *B. castaneus*, has exactly the form and appearance of *gracilis*, but he shows white tubes in section.

NORTH CAROLINA. Highlands. No. 8927. In humus under hemlock, July 27, 1931. Spores fleshy brown in light print, more ochraceous in heavy print, distinctly fusiform, 4.8–6.5 x 11.5–14μ. No. 9635. Mixed mountain woods, Aug. 22, 1933. No. 12011. Mixed woods in Primeval Forest, July 13, 1939. No. 12218. Under rhododendron and hemlock, Aug. 23, 1939.

Blowing Rock. No. 5697. In mold in deciduous woods, Aug. 22, 1922. Spores burnt umber in heavy print when fresh, 5.5–6.4 x 12–15μ.

Haywood County. No. 8035. In mixed woods, Aug. 4, 1926.

Also many other collections in our herbarium from above places.
Asheville. Beardslee.
Pisgah Forest. Murrill.

Boletus Vanderbiltianus Murrill. Torreya **8**: 215–216. 1908.

Plate 61, fig. 9

We have not collected this species and give below the original description.

Pileus subconical, 2–3 cm. broad, 1–2 cm. thick; surface smooth, dry, conspicuously ornamented on the umbo with dense, pointed, imbricated, dark purple scales, which become gradually smaller and give place to minute purplish specks near the margin, the color changing from atropurpureous to latericeous; margin thin, undulate, concolorous, with a distinct inflexed sterile portion 1 mm. broad; context thick, fleshy, firm, cream-colored, unchangeable, sweet to the taste; tubes adnate, slightly decurrent on one side, salmon-colored near the margin, incarnate next to the stipe, unchangeable within, the mouths becoming incarnate as the spores mature, mouths angular, 1 mm. or less broad, elongated to 2 mm. near the stipe, edges thin, entire; spores oblong-ellipsoid, smooth, pale ochraceous-brown, 9–12 x 2–3μ; stipe curved, cylindrical, slightly enlarged above, delicately pruinose, not reticulated, deep salmon-colored, changing to incarnate, finely purplish-dotted like the margin of the cap, solid and cream-colored within, 2–3 x 0.5 cm.

NORTH CAROLINA. Pink Bed Valley. Type specimens collected by a road in thin oak woods.

Roan Mountain. In frondose woods. Reported by Hesler (Rept. Reelfoot Lake Biol. Station **5**: 169. 1941).

Boletus chromapes Frost. Bull. Buf. Soc. Nat. Sci. **2**: 105. 1874.

Frontispiece, fig. 3, and pl. 61, fig. 10

Cap about 5–9.3 cm. broad, convex, somewhat pitted, dry, faintly tomentose with felted fibers or merely dull and glaucous to the eye, rose colored all over when young, later with pale brownish or buffy areas; margin thick, irregular. Flesh about 6–10 mm. thick near stem, white or faintly rose, grub channels sordid; odor none, taste mild, the cap surface usually distinctly acid to the tongue, but not so in some cases.

Tubes 5–8 mm. long, conspicuously depressed at stem, almost free, small, 2–3 to a mm., white at first then yellowish or pallid, becoming flesh colored then brownish in age, at times rosy when bruised.

Stem up to 10 cm. long, 1–2 cm. thick, crooked, equal or slightly larger below, scabrous dotted above and smooth below or dotted all over, the dots sometimes in the form of a faint reticulum, white at very top (rarely deep rose to very top), rosy or rarely whitish in middle region, bright chrome yellow below; flesh firm, solid, light above, shading to deep chrome yellow below; mycelium chrome yellow.

Spores (of No. 10209) rosy brown or dull salmon, oblong-elliptic, smooth, 3.8–5 x 9.3–12.5μ.

This is a beautiful species, easily recognized by its rosy cap, scabrous dotted stem which is bright chrome yellow below, and the yellow mycelium. It is fairly common but is usually found singly.

COLOR PLATES

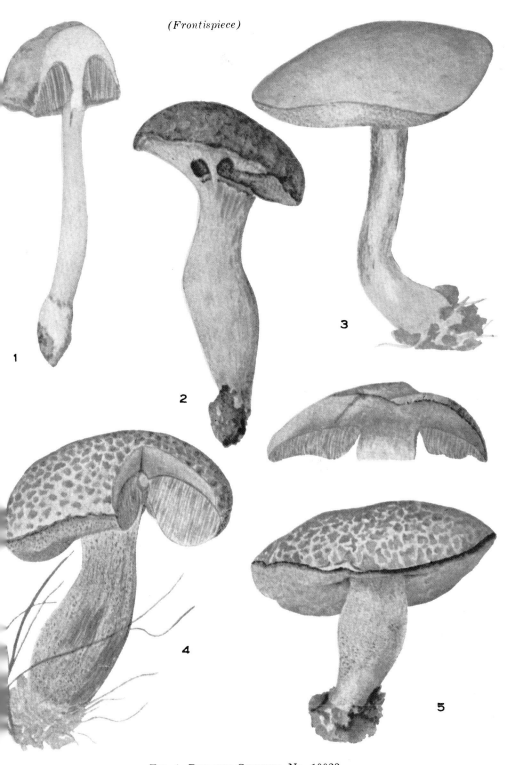

FIG. 1. BOLETUS CURTISII. No. 10023.
FIG. 2. B. RAVENELII. No. 4521.
FIG. 3. B. CHROMAPES. No. 3334.
FIGS. 4-6. B. RIMOSELLUS. Nos. 10666 and 4615. The stem is usually nearly
equal and often relatively longer.

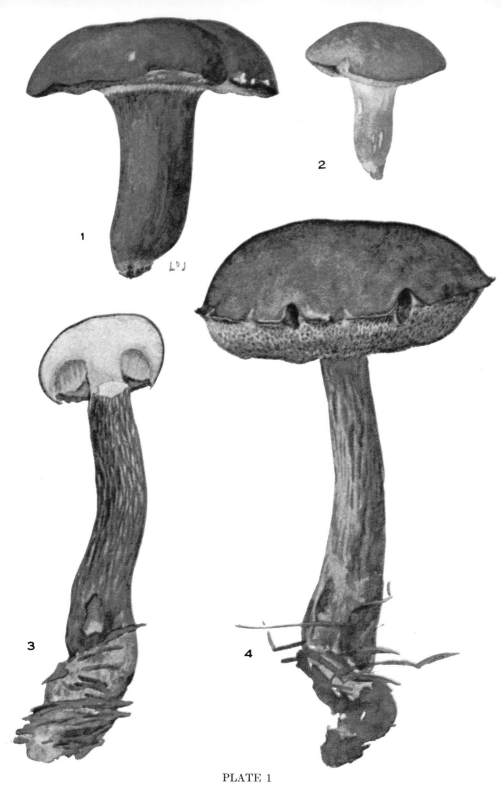

PLATE 1

Figs. 1 and 2.   Boletus subsanguineus.   No. 12812.   This is an unusual form with duller
   cap and brown stem.
Figs. 3 and 4.   B. projectellus.   Nos. 13193 and 13201.

PLATE 2

Figs. 1–3. Boletus auriflammeus. Highlands, N. C., Aug. 27, 1939.
Figs. 4, 5. B. Betula. Nos. 10681 and 10677, respectively.
Figs. 6–8. B. viridiflavus. Figs. 6 and 7, No. 10667; fig. 8, No. 9863.

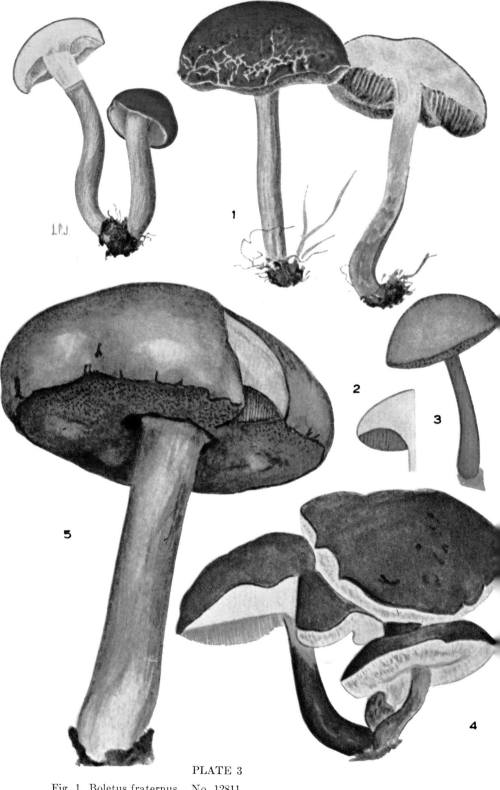

PLATE 3

Fig. 1. Boletus fraternus. No. 12811.
Figs. 2, 3. B. rubinellus. No. 3606.
Fig. 4. B. indecisus. No. 9869.
Fig. 5. B. luridus. No. 3329. Note: Stem usually more yellow.

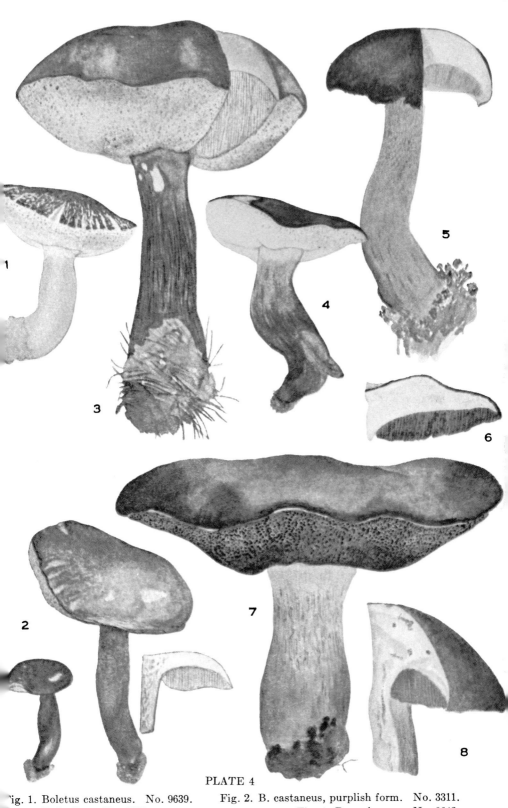

PLATE 4

Fig. 1. Boletus castaneus.   No. 9639.   Fig. 2. B. castaneus, purplish form.   No. 3311.
Fig. 3. B. badius.   No. 9623.   Fig. 4. B. auriporus.   No. 9642.
Figs. 5–8. B. auripes.   Fig. 5, No. 9817; Figs. 6 and 7, No. 4379; fig. 8, No. 4475.   The stem
    is usually brighter yellow in youth.

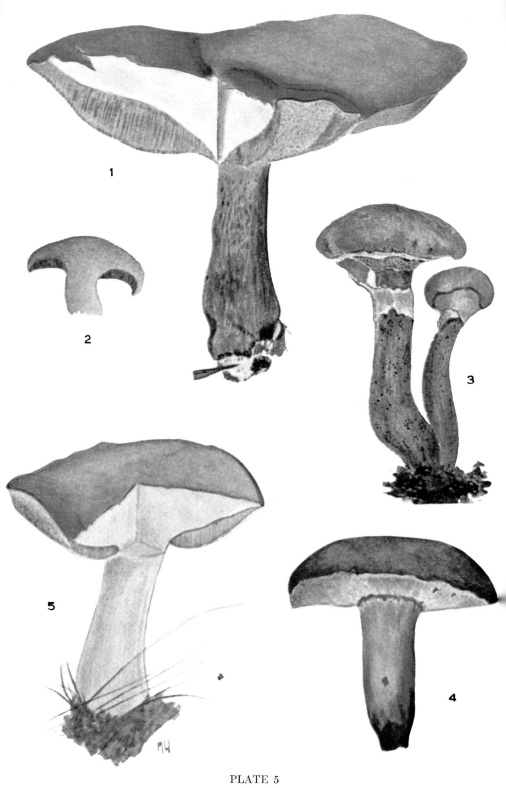

PLATE 5

Fig. 1. Boletus felleus. No. 10664. The stem is often less brown.
Figs. 2, 3. B. luteus. No. 3515.
Figs. 4, 5. B. pallidus. Nos. 4458 and 9820, respectively.

ILLUSTRATIONS: Atkinson. Mushrooms, pl. 53. 1900 (pl. 59 of 2nd ed., 1901). Not in color.
Farlow. Icones Farlowianae, pl. 87.

NORTH CAROLINA. Chapel Hill. No. 2208. Mixed woods, June 22, 1916. The spores of this collection were very variable in size, 4–6 x 9–15μ, nearly light ochraceous salmon (Ridg.) but a little darker, toward avellaneous. No. 3072. In low woods, May 20, 1918. No. 3334. In damp mixed woods, June 10, 1919. Typical. Spores 4.2–5.5 x 10–14μ. No. 10298. Mixed woods, Oct. 17, 1936.

Highlands. No. 10209. Mixed mountain woods with hemlocks, Aug. 23, 1936. No. 10541. On bank by road, Aug. 19, 1937. Spores fleshy brown, 3.8–5.2 x 10–12.8μ. No. 11753. Mixed woods, July 23, 1940. No. 12144. By road around Ravenel Lake, Aug. 11, 1939. Spores oblong-elliptic, 4–5 x 10–12.8μ.

Jackson County. No. 10940. In deciduous woods in Whiteside Cove, Aug. 17, 1938.

Also other collections from Highlands and Chapel Hill.

Asheville. Common. Beardslee.

Pink Bed Valley, Pisgah Forest. Murrill.

Boletus subsanguineus Peck. Bull. Torr. Bot. Club **27**: 17. 1900.

? *B. Ballouii* Peck. Bull. N. Y. St. Mus. **157**: 22–23, pl. 8. 1912.

Plate 1, figs. 1, 2; pls. 12, 13; pl. 61, fig. 11

Cap 5–12 cm. broad, convex but irregular and pitted and sometimes depressed in center, glabrous, slightly viscid, margin narrowly extended as a membrane, color brilliant and peculiar, from apricot orange to bittersweet or flame scarlet (Ridg.). Flesh up to 2.5 cm. thick near stem, firm, white or nearly so, turning lavender-straw, then darker vinaceous brown; taste subacid, odor slight.

Tubes short and small, up to 8 mm. long and about 2 to a mm., squarely adnate or depressed, often decurrent by lines, creamy white, then deeper flesh or straw color and brown when rubbed or on drying; tube surface sometimes pitted and irregular.

Stem up to 7 cm. long, usually short, up to 3 cm. thick at the flaring top and tapering downward to a point at base, white or yellowish at top and below, usually streaked with cap color in central region (sometimes white all over if protected, and in one of our plants brown except for narrow yellow band at top); marked at top by descending lines; flesh like that of cap, solid but becoming spongy and often hollowed by grubs at base.

Spores (of No. 8568) yellow-ochre, ovate-elliptic, broader near mucro end, thick-walled, 3.5–4 x 7–8.5μ.

This is a rare plant, having been reported from only a few places (Pennsylvania, New Jersey, North Carolina, Alabama, and also New York and Tennessee, if *Ballouii* is included as a synonym) since its original discovery. It is a handsome and conspicuous species, easily recognized by the bittersweet color of the cap, small, short, pale tubes which turn brown on being wounded or drying, and the short, thick-walled spores.

Two of our collections of this species came from the same spot (in a periwinkle bed under a beech tree) but several years apart. The first one and some plants of the second collection were typical *subsanguineus*, with the brilliant cap and whitish stem streaked with the cap color. Other plants of the later collection were much duller in cap color and one had the stem leaf brown all over except the apex (see Plate 1). This leaves practically no distinction except viscidity, which is not great in any case in normal weather, between this species and *B. Ballouii*, and we think they are very probably the same.

ILLUSTRATIONS: McIlvaine. Amer. Fungi, pl. 116, fig. 4.
Murrill. Mycologia **2**: pl. 19, fig. 4. 1910.

NORTH CAROLINA. Chapel Hill. No. 2289. In pine woods, June 28, 1916. Spores light ochre, usually broader near proximal end, 3.4–4.4 x 6–8μ. No. 2676. In oak grove, July 15, 1917. No. 5202. In pine needles in a road, June 19, 1922. Spores 3.5–4 x 6.5–9μ. No. 8568. In a periwinkle bed under a beech tree, July 13, 1931. No. 10026. In a hollow under a stump in almost complete darkness, Oct. 5, 1935. These specimens were distinctly cespitose, and were brilliantly colored. No. 11111. In path by Battle Branch, July 22, 1939. A poor specimen with cap surface partly eaten off but unmistakably this species. No. 12812. In a periwinkle bed under a beech tree, June 17, 1942.

Boletus Housei (Murrill) n. comb.
Ceriomyces Housei Murrill. N. Amer. Fl. **9**: 145. 1910.

Plate 61, fig. 12

We have never collected this interesting little species, but the original collections were made in our state (see below). The type now shows the cap rich brown, felted-tomentose; tubes very short, small. The spores are (our measurements) oval to short-elliptic, some broader near proximal end, smooth, 4–5.5 x 7.4–9.3μ, a few larger.
Added below is the original description.

Pileus convex above, nearly plane below, 3–4 cm. broad, 1 cm. thick; surface smooth, dry, minutely tomentose, chocolate-red with a velvety sheen; margin concolorous above, slightly overlapping the tubes, reddish beneath; context firm, solid, white, unchanging; tubes decurrent, never depressed, clear-yellow when young, dull-yellow with age, not changing when wounded, 2–4 mm. long, mouths of medium size, circular to oblong, never angled, edges thin, entire; spores smooth, oblong-ellipsoid, yellowish, with a large hyaline nucleus, 7–9 x 4–5; stipe central, cylindric, equal, subglabrous, yellow and distinctly reticulate above, dull chocolate-brown below, the base frequently mottled with yellow, solid and unchanging within, 3–5 cm. long, 5–8 mm. thick.

Type collected at the Pink Beds, North Carolina, July 6, 1909, on mossy banks in deciduous thickets, by H. D. House.

Boletus scaber Bull. Herb. Fr., pl. 132. 1782.

Plate 14 and pl. 61, fig. 14

Cap 4–13 cm. broad, convex to flat, often pitted or rugose, sometimes areolated, glabrous or minutely felted-tomentose (rarely with small tufts of tomentum), somewhat viscid when wet; color variable, from pallid straw through antimony yellow, tawny brown or grayish brown to blackish brown, and normally dark brown when bruised. Flesh 6–10 mm. thick near stem, white or creamy, unchanging or usually turning smoky rose or even brick red when cut and after a time blackish brown if strongly bruised; taste mild, odor none.

Tubes usually long, up to 18 mm., small, 2 or 3 to a mm., strongly convex on surface, deeply depressed at stem and free or nearly so, white when young, then tan or light brownish drab with tint of flesh color, darker when bruised.

Stem up to 11 cm. long, often crooked, subequal or tapering upward, relatively slender, surface color nearly white or grayish or pallid, conspicuously marked with reddish brown or blackish scabrous dots or ridges which vary in intensity (sometimes pale), and appearing as if a cottony surface had been quickly scorched or held in sooty smoke; flesh solid, whitish to brownish and sometimes turning bluish at base when broken.

Spores (of No. 9609) medium brown (Dresden brown in heavy print), smooth, *fusiform*, variable in size but always large, 4.8–6.5 x 15–19 (–21)μ.

This is one of our commonest and most variable species. Its most obvious character is the strongly scabrous-dotted stem which is dry, the dots not being formed by agglutinated resinous drops as in *B. granulatus*. Other distinguishing characters are the small, deeply depressed, white to tan or fleshy-gray-brown tubes, and the large fusiform spores. The various color forms have all been given varietal or even specific names. In his monograph (pp. 148–49), Peck gives ten varieties, seven of which are based on cap color. Snell (Mycologia **26:** 349. 1934) segregates several species in the *scaber* group and describes as *B. leucophaeus* Pers. a plant with dark brown to blackish, tomentose cap, and stem "somewhat darker than that of *B. scaber*, more rugose, with asperities nearly black." Our specimens from Rabun County, Georgia, are tomentose but only one collection has the dark cap, and furthermore the very dark dots on the stem are characteristic of our plants in most of the color forms. Except for the white form (*B. niveus*), we are unable to separate consistently any group, and are treating them all under the species *scaber*.

ILLUSTRATIONS: Bresadola. Icon. Mycol. **19:** pl. 936. 1931.

Bulliard. Herb. Fr., pl. 132.

Cordier. Champ. Fr., pl. 37. 1870.

Fries. Sveriges Svampar, pl. 14.

Gibson. Our Edible Toadstools and Mushrooms, pl. 21.

Gillet. Champ. Fr., Hymén., pl. 77.

Güssow and Odell. Mushrooms and Toadstools, pl. 96 (not in color).

Krieger. Mushroom Handbook, pl. 10. 1936.

McIlvaine. Amer. Fungi, pl. 118, fig. 4. (Stem exaggerated.)

Murrill. Journ. N. Y. Bot. Gard. **9:** pl. 54, fig. 5, 1908. Also in Mycologia **1:** pl. 1, fig. 5. 1909.

Palmer. Mushrooms of America, pl. 7, fig. 3. 1885.

Peck. Rept. N. Y. St. Mus. **48:** pl. 35. 1894 (1895).

NORTH CAROLINA. Chapel Hill. No. 1136. Low damp woods, July 12, 1914. Spores fusiform, 4.5–5.6 x 13–18.5 (–20)μ. No. 2450. In a swamp, Sept. 29, 1916. No. 4585. Mixed woods by Fern Walk, July 29, 1920. Highlands. No. 9572. In mossy grass, Aug. 26, 1932. Spores 5–6.5 x 14–18.5μ. No. 9609. By road around Ravenel Lake, Aug. 15, 1933. No. 10545. In mixed woods, Aug. 18, 1937. No. 12068. Moist soil near Trillium Lodge, Aug. 3, 1939. No. 12096. By trail to Kalalanta, Aug. 6, 1939. No. 12490. On roadside bank, Aug. 3, 1941. No. 12847. In sandy humus by road, July 21, 1942. Stem drab brown, its surface split into striations, flecks minute and inconspicuous.
Haywood County. No. 8079. Mixed woods by Pisgah Creek, Aug. 7, 1926. No. 10977. Sandy deciduous woods, Pink Beds, Aug. 23, 1938.
Also other collections in our herbarium from Chapel Hill and Highlands. Blowing Rock. Atkinson.
Low and middle districts. Curtis.

GEORGIA. Rabun County. No. 11921. Rich ravine on Big Creek, Aug. 22, 1940. No. 12409. Same locality as above, July 20, 1941. Both these collections were of the form with scabrous-tomentose cap.

Boletus niveus Fr. Obs. Myc. **1**: 111. 1815.

Plate 15 and pl. 61, fig. 15

Cap 3–10 cm. broad, convex to hemispheric, even or pitted, glabrous, sub-viscid, varying from pure milk white all over to faintly vinaceous pink or pale straw color. Flesh 6–10 mm. thick near stem, rapidly thinning to a sharp margin, white or nearly so, soft and delicate, almost tasteless (slightly acid), odor none.

Tubes 7–10 mm. long, about 2 to a mm., mouths not stuffed, deeply depressed at the stem and easily separating from it, white or nearly so, then light fleshy brown or clay-gray.

Stem long and slender, 7.5–11 cm. long, 5–7 mm. thick, equal or slightly tapering upward, pure white or stained with light vinaceous brown, entire surface covered with scurfy particles and lines which may be more or less reticulated above; flesh whitish, solid, fibrous; stem base connected with white, ropy mycelium.

Spores (of No. 12468) light brown in a faint print, elliptic-fusiform, smooth 4–5.3 x 13–16(–18.5)μ.

This species is very close to B. scaber and is often considered a form or variety of it. Fries himself treated it as a variety in his Hymenomycetes Europaei, and Peck described it as a variety at one time (N. Y. St. Mus. Rept. **38**: 110. 1885), then later as a species (N. Y. St. Mus. Bull. **122**: 140-141. 1908). There are intergrading forms, but typically the present species is more delicate, as well as differently colored, and has a less scurfy stem. Peck's B. albellus (N. Y. St. Mus. Rept. **41**: 77. 1888) is most probably the same as the smoother-stemmed specimens of the present species.

ILLUSTRATIONS: Peck. Bull. N. Y. St. Mus. **122** (61st Rept.): pl. 113. 1908.

NORTH CAROLINA. Chapel Hill. No. 4456. In sphagnum bed with base of plant in water, July 20, 1920. Spores long-elliptic to fusiform, 4.2–5 x 12.5–16μ. No. 4480. By Battle Branch, July 21, 1920. No. 4512. In damp soil among decaying leaves, July 25, 1920. No. 4528. In mixed woods, July 26, 1920.

Highlands. No. 12468. By trail to Trillium Lodge, July 31, 1941. Plant milk white all over when fresh. No. 13012. In a pasture, Aug. 20, 1942.

TENNESSEE. Near Gatlinburg, Aug. 21, 1939.

Boletus Ravenelii B. and C. Ann. Mag. Nat. Hist. II, **12**: 429. 1853.

Frontispiece, fig. 2; pl. 16; pl. 61, fig. 16

Cap up to 7.5 cm. broad, convex or nearly plane, usually dry but slightly viscid when moist, orange red or more brownish red in central region of cap, lighter and more yellow on the margin, covered all over when young with a bright lemon yellow or strontian yellow (Ridg.) fibrous powder which largely disappears by maturity, surface under the powder delicately felted-fibrous. Flesh whitish or yellow, becoming light blue then drab brown or dull yellowish when wounded; taste distinctly acid, odor quite peculiar, somewhat like hickory leaves.

Tubes up to 7 mm. long, about 2 to a mm., even, nearly circular, adnate, more or less depressed around the stem, about lemon yellow when young, then grayish yellow and finally yellow brown when dry, turning greenish blue, then drab brown or blackish when wounded.

Veil obvious as a soft fibrous yellow flocculent membrane that remains for a time as a pendent margin on the cap and as collapsed fibers near the top of the stem.

Stem 4.5–14.5 cm. long, 4–12 mm. thick, nearly equal or variously swollen, solid, surface covered with the same sulphur yellow powder as the cap, the base showing the whitish or yellow stringy mycelium.

Spores (of No. 9606) smoky olive in a good print, ovate-elliptic, narrowed toward the distal end, smooth, 4.2–4.8 x 8.5–10μ.

This is a peculiar and beautiful species easily recognized by the flocculent yellow veil and yellow powder that dusts the plant. It often grows in deep shade.

ILLUSTRATIONS: Farlow. Icones Farlowianae, pl. 78. 1929.

NORTH CAROLINA. Chapel Hill. No. 2699. On ground under pines, July 16, 1917. Spores subelliptic, broader toward mucro end, 4.3–5.2 x 9.3–11.2μ. No. 4613. Under pines, July 31, 1920. No. 11107. On a very rotten log, July 20, 1939.

Highlands. No. 8939. By Dillard road, July 28, 1931. No. 9580. In mixed mountain woods, Aug. 28, 1932. Spores medium brown, with olive tint, 4–5 x 9–11μ. No. 9606. Under rhododendron and hemlock, Aug. 15, 1933. No. 11925. In mixed mountain woods, Aug. 23, 1940.

Also other collections from above places.

Macon County. No. 10906. In Coweeta Experiment Forest, Aug. 12, 1938.

Jackson County. No. 12194. In humus under beech, Aug. 21, 1939.

Transylvania County. No. 12757. In rhododendron and kalmia woods, by Horsepasture River, Sept. 3, 1941.
Blowing Rock. Atkinson and Schrenk.
Pink Bed Valley, Pisgah Forest. Murrill.

SOUTH CAROLINA. Hartsville. No. 17. On ground among rotting pine rails, Sept. 9, 1916.

Boletus hemichrysus B. & C. Ann. Mag. Nat. Hist. II, **12:** 429–430. 1853, Also in Grevillea **1:** 35. 1872.

Plate 61, fig. 17

We have not collected this species in North Carolina, but Curtis reported it here, and the type locality is in South Carolina. We take the following description from Peck (Bull. N. Y. St. Mus. **2,** No. 8: 103-4. 1889):

Pileus convex, at length plane or irregularly depressed, floccose-squamulose, covered with a yellow powder, sometimes rimose, bright golden-yellow, flesh thick, *yellow*; tubes adnate or decurrent, yellow, becoming reddish-brown, the mouths large, angular; stem short, irregular, narrowed below, sprinkled with a yellow dust, yellowish tinged with red; mycelium yellow; spores oblong, minute, dingy-ochraceous.
Var. *mutabilis*. Flesh slightly changing to blue where wounded; stem reddish, yellow within, sometimes eccentric; spores oblong-elliptical, 3–4 x 7.6–8.9μ (his measurements were given in fractions of an inch).
Pileus 1.5 to 2.5 in. broad; stem about 1 in. long, 3 to 6 lines thick.

This species grows on the roots and stumps of pine. It is rare but has been found in New York, New Jersey, Florida, and Alabama, as well as the Carolinas. Dr. Dearness has reported the variety as growing "in cleft of a living trunk of *Quercus rubra* L., Rondeau Park, Ontario." This species seems near *B. sulphureus* Fr., which grows in clusters on sawdust (pine, according to Rea), but the tubes of the latter are shorter and smaller, and the stem much thicker.

We have in our herbarium only one specimen of this species, found on a pine stump at Green Cove Springs, Florida, by Murrill. In the dried state the cap is 7.6 cm. wide; tubes 10 mm. long, distinctly decurrent, mouths irregular, radially elongated near stem but not large; stem about 7 cm. long. The size of the tube mouths and length of stem thus depart from the usual description, but it is otherwise typical and undoubtedly the present species.

Boletus auriflammeus B. & C. Grevillea **1:** 36. 1872.

Plate 2, figs. 1–3; pl. 17; pl. 61, fig. 18

Single or cespitose; cap 2–7 cm., rarely 10.8 cm. broad, convex, rarely plane in age, regular, rich brownish orange in youth, becoming more chrome yellow (about Cadmium yellow, Ridgway) on margin or all over at maturity, pulverulent and strongly felted-tomentose, the felt becoming finely areolated, dry at maturity but slightly viscid when young; margin incurved. Flesh up to 2 cm. thick, cream colored, sometimes with pinkish tints near surface, unchanging; odorless and mild or with an acid taste.

Tubes medium to large, 1–2 mm. wide, up to 1.5 cm. long, depressed at stem but attached and decurrent, mouths when quite young deep chrome yellow, then bright crimson all over or in splotches, the crimson not due to powder, finally greenish yellow or darker with areas of crimson, sometimes almost no crimson present.

Stem up to 8 cm. long and 1.5 cm. thick, subequal, larger above or below, pinched at base and firmly rooted by strong white mycelial plates and cords, surface a beautiful chrome yellow all over, pulverulent, and strongly reticulated above or all over, the areas between long and narrow; flesh solid, firm, like that of cap.

Spores (of No. 10444) distinctly olivaceous, evenly elliptic, smooth, 3.7–4.5 x 8.5–11μ.

This is a rare and beautiful species, found first by Dr. M. A. Curtis, in North Carolina, probably at Hillsboro. The brilliant colors are indefinitely retained on drying. Specimens which show practically no crimson color on the tube mouths when collected will usually acquire this character after some exposure. Plants of this species, especially the stems, will stain the fingers yellow.

NORTH CAROLINA. Chapel Hill. No. 430. In woods, mostly deciduous, Oct. 8, 1912. No. 1242. In mixed woods, Sept. 22, 1914. No. 1757. In oak woods, Sept. 12, 1915. No. 11613. By Battle Branch below the theater, Aug. 31, 1940.

Highlands. No. 9638. In sandy clay soil, Aug. 19, 1933. Spores olive brown, 3.7–4.3 x 8.5–11μ. No. 10444. On bank at entrance to Sloan place, July 23, 1937. No. 10868. On a bank under chestnuts, Aug. 6, 1938. No. 12574. In deep humus, Aug. 14, 1941. Spores light olive in a medium print, elliptic, smooth, 3.8–4.5 x 8.5–10.5μ.

Also many other collections from Chapel Hill and Highlands.

Franklin County. No. 12990. Mixed pine woods, Aug. 18, 1942.

Asheville. Beardslee.

Pisgah Forest. Murrill.

GEORGIA. Rabun County. No. 11915. By Big Creek, Aug. 22, 1940.

Boletus griseus Frost. Rept. N. Y. St. Mus. **29**: 45. 1878.
? *B. flexuosipes* Peck. Bull. N. Y. St. Mus. **2**, No. 8: 130. 1889.

Plate 18 and pl. 62, fig. 1

Cap 5–13(–16) cm. broad, convex, buffy gray or drab gray all over or darker in center, dry, delicately tomentose in youth, like chamois, becoming quite glabrous in part; narrow margin free. Flesh rather thick, up to 1.5 cm. near stem, firm, grayish white or dull yellowish, becoming pinkish or brown on long exposure when cut; taste mild, faintly sweetish, odor mild, a delicate fruit fragrance.

Tubes small, about 2 to a mm., irregular, 5–14 mm. long, typically adnate but sometimes depressed around the stem and also slightly decurrent, whitish when young, then pallid gray-clay at maturity, brown when bruised.

Stem 5–8 cm. long, about 1.3–1.5(–2.8) cm. thick, subequal, often crooked and strongly pointed at the bent base; surface distinctly reticulated all or nearly all over, the ground color being pallid grayish or yellowish to distinctly yellow and the reticulations darker, brown when bruised.

Spores (of No. 8912) dull clay brown, Dresden brown (Ridg.), evenly elliptic, 3.5–4 x 9–12μ.

This is a rare plant in Chapel Hill but more common in the mountains. It is characterized by its nearly smooth, dry, buffy gray or darker cap and its stem distinctly reticulated with darker lines over a pale gray or yellowish surface. The yellowish ground color of the stem usually shows well in the dried state.

We are not sure of the identity of *B. flexuosipes*, which was described from North Carolina, but think it very probable that Murrill was right in placing it under the present species. The type cannot be found, but the description is in close agreement.

ILLUSTRATIONS: Hard. Mushrooms, fig. 302. 1908. (Not in color.)

NORTH CAROLINA. Chapel Hill. No. 8236. In upland deciduous woods, Sept. 23, 1927. No. 10020. Among shrubbery, Sept. 13, 1935. Spores dull brown with slight olive tint, 3.6–4 x 10–13μ. No. 11116. Battle Park, Aug. 3, 1939. No. 11607. Mixed woods in pasture, Aug. 25, 1940.
Highlands. No. 8912. Under deciduous trees, July 26, 1931. No. 9764. In grass in a yard, Aug. 12, 1934. Spores subelliptic, one side slightly more swollen, 3.5–3.8 x 9.5–12.5μ. No. 10816. In open deciduous woods, July 27, 1938. No. 11772. In deciduous woods, July 28, 1940. No. 11900. In open deciduous woods, Aug. 20, 1940. Spores clay brown with slight olive tint, 3.5–4 x 10–12.5μ. Also other collections from Highlands.
Chatham County. No. 10786. In deciduous woods on right of road from Chapel Hill to Pittsboro, July 5, 1938.
Asheville. Beardslee.
Blowing Rock. Atkinson.
Pink Bed Valley, Pisgah Forest. Murrill.

Boletus retipes B. and C. Grevillea **1**: 36. 1872.
B. ornatipes Peck. Rept. N. Y. St. Mus. **29**: 67. 1878.

Plate 19 and pl. 62, fig. 2

Single or often cespitose; cap 6–14(–20) cm. broad, convex, rather thick, dry, firm, varying from shades of yellow (dull mustard, yellow ocher, etc.) through yellow brown, such as old gold or Dresden brown (Ridg.), to gray-drab, with or without a tint of olive, subtomentose or smooth at maturity, often with a dry yellow powder, normally not viscid but rarely so in wet weather; narrow sterile margin (about 1 mm.). Flesh thick and firm, pale or clear yellow when cut and turning deep golden yellow, slightly or distinctly bitter, as is the cap surface when touched by the tongue.

Tubes about 1 cm. long and 0.5–1 mm. wide, rarely larger, adnate but often deeply depressed around the stem, not truly stuffed when young but so crowded and folded together as to obliterate the openings, deep clear yellow at first, becoming golden yellow with olive tint in age and turning slowly brownish or reddish brown when bruised; tube surface slightly pitted from unequal tube lengths. Stem up to 10 cm. long and 2.5 cm. thick in center, nearly equal or somewhat tapering either way, colored like the tubes and *strongly reticulated* all over or with base smooth, sometimes with yellow surface powder, and with olivaceous gold mycelium at base; flesh solid and firm, golden yellow.

Spores (of No. 10515) bright yellow olive (darker and more rusty brown in very heavy prints) or about Isabella color (Ridg.), rather evenly elliptic except for oblique mucro, 3.7–4.2 x 10–12.5μ.

This is one of the commoner species, both in Chapel Hill and Highlands, growing in woods and on roadside banks. The average large size, colors, and especially the strongly reticulated stem are distinguishing features. The variable cap color runs into two distinct forms, yellow and gray, and the flesh is golden yellow on exposure. The plant stains the hands yellow when handling it.

ILLUSTRATIONS: Farlow. Icones Farlowianae, pl. 83. (As *B. ornatipes*).
Güssow and Odell. Mushrooms and Toadstools, pl. 95 (not in color).
Murrill. Mycologia **7**: pl. 160, fig. 7. 1915.
Peck. Bull. N. Y. St. Mus. **54**: pl. 80, figs. 1–5. 1902. (As *B. ornatipes*).
Also in Rept. **55**, same plate. 1903.

NORTH CAROLINA. Chapel Hill. No. 236. In Battle Park, near branch, Sept. 21, 1905. Spores 3.7–4.8 x 9.3–13μ. No. 710. Battle Park, June 20, 1913. Spores 4–5 x 9–12μ. No. 1644. In leaves, mixed woods, July 26, 1915. Fine plants all arising from a single rhizomorph. Cap shining in places, dull and slightly powdery-tomentose elsewhere. No. 9813. In sand-clay soil by Gimghoul Road, Sept. 25, 1934. No. 11609. June 15, 1940. Very early. Highlands. No. 8928. In humus by Ravenel Lake, July 27, 1931. Spores ochraceous with olive tint, 3.6–4.2 x 8.5–12μ. No. 10515. On bank by road, Aug. 11, 1937. No. 12428. In deciduous woods above Sunset Rock, July 24, 1941. Very small specimen, only 3.8 cm. wide, but otherwise typical. No. 12573. On bank by road to Sunset Rock, Aug. 14, 1941. Cap distinctly tomentose.
Haywood County. No. 8080. In rhododendron woods by Pisgah Creek, Aug. 7, 1926.
Transylvania County. No. 12767. Mixed mountain woods by Horsepasture River, Sept. 3, 1941.
Also many other collections from Chapel Hill and Macon County.
Blowing Rock. Atkinson and Schrenk.
Pink Bed Valley, Pisgah Forest. Murrill.
Middle district. Curtis.

Boletus auripes Peck.   Rept. N. Y. St. Mus. **50**: 107.   1897.

B. crassipes Peck.   Bull. Torr. Bot. Club **27**: 19.   1900.

Plate 4, figs. 5–8, and pl. 62, fig. 3

Cap 7–15 cm. broad, rarely up to 22 cm., convex to plane or with center slightly depressed, in youth a very dark, velvety, handsome chestnut brown, at maturity becoming much lighter clay color (Ridg.) with olive tint, surface like kid, taking the imprint of a finger, sometimes minutely rimose in age, dry, with narrow sterile margin.   Flesh soft, 1.3–1.5 cm. thick (up to 4 cm. in our 22 cm. plant), *yellow* to creamy yellow; taste mild and pleasant, odor mild.

Tubes up to 3 cm. long in the large plants, 1–3 to a mm. (many more small than large), depressed around the stem, almost free (rarely adnate), creamy yellow and conspicuously stuffed when young, appearing as if covered by a yellow membrane, passing through clear chrome yellow to yellow-brown in age.

Stem up to 9 cm. long, up to 3.8 cm. thick above when somewhat flattened, tapering downward or in some cases enlarged near base, clear *golden yellow*, glabrous, reticulated above and lightly so downward with slightly darker fibrils, becoming duller brownish yellow on handling or exposure; flesh yellow.

Spores (of No. 9805) strongly olive when fresh, cylindrical-elliptic or slightly sway-backed, smooth, 3.7–4.2 x 11–13μ.

Characterized by deep brown velvety cap when young, becoming much paler at maturity, bright yellow tubes, stem, and flesh, and stem reticulated with darker lines above.   Some forms of *retipes* approach this in appearance, but in that species the color of tubes and stem is much less bright yellow, the stem is more strongly reticulated, and the tubes are not stuffed.

ILLUSTRATIONS: McIlvaine.   Amer. Fungi, pl. 116, fig. 5 (as *B. crassipes*).

NORTH CAROLINA.   Chapel Hill.   No. 3118.   In pasture by New Hope Creek, June 22 and 23, 1918.   Spores elliptic to subventricose, 3.4–4.2 x 10–13μ. No. 4379.   Damp mixed woods, July 9, 1920.   Spores 3.2–4.2 x 9.2–12.5μ. No. 4475.   Under magnolia tree in arboretum, July 21, 1920.   No. 9805. Under willow oak, Sept. 24, 1934.   No. 9817.   Same spot as above, Sept. 21, 1934.

Highlands.   No. 9842.   In open place by "Trillium Lodge," Aug. 29, 1934. No. 10571.   On a lawn, Aug. 23, 1937.   Spores strongly olive, 3.7–4.5 x 10–13μ.   No. 12618.   In grass in Episcopal churchyard, Aug. 18, 1941. One cap was 23 cm. wide.   No. 12889.   Same spot as above, July 29, 1942.   Pores covered as with a blanket.

Also many other collections from Chapel Hill and Highlands.

GEORGIA.   Rabun County.   No. 11956.   In rich cove by Big Creek, Aug. 27, 1940.

Boletus affinis Peck.   Bull. Buf. Soc. Nat. Sci. **1**: 59. 1873.   Also in Rept. N. Y. St. Mus. **25**: 81.   1873.

Plate 20 and pl. 62, fig. 4

Single, gregarious or slightly cespitose; cap up to 14 cm. broad, usually about 6–8 cm., convex, then plane with slight irregularities and rugose patches, about bay (Ridg.), or darker (sepia) when young, with lighter àreas shading into hazel or yellowish brown, subtomentose or practically glabrous, dry. Flesh 1–1.5 cm. thick near stem, rather firm, white, unchanging when cut but old grub channels yellowish or dull reddish.

Tubes up to 1.5 cm. long, small to medium, 2 or 3 to a mm., squarely attached or depressed at stem, mouths angular or roundish, apparently lightly stuffed but only tightly packed and folded, white or pale flesh in youth, becoming sordid yellowish buff in age, turning yellow or brownish when bruised; tube surface slightly pitted from uneven tube length.

Stem 4–5(–8) cm. long, 1–2.5 cm. thick at top, tapering downward and pointed at base, color of tubes at top and bottom (or more white at base), concolorous with cap or paler in central region where the color may be in streaks, sometimes minutely tomentose below; flesh solid, white.

Spores (of No. 9749) rich *rusty ochre*, no tint of olive, long-elliptic to subventricose, 3.4–4 x 8.5–12μ.

The reddish brown or yellowish brown cap, paler stem, white, unchanging flesh, small, yellow-brown tubes (whitish in youth), and bright rusty ochre spores are distinguishing characters. If well dried the plants retain a characteristic bright tint of rusty brown. When fresh they do not disintegrate readily and remain in good condition for several days, even in wet weather.

We have compared our specimens with Peck's and find them identical. The average smaller size, the ochraceous instead of greenish tubes and spores, and the smoother stem which tapers downward to a point at base separate this from *B. edulis*. See *B. indecisus* for comparison with that species.

ILLUSTRATIONS: Peck. Rept. N. Y. St. Mus. **49:** pl. 48, figs. 6–13. 1895 (1896)· Mem. N. Y. St. Mus. **3,** No. 4 (Edible Fungi): pl. 66, figs. 7–11. 1900.

NORTH CAROLINA. Chapel Hill. No. 1625. On rotting wood, July 21, 1915. Spores 3.5–3.8 x 9.3–13μ. No. 4563. Mixed woods, July 25, 1920. Spores 3.6–4.8 x 8–12μ, a few larger. No. 11617. Mixed woods, Battle Park, Sept. 1, 1940.

Highlands. No. 9616. By road in open mixed woods, Aug. 16, 1933. Spores slightly ventricose, 3.7–4.5 x 10–12μ. No. 9749. By road around Ravenel Lake, Aug. 10, 1934. No. 10196. On bank by Ravenel Lake, Aug. 22, 1936. Typical. Spores bright rust color, 3.6–4 x 9.5–13μ. No. 12434. Under hemlock hedge, July 25, 1941.

Also many other collections in our herbarium from Chapel Hill and Highlands. Henderson County. Near East Flat Rock. No. 10490. Macon County. Standing Indian. No. 10963. Pisgah Forest. No. 10988.

TENNESSEE. Near Gatlinburg. No. 12188. At foot of a birch tree, Aug. 21, 1939.

Boletus affinis var. **maculosus** Peck. Rept. N. Y. St. Mus. **32:** 57. 1879. ?*B. leprosus* Peck. Bull. N. Y. St. Mus. **2,** No. 8: 135. 1889.

Plate 20 (lower left fig.) and pl. 62, fig. 5

This variety differs mainly in having whitish or yellowish spots scattered irregularly over the cap, but in some collections there are certain other slight differences, such as in the cap color which may be seal brown (like that of *Lac-*

tarius ligniotus) or olive brown, and also the spores may show an olivaceous tint, never seen in those of the species.

Boletus leprosus was described from North Carolina, but the type has been lost and we feel uncertain of its identity. It may be the same as the present variety but there are some discrepancies. However, it is well to remember that the description by Peck was apparently based on only one collection (sent him in the dried state), together with notes, made by C. J. Curtis, and further study of the fresh condition might have made it necessary to amend the original description.

ILLUSTRATIONS: Peck. Rept. N. Y. St. Mus. **49:** pl. 48, figs. 14–16. 1896. Mem. N. Y. St. Mus. **3,** No. 4 (Edible Fungi): pl. 66, figs. 12–14, 1900.

NORTH CAROLINA. Highlands. No. 8826. In mixed woods, July 23, 1931. No. 9598. By trail to Primeval Forest, Sept. 1, 1932. Spores ochraceous with faint olive tint, 3.5–4 x 10–13μ. No. 11899. In deciduous woods, Aug. 20, 1940. No. 12435. Rich mixed woods, July 25, 1941. Spores yellow-ochre with no olive tint. Also other collections from Highlands.

Boletus edulis Bull.   Herb. Fr., pl. 60, 1781; pl. 494, 1790.

Plate 21 and pl. 62, fig. 6

Cap medium to quite large, up to 22 cm. wide, convex, often rugosely pitted, glabrous, dry, slightly viscid when moistened, color varying from light buff or biscuit color, sometimes with greenish yellow margin, to deep reddish buff or yellow brown, surface dull or shining in places, sometimes rimose-areolated in age. Flesh thick, up to 2 cm., white and unchanging; taste pleasant, sweet and nutty, odor none or slight.

Tubes up to 2 cm. long, mouths small, 2–3 to a mm., depressed, often deeply so, white and conspicuously stuffed in youth as if covered by a complete white membrane, becoming greenish yellow, maturing from the stem outward, finally clay brown.

Stem 6–14 cm. long, stout, subequal or enlarged below, rarely above, whitish to concolorous with cap but usually paler, partially or wholly reticulated, very rarely smooth; flesh solid and firm, white or yellowish.

Spores (of No. 11888) deep olive brown in a thick print, fusiform-elliptic, smooth, 4–5 x 12–14.8μ.

This is a common and well known edible species, distinguished by buff to reddish brown, glabrous cap, white, unchanging flesh, small, white, conspicuously stuffed tubes when young, and the rather large olivaceous spores. See *B. separans* and *B. variipes*, which are very near, for comparisons.

This species has been so frequently illustrated that we list below only a few pictures, which are easily accessible and seem to show rather well the plants as we find them.

ILLUSTRATIONS: Boyer. Champ. Comest., pl. 43. 1891.
Bulliard. Herb. Fr., pls. 60 and 494.
Cooke. Brit. Edible Fungi, pl. 10, fig. 33.
Dufour. Atl. Champ., pl. 55. 1891.

Gibson. Our Edible Toadstools and Mushrooms, pl. 20. 1895.
Kallenbach. Die Pilze Mitteleuropas 1: pl. 54.
Krieger. Nat. Geog. Mag. 37, No. 5: pl. 4, May 1920; also Mushroom Handbook, pl. 7. 1936.
Palmer. Mushrooms of America, pl. 7, fig. 2. 1885.
Peck. Rept. N. Y. St. Mus. 48: pl. 36, figs. 8–12 (these may include the *separans* form); 51: pl. 54, 1898; N. Y. St. Mus. Mem. 3, No. 4: pl. 65, 1900.
Rolland. Atl. Champ. Fr., pl. 81. 1910.

NORTH CAROLINA. Chapel Hill. No. 737. In rich woods, summer, 1913. No. 11088. In wooded pasture, July 12, 1939. Spores ventricose-elliptic, smooth, 4.3–5 x 12–14.5μ. No. 11596. In mixed woods, Aug. 25, 1940. Highlands. No. 11784. In open woods near Kettle Rock, July 29, 1940. No. 11838. In deciduous woods near Camp Calhoun, Aug. 8, 1940. No. 11888. Low flat deciduous woods, Aug. 18, 1940. Toxaway Station. In deciduous open grove, Aug. 24, 1940. Also many other collections from Chapel Hill and Highlands in our herbarium.

GEORGIA. Rabun County. No. 11953. In rich ravine by Walhalla road, Aug. 27, 1940.

Boletus separans Peck. Bull. Buf. Soc. Nat. Sci. 1: 59. 1873. Also Rept. N. Y. St. Mus. 25: 81. 1873.

Plate 22 (above) and pl. 62, fig. 9

This was first considered by Peck to be a marked variety of *B. edulis*, and in some cases it is certainly difficult to separate them. However, we think it will do no harm to retain Peck's name, as the extreme forms of the two are quite distinct in appearance. The typical form of *separans* is distinguished by brownish lilac or purplish red cap, adnate tubes which separate from the stem, often leaving fibers connecting them or sticking out from the stem as small free bristles, and the rhubarb or more strongly lilac colored stem. We have also noticed in some of our collections the strong acid odor which Peck mentions for the dried plants. Other slight differences which are probably of no significance are that in *separans* the stem is more often enlarged *upward* than it is in *edulis*, and there is apparently less greenish tint in the tubes and spores. Nevertheless intergrading forms occur and make the specific distinctions rather obscure.

Spores (of No. 9826) ochraceous brown with little or no olive, subfusiform, smooth, 4.2–5.8 x 11–14.8μ.

ILLUSTRATION: McIlvaine. Amer. Fungi, pl. 118, fig. 1 (stem longer than in our plants).

NORTH CAROLINA. Chapel Hill. No. 11618. In pasture, Aug. 25, 1940. Highlands. No. 9826. In open old field, Aug. 25, 1934. No. 10492. On bank by road, Aug. 11, 1937. Cap 31 cm. broad. Spores subfusiform, 4.5–5.5 x 11.5–15μ. No. 10530. On lawn of Tricemont Terrace, Aug.

13, 1937. No. 10597. In open grassy chestnut woods, Aug. 26, 1937. No. 11785. In deciduous woods near Kettle Rock, July 29, 1940. No. 11895. Low deciduous woods, Aug. 17, 1940. Also numerous other collections from Highlands in our herbarium.

Transylvania County. No. 12758. In rhododendron-kalmia woods, by Horsepasture River, Sept. 3, 1941.

Boletus variipes Peck. Rept. N. Y. St. Mus. **41**: 76. 1888.
B. Atkinsoni Peck. Bull. N. Y. St. Mus. **94**: 20. 1905.

Plate 23 and pl. 62, figs. 7, 8

Cap up to 12.5 cm. broad, convex to nearly plane or irregular, dry, minutely tomentose to squamulose, usually areolated, the tomentum sometimes gathered all over into small flakes or warts as in *Scleroderma lycoperdoides*; color light grayish brown or more yellowish, nearly clay color (Ridg.), sometimes with vinaceous areas toward the margin, which is thin, sterile and inflexed. Flesh up to 2 cm. thick, soft, often almost cottony when dry, white and unchanging or slowly pinkish; taste mild and pleasant, odor faintly sweetish.

Tubes up to 1.8 cm. long, small to medium, 0.4–1 mm. wide, typically adnate but varying to depressed or slightly decurrent, subrotund, at first white and distinctly stuffed, then greenish yellow.

Stem up to 15 cm. long, usually less, and 2.5 cm. thick above, enlarging downward or rarely subequal, concolorous or usually a peculiar pallid liver color, rarely stained with rose, often white toward base, conspicuously lined and with faint to distinct reticulum of darker fibrils all over or at least above; flesh solid.

Spores (of No. 10141) distinctly olive brown in a good print, smooth, subventricose to elliptic, 4–4.8 x 11–13μ.

This species is very close to *B. edulis*, from which it differs in tomentose to squamulose cap, more grayish brown color, and adnate tubes. The squamulose cap and different colors also separate it from *B. separans*.

ILLUSTRATIONS: Peck. Bull. N. Y. St. Mus. **94**: pl. R (as *B. Atkinsoni*). 1905.

NORTH CAROLINA. Chapel Hill. No. 10141. In Battle Park, deciduous woods, July 14, 1936. No. 10632. On roadside bank in deciduous woods, Sept. 5, 1937. No. 11595. In mixed woods, Aug. 25, 1940.

Highlands. No. 8918. Under rhododendron in a yard, July 27, 1931. Spores 3.8–5 x 11–13.5μ. No 9827. On a clay bank by road, Aug. 26, 1934. Spores 3.8–4.8 x 10–12.5μ. No. 11885. Mixed upland woods, not coniferous, Aug. 18, 1940.

Also a number of other collections from Chapel Hill and Highlands.

Jackson County. No. 12922. On bank by Chattooga River, Aug. 7, 1942.

SOUTH CAROLINA. Near Walhalla. No. 12125. In deciduous woods, Aug. 9, 1939.

GEORGIA. Rabun County. No. 12420. At parking place near top of Rabun Bald Mt., July 22, 1941.

Boletus eximius Peck. Journ. Myc. **3**: 54–55. 1887.

B. robustus Frost. Bull. Buf. Soc. Nat. Sci. **2**: 104. 1874. (Not *B. robustus* Fr.)

B. scabripes Peck. Bull. Torr. Bot. Club **29**: 555. 1902.

Plate 24 and pl. 62, fig. 10

Cap up to 12 cm. broad, hemispheric when young, continuing strongly convex or becoming plane, rather regular but characteristically somewhat pitted, surface glabrous, taking the imprint of a finger, not viscid except in very wet weather, then becoming slimy and staining the fingers yellow, color at all ages brownish purple with a distinct whitish bloom that disappears after heavy rains, margin free, whitish and typically inturned when young. Flesh up to 2 cm. thick, rather firm, whitish or pale brownish with purplish tints above, grub channels dar¹ brown; odor of rotting wood or rancid oil and taste similar or bitterish.

Tubes up to 1.7 cm. long, very minute, about 3 to a mm., tissue between openings quite thick, mouths practically closed in youth, dark brownish purple to nearly black (tube flesh the same color), usually darker than the cap but of the same tone or less reddish and retaining this color until maturity, then ochraceous brown with purple tints in places, the tube surface showing a strong tendency to be quite irregularly pitted and folded in areas.

Stem 4.5–9 cm. long, 1.3–2.8 cm. thick, crooked, nearly equal but slightly smaller at top and bottom, often somewhat flattened or grooved, color same as of tubes but given by minute purplish flecks or scales over a much paler purplish gray background, the scales sometimes so numerous as to make the stem quite dark, the entire effect being that of purplish gray with darker flecks; flesh firm and solid, colored like the surface; base firmly attached by obvious white mycelium which holds the earth.

Spores (of No. 10192) strongly yellow-brown or in thick plac es on print red-brown (no tint of olive), becoming more red-brown in the herbarium, rod-elliptic, smooth, 3.4–4 x 11–14(–14.8)μ.

This is a handsome species strongly marked by the grayish purple-brown stem entirely covered with minute flecks and by the color of the tubes and tube flesh. The spores of No. 10812 were deep rust brown in a heavy print where evenly scattered over the paper but where there were piles of spores they were distinctly purplish.

ILLUSTRATIONS: Farlow. Icones Farlowianae, pl. 84.

Peck. Bull. N. Y. St. Mus. **54**: pl. 80, figs. 6–12. 1902. Also in Rept. **55**, same plate. 1903 (for 1901).

NORTH CAROLINA. Highlands. No. 9522. By Ravenel Lake, Aug. 21, 1932. No. 10192. Under hemlock hedge by Ravenel Lake, Aug. 22, 1936. No. 10812. On rhododendron bank, July 26, 1938. Spores long-elliptic, smooth, 3.8–4.5 x 11–13μ. No. 12487. In mixed deciduous and pine woods, Aug. 2, 1941. Also many other collections from Highlands. Transylvania County. No. 12718. On a hemlock root by Horsepasture River, Aug. 28, 1941.

GEORGIA. Rabun County. No. 12553. Mixed woods by Bascom Caves, Aug. 12, 1941.

Boletus piperatus Bull. Herb. Fr., pl. 451, fig. 2. 1789.

Plate 25 and pl. 62, figs. 11, 12

Cap 1.8–5.5 cm. wide, hemispheric, fibrous-felted but soon glabrous except on margin, slightly viscid, terra cotta red all over. Flesh thick for size of cap, 5 mm. at edge of stem, sordid cream color or with tint of rose, slightly darker when cut, rather firm and solid; taste remarkable, extremely peppery like red pepper.

Tubes irregular in size and shape, about 3 mm. long, 2–3 to a mm. when young, but those near the stem becoming much larger with mouths elongated radially, adnate to decurrent, not stuffed when young, deep reddish brown, sometimes with purplish tint toward the margin, becoming darker when bruised, *flesh of tubes* also reddish brown.

Stem about 4 cm. long and 4.5 mm. thick, nearly equal at maturity or pointed at base, often bent, color of cap but slightly paler, almost smooth, not reticulated, base with a ball of bright golden yellow mycelium; flesh solid, yellowish with tints of reddish especially at top.

Spores (of No. 8140) deep brown, elliptic-subfusiform, smooth, 3–3.5 x 6–9μ.

This species is rare with us, but when found is easily determined by its small size, red tubes, and especially by the peppery taste. See *B. rubinellus* for further discussion.

ILLUSTRATIONS: Batsch. Elenchus Fungorum, pl. 25, fig. 128 (as *B. ferruginatus*).
Bulliard. Herb. Fr., pl. 451, fig. 2.
Dufour. Atlas Champ., pl. 60, fig. 132. 1891.
Farlow. Icones Farlowianae, pl. 77, lower right figs.
Flora Danica, pl. 1850, fig. 2.
Konrad and Maublanc. Icon. Selectae Fung., pl. 419, fig. 1.
Rolland. Atlas Champ. Fr., pl. 79, fig. 176. 1910.
Sowerby. Engl. Fungi, pl. 34.

NORTH CAROLINA: Haywood County. No. 8004. In mixed rhododendron woods, Aug. 3, 1926. Spores subelliptic, ends slightly pointed, 3.5–3.8 x 7.4–9.5μ. No. 8012a. Mixed woods by Crawford's Creek Aug. 4, 1926. No. 8039. In deciduous woods, by Cold Creek, Aug. 6, 1926. Spores 3–3.5 x 6.5–9μ. No. 8140. On earth, mixed woods by Crawford's Creek, Aug. 2, 1926.
Low and middle districts. Woods. Curtis.
"In humidis graminosis." Schweinitz.

Boletus rubinellus Peck. Rept. N. Y. St. Mus. **32**: 33. 1879.
B. rubritubifer Kauff. Bull. N. Y. St. Mus. **179**: 88–89. 1915.

Plate 3, figs. 2, 3, and pl. 62, figs. 13, 14

Cap 2–4.2 cm. broad, strongly convex, dry, not viscid except in quite wet weather, dull or subshining, with the appearance of leather and very finely punctate-tomentose under a lens, color buffy leather with a reddish tint, especially in center, more reddish in youth; margin very thin, projecting a little beyond the tubes. Flesh relatively thick, rapidly thinning to the margin, tender, pale yellowish, at times with a rosy tint near the tubes; taste mild and very pleasant, odor none.

Tubes 4–6 mm. long, shorter at stem and margin, squarely attached at stem or depressed there, irregular, the mouths about 0.4–1 mm. wide; color a deep red, about Pompeian red throughout, *flesh of tubes as well as mouths.*

Stem short, small, 2–3.5 cm. long and 5–6 mm. thick, equal, glabrous-looking but finely punctate under a lens, the upper end more strongly so, color of tubes all over or with yellowish areas; flesh pale yellowish, firm, succulent, solid.

Spores (of No. 9858) rusty brown, narrowly elliptic, smooth, 3–3.8 x 8.5–12μ.

We have compared our specimens with a collection from Friendship, Maine, in the Peck Herbarium and find them alike in appearance and spores. Peck's colored figures in his herbarium (unpublished) show the tube flesh as well as the mouths red. Beardslee also mentions the fact that the tubes are red within in *B. rubinellus* (*in* Lloyd, Myc. Notes, p. 543. 1916). This leaves no distinction of importance between *B. rubinellus* and *B. rubritubifer.* Kauffman's original description of the latter says stem "dingy apricot yellow," while Peck described the stem of *rubinellus* as "yellow with reddish stains." In a later and fuller description (Bull. N. Y. St. Mus. **2,** No. 8: 101. 1889) Peck gave the stem as "colored like the tubes, . . . sometimes yellow at thè base."

The species, as we have it, is characterized by small size, quite convex cap, which is subtomentose, leather colored to reddish, mild taste, and by the tubes in which the *flesh* is red. The species is very close to *piperatus,* differing mainly in mild taste, more tomentose cap, and longer spores. There is also usually a slight difference in the colors of the cap. Since Bulliard's original illustration shows the flesh of the tubes as red as the mouths, and the taste of the European *piperatus* is said to be sometimes mild, *rubinellus* may be only a form. The bruised flesh of both species may turn paper bright rose.

ILLUSTRATIONS: Farlow. Icones Farlowianae, pl. 77, lower left figs.

Peck. Bull. N. Y. St. Mus. **1,** No. 2: pl. 2, figs. 20–22. 1887. (Not in color.)

NORTH CAROLINA. Chapel Hill. No. 3606. Under pines in a pasture, Nov. 6, 1919. Spores rather narrowly elliptic, 3.2–3.7(–4) x 9–12.5μ. No. 5199. In pine needles, June 13, 1922. No. 9858. Under pines, Sept. 22, 1934. No. 11614. By path in Battle Park, mixed woods, Aug. 31, 1940. Spores medium brown, 3.4–3.7 x 8.5–12μ.

Boletus parvus Peck. Bull. Torr. Bot. Club **24**: 145–146. 1897.

Plate 62, fig. 15

Since we have collected this species only once and our notes are incomplete, we give below the original description.

Pileus convex, becoming plane, often slightly umbonate, subtomentose, reddish, flesh yellowish white, slowly changing to pinkish where wounded; tubes nearly plane, adnate, their mouths rather large, angular, at first bright red, becoming reddish-brown; stem equal or slightly thickened below, red; spores oblong, .0005 in. long, .00016 broad. Pileus 1–2 in. broad; stem 1–2 in. long, 2–3 lines thick.

Grassy woods. Auburn, Alabama. July. Underwood.

Our specimens were about 4–6 cm. broad, cap subtomentose, red, then fading. Flesh yellowish and drying more yellow.

Tubes rather large for the size of the cap, angular and irregular, adnate, red in youth, then dull olivaceous, turning bluish.

Stem up to 4 cm. long, enlarged downward, red all over, pruinose, not reticulated.

Spores (of No. 11967) dark olive in mass but very pale (surprisingly so) under the microscope, *oblong*-elliptic, smooth, 3–4 x 8–11μ.

Murrill placed this species in the doubtful list, but since we have found a plant which anwers the description in all essentials, and we know of no other small plant except *rubinellus* and *piperatus* with tubes red in youth, we are referring it here.

NORTH CAROLINA. Highlands. No. 11967. In grassy deciduous woods at Kettle Rock, Aug. 23, 1940.

Boletus vermiculosus Peck. Rept. N. Y. St. Cab. **23:** 130–131. 1873.

Plate 26 and pl. 62, fig. 16

Cap 5.5–11.5 cm. broad (rarely up to 15 cm.), convex then irregularly expanded and often with an upturned margin, surface dull, smooth or finely felted-tomentose with a velvety appearance and not taking the imprint of a finger; when young dark brown or red-brown with a yellow olivaceous tint all over, the free margin and very young marginal tubes yellow, becoming paler and distinctly yellow toward the margin when mature. Flesh about 1–1.5 cm. thick, rather firm, slimy to the tongue, pale to bright yellow, turning immediately dark blue when cut, fading to soiled whitish, but old grub channels red or yellow; odor and taste none.

Tubes 5–12 mm. long, strongly depressed at stem, very small, about 2.5–3 to a mm., mouths not stuffed when young, a deep rich brown, becoming dull brownish yellow with tint of olive, flesh yellow, turning deep blue then blackish brown when bruised, tube surface often pitted and ridged.

Stem crooked or straight, 6–9 cm. long, including the rooted part and 1–2 cm. thick, usually but not always slender in proportion to length, color bright or dull yellow or brownish, usually delicately streaked with darker brown lines above and squamulose-dotted with brown flecks below, rarely reticulated above; flesh very hard, solid and firm, yellow then deep blue when wounded, wounds later becoming dull red; base usually inserted for a cm. or more, the white mycelium holding the earth firmly.

Spores (of No. 10193) dark and strongly olive, rather evenly elliptic, smooth, 3.6–4.2 x 9.3–12.5μ.

Peck gave this species the name *vermiculosus* because the earlier specimens found by him were infested by grubs, but he later said that the name was inappropriate. Murrill lists it as a synonym of *luridus*, but, while intermediate forms do occur, we find so many specimens which agree perfectly with Peck's description and with his plants at Albany and differ from *luridus* that we feel justified in keeping the name. These differences are as follows: brown tube mouths, smaller average size of plants, dry cap, thinner flesh, and usually slenderer stem.   In some of our specimens the tubes mouths when young were almost black-brown and the darker color is always obvious.   Both species are quite hard in the dry state.

Our Nos. 12386 and 12541 entered below are intermediate between the present species and *luridus*, having the more slender form and dry cap of *vermiculosus* but with more red in cap, tubes, and stem than in the form described above.

ILLUSTRATIONS: Atkinson.   Mushrooms, pl. 54.   1900 (pl. 60 of 1901 ed.).   Not in color.

NORTH CAROLINA.   Chapel Hill.   No. 483.   In woods, mostly deciduous, Oct. 3, 1912.   No. 503.   As above, Oct. 5, 1912.   In this collection the flesh of some plants was whitish and of others yellowish.   Spores deep brown with olive tint, 3.6–4.3 x 9.3–11.5μ.

Highlands.   No. 8942.   By Dillard road, July 28, 1931.   No. 10193.   By road around Ravenel Lake, under hemlock hedge, Aug. 22, 1936.   No. 11794. On east side of Ravenel Lake, Aug. 1, 1940.   No. 12359.   Same place as No. 10193, July 12, 1941.   No. 12386.   On grassy bank nearly opposite the museum, July 17, 1941.   No. 12541.   In grass under trees, Aug. 10, 1941.   Spores very dark, elliptic-subventricose, 4–5.5 x 10–13μ.

Also other collections from Chapel Hill and Highlands.

Macon County.   No. 10901.   By Gold Mine road, Aug. 11, 1938.

Polk County.   No. 11965.   Pearson's Falls, Aug. 24, 1941.

Carteret County.   Harker's Island.   No. 12810.   May 10, 1942.

Transylvania County.   No. 12764.   In deciduous woods by Horsepasture River, Sept. 3, 1941.

Blowing Rock.   Atkinson.

GEORGIA.   Rabun County.   No. 12412.   In deciduous woods by Big Creek, July 20, 1941.

Boletus luridus Schaeffer.   Fung. Bavar., p. 78, pl. 107.   1772.

Plate 3, fig. 5; pl. 22 (below); pl. 62, fig. 17

Gregarious, sometimes cespitose; cap up to 27 cm. wide, usually about 8–12 cm., very firm and solid, slow to decay, convex, minutely subtomentose or smooth, dry or more often somewhat viscid, color variable, some shade of reddish brown or brick red with blackish streaks and areas or olivaceous brown; narrow margin free and incurved in youth.   Flesh thick, up to 2.7 cm. near stem, yellow or nearly white (about like apple meat), changing immediately to blue when cut (rarely changing only slightly); taste pleasant, odor acid.   In old cuts, worm holes, etc., the flesh is reddish.

Tube mouths deep red, not stuffed when young but tightly packed, small, 2–3 to a mm., round, tubes up to 1.5 cm. long in large plants, free from the stem or barely reaching it, the mouths losing much of the red at maturity (rarely the mouths may be yellow in youth, becoming red toward maturity); tubes yellow or greenish yellow inside and turning greenish blue when cut, then fading back to reddish or sordid on long exposure.

Stem as long as the width of the cap or shorter, usually stout and if flattened may be up to 6 cm. wide, subequal or enlarged above or below, smooth or with punctations or light reticulations which are usually reddish, color clear yellow at the top, deepening, often quite abruptly, to nearly the cap color below or yellow all over (rarely red all over); flesh solid, yellow, changing quickly to blue, but old grub channels red.

Spores (of No. 9772) olivaceous smoky in a good print, rather evenly elliptic, 3.7–4.4 x 9.5–12.5μ. The olivaceous tint may be soon lost in the herbarium.

Boletus luridus, like *B. bicolor*, belongs in a difficult and confused group. The plants which we are treating here do not agree well with European descriptions and figures. The stems of our specimens almost never have the distinct reticulations mentioned and pictured in Europe for *luridus*. Some early students of the genus in America (as Curtis and Peck) recognized *Satanas*, *luridus*, and *purpureus* as separate species all occurring in this country. These were distinguished on the basis of the variable colors of cap and stem, the whiteness or yellowness of the flesh, and change to blue or red when wounded. Curtis listed all three from North Carolina, but we have no way of knowing what his interpretations were. Murrill makes *Satanas* a synonym of *luridus* but does not mention *purpureus*. Among a number of other species, he reduces to synonymy *B. vermiculosus*, which we consider distinct enough to be treated separately in this work. Snell (Mycologia **25**: 227. 1933) gives notes attempting to separate *luridus* and *erythropus*, but the characters which he gives are in our plants not segregated. For instance, fruit-bodies in the same collection may show stems glabrous or punctate with reddish tomentose dots and caps brownish or red. Snell mentions one fact not ordinarily recognized which we find to be true of our plants, namely, that in some rare cases the mouths are not red in youth but become so toward maturity. In most cases the red fades out somewhat after maturity.

With all its variations the species, as we are treating it, is characterized by large size, reddish or brownish cap, firm, solid flesh changing immediately to blue, small tubes with red mouths, and stem which usually has a ground color of yellow with areas of the cap color below and with or without reddish dots or light reticulations. The spores in our specimens are distinctly smaller than the dimensions given by Farlow, Murrill, and most European authors. We have only one collection in which the spores approach the sizes they give. However, Rea gives for *luridus* the same spore sizes as in ours.

The nomenclature of the species in this group is further complicated by the fact that the plant interpreted by Fries (Obs. Myc. **2**: 243. 1818) as *B. erythropus*, and later reduced by him to a variety of *luridus*, is not now considered in Europe to be the same as the plant so named by Persoon, to which Fries referred (see Kallenbach, Konrad and Maublanc, Gilbert, etc.).

ILLUSTRATIONS: Bulliard. Herb. Fr., pl. 100 (as *B. tuberosus*).
　　Farlow. Icones Farlowianae, pl. 85 (as var. *erythropus*).
　　Gillet. Champ. Fr., Hymén., pl. 65.
　　Greville. Scot. Crypt. Fl. **3**: pl. 121.
　　Murrill. Mycologia **4**: pl. 68, fig. 1. 1912.
　　Palmer. Mushrooms of America, pl. 11, figs. 3, 4.

NORTH CAROLINA. Chapel Hill. No. 83. In mixed woods, Oct. 4, 1911. No. 239. Mixed woods, Oct. 28, 1910. Spores elliptic-subventricose, smooth, 3.8–4.8(5.5) x 11–15(18)μ, larger than in our other collections. No. 3329. In low mixed woods, June 10, 1919. Spores evenly elliptic except for oblique mucro, 3.7–4.8 x 9.5–12.5μ. No. 10676. In Battle Park, Sept. 18, 1937. No. 11090. In deciduous woods, July 15, 1939. In this collection the tube mouths of the youngest plant showed practically no red, those of the middle sized one were quite red, and those of the largest slightly so. No. 11608. In a pasture, Aug. 25, 1940. Some stems in this collection were red-tomentose, others smooth and yellow except at base. Highlands. No. 8969. On a roadside bank, July 29, 1931. Spores 3.6–4.8 x 9–11.5μ, a few larger. No. 9505. In mixed mountain woods near the laboratory, Aug. 19, 1932. No. 9772. In open hillside pasture under oaks, Aug. 12, 1934. No. 11008. In mixed woods, Aug. 28, 1938. Very large specimens, up to 27 cm. wide. Spores oblong-elliptic, 3.7–4 x 9.3–11μ. Also many other collections from Chapel Hill and Highlands.
Chatham County. No. 10784. In deciduous woods on right of road to Pittsboro from Chapel Hill, July 5, 1938.
Jackson County. No. 12136. In mixed woods in Whiteside Cove, Aug. 10, 1939. Spores bright olive when fresh, 3.6–4 x 9–11μ.
Asheville. Beardslee.
Middle district. Schweinitz and Curtis.
Pisgah Forest. Murrill.

Boletus Satanas Lenz var. **americanus** n. var.

Cap 9–15 cm. broad, convex, dull, dry, with texture of leather but with margin punctate-tomentose, color very pale pallid straw buff or pinkish buff (Ridg.), in one plant with distinct tint of dull olive over the other colors; margin free, broad, strongly inturned. Flesh up to 2.5 cm. thick, dull white, turning blue in places then back to white or if crushed becoming about color of cap; taste slight or bitter-acid, odor none.

Tubes up to 2 cm. long, very small, nearly or quite free, the mouths a fine deep red, Morocco or Etruscan red (Ridg.) when young, becoming a lighter, more orange red or brownish after maturity, turning greenish brown when rubbed; tube flesh yellow or greenish gray; tube surface deeply pitted in some plants.

Stem up to 9 cm. long and 2.3 cm. thick, equal except for slightly enlarged base, nearly glabrous above, minutely flecked downward, not reticulated, color of tube mouths or paler above, greenish brown downward; solid.

Spores (of No. 12872) buffy olive with grayish tint, elliptic, 3.7–4.4 x 8.9–12.5μ.

This plant is near the European *B. Satanas*, but the latter is said to be strongly characterized by the bulbous stem with a red reticulum, whereas in the present variety the stem is nearly equal and not reticulated, and also the bruised flesh turns blue instead of rosy or violaceous. The most striking character of both this and the European *Satanas* is the very pale, *whitish* cap.

NORTH CAROLINA. Highlands. No. 12695. In deciduous woods on Fodderstack Mt., Aug. 25, 1941.

GEORGIA. Rabun County. No. 12872. In mixed woods by Big Creek, July 27, 1942.

Boletus Frostii Russell *in* Frost. Bull. Buf. Soc. Nat. Sci. **2:** 102. 1874.
B. alveolatus B. & C. *in* Frost. Ibid., p. 102.

Plate 27 and pl. 62, fig. 18

Cap 6–10 cm. broad, convex, smooth or delicately pruinose, dull or shining in places, viscid, usually blood red all over but sometimes with paler, more yellowish areas toward the margin, especially in age. Flesh pallid or yellowish, 1–2 cm. thick near stem, turning bluish when cut; odor none and taste of flesh mild but cuticle usually acid to the tongue.

Tubes small, 2 or 3 to a mm., round, 7–11 mm. deep, "stuffed" when young, attached but usually depressed at stem, partly decurrent, mouths deep red at all ages; flesh greenish yellow, dirty blue when wounded.

Stem 4–11 cm. long, very variable in length and thickness, tapering upward from a somewhat bulbous base, from 7 mm. above to 2.7 cm. thick below, blood red, sometimes yellow at base, lacerate-reticulate above, more shallowly reticulated below, firm, solid, changing slowly to blue or blackish when wounded; base may be bent and pointed.

Spores (of No. 508) yellow-brown after standing (prints observed fresh are distinctly olivaceous), fusiform, 4–4.8 x 13.5–16μ.

This beautiful species is characterized by blood red color all over externally (except at base of stem), viscid cap, small tubes and strongly reticulated stem.

Our collections from Highlands, N. C., entered under this species, differ from the typical form in the following respects: stem much less strongly reticulated and only at the top, lower part of stem delicately streaked longitudinally or only velvety-tomentose, and the smaller, more evenly elliptic spores. Also the cap, tubes, or stem of these plants may show more blackish than bluish areas where rubbed.

ILLUSTRATIONS: Farlow. Icones Farlowianae, pl. 86.
Gibson. Edible Toadstools and Mushrooms, pl. 24 (above). 1895. (As *B. alveolatus.*)
Palmer. Mushrooms of America, pl. 11, fig. 2. 1885. (As *B. alveolatus.*)
Peck. Bull. N. Y. St. Mus. **116:** pl. 108. 1907.

NORTH CAROLINA: Chapel Hill. No. 508. In woods on hillside, Oct. 5, 1912. No. 1114. In mixed woods, July 10, 1914. Spores fusiform, sometimes slightly sway-backed, 3.8–5 x 13–18μ. No. 1147. In a sphagnum bed, July 16, 1914. Spores long-elliptic, subfusiform, and slightly curved at distal end, 4–5.5 x 12.5–16μ.
Haywood County. No. 8112. In mountain woods by Cold Creek, Aug. 8, 1926.
Highlands. No. 9591. In mixed mountain woods, Sept. 1, 1932. Spores distinctly olivaceous, rather evenly elliptic, 3.5–4.2 x 9.8–12(–13)μ. No. 9814. In mixed woods, Aug. 18, 1934. Spores elliptic, 3.6–4.2 x 10–12.5μ. No. 10260. In the Primeval Forest, Aug. 30, 1936.
Macon County. No. 10880. In clump of grass on rocky face of White Rock Mt., Aug. 7, 1938.
Also other collections in our herbarium from Chapel Hill and Highlands.

Boletus Morrisii Peck.   Bull. Torr. Bot. Club **36**: 154.   1909.

Plate 28 and pl. 63, fig. 1

Cap up to 9.5 cm. broad, convex, glabrous at maturity, dry, dull or with center somewhat shining, very dark in youth and often olive tinted with a bloom, remaining darker in center, which at maturity may be olive brown or reddish brown, fading out irregularly toward the margin to a peculiar olive gold, or brick red with only the very margin orange yellow; cuticle red and surface turning deep red when bruised, sometimes so after heavy rain; a thin free margin present.   Flesh up to 1.4 cm. thick, soft, light clear yellow, not turning blue but slowly reddish in places when cut or in age, bright yellow when properly dried; tasteless and odorless.

Tubes up to 1 cm. long, very small, 3 (rarely 2) to a mm., deeply depressed at stem, rarely not so, "stuffed" in youth, mouths in youth clear egg yellow all over or only marginal ones yellow and others clear brownish red, becoming bright greenish yellow, then orange brown, turning red when bruised.

Stem up to 7.5 cm. long and 1.5 cm. thick in center, crooked, enlarged below, surface color bright greenish yellow, thickly set with red punctate squamules; mycelium yellow; flesh solid, fibrous, yellow or with vinaceous red areas.

Spores (of No. 10910) distinctly olive, elliptic to subfusiform, smooth, 3.7–4.2 x 10–13.5μ.

A well marked species that seems rare with us.   The colors of the cap, the bright lemon yellow stem dotted with red squamules, and the small tubes which may be red or orange are distinguishing characters.   *Boletus rubropunctus* also has a stem with reddish flecks over a yellow or yellowish surface, but in that species the cap is quite viscid, the color of the cap is different, and the spores are larger.   Our plants have been compared with Peck's and agree perfectly.   The colors are well retained on drying.

According to Murrill (Jour. N. Y. Bot. Garden **10**: 265.   1909), this species has been reported in this country by Morgan and others as *B. radicans* Pers., a closely related species of Europe.

NORTH CAROLINA.   Highlands.   No. 9015.   By trail up Mt. Satulah, July 31, 1931.   Spores olivaceous, 3.7–4.5 x 11–14.2μ.

Macon County.   Coweeta Expt. Forest.   No. 10910.   By trail to Reynolds Knob, Aug. 12, 1938.

GEORGIA.   Rabun County.   No. 11955.   In rich cove on Big Creek by Walhalla road, Aug. 27, 1940.   No. 12640.   Under rhododendron by Clear Creek, Aug. 22, 1941.   Spores elliptic to subfusiform, 3.8–4.5 x 11–12.8μ.

Boletus rimosellus Peck.   Bull. N. Y. St. Mus. **2**, No. 8: 127.   1889.
B. rugosiceps Peck.   Bull. N. Y. St. Mus. **94**: 20.   1905.

Frontispiece, figs. 4–6; pl. 29; pl. 61, fig. 13

Cap up to 13.5 cm. broad, convex or flat at maturity, dull, dry, minutely felted-tomentose or glabrous, becoming beautifully rimose all over at maturity and often pitted, deep reddish brown or brownish tawny on the areolae, paler and tawny buff in the cracks.   Flesh up to 1.4 cm. thick near stem, rather tough, nearly white or creamy, in young plants becoming vinaceous pink after a few minutes, in age only slightly changing but grub channels and often the region over the stem pinkish brown; taste none, odor faintly oily fragrant. There is a very characteristic tendency to a greenish line between the tubes and flesh in mature plants, or, in its absence, to green stains here and there near the tubes.

Tubes about 1–2.2 cm. long, *small*, about 2 to a mm., round, deeply depressed at stem and in age usually receding and leaving lines on the stem; mouths in youth pale yellow, or pallid olive cream, then yellow-brown with tint of olive, or in some cases brownish ochraceous when young, dark brown when bruised or in age, lightly stuffed when young. Flesh of tubes pale yellow.

Stem relatively stout, often swollen below or in middle, up to 9 cm. long and 2 cm. thick in center, swollen part up to 2.8 cm., or stem nearly equal and more slender in some, base more or less pinched to a yellowish mycelium; surface dull yellow or concolorous with cap, closely covered with small brownish scabrous dots, surface under dots longitudinally fibrous. Flesh of stem concolorous with that of cap and often vinaceous red in areas disturbed by grubs.

Spores (of No. 12605) deep brown with tint of olive, smooth, fusiform-elliptic, 4.5–5.8 x 14–19.6μ.

The type of this species was found in North Carolina by C. J. Curtis and sent to Peck, who described it from one dried specimen and Curtis's notes, saying in the description that more collections would probably necessitate some modifications of the description. Murrill (N. Amer. Flora **9**: 151) puts the species in the doubtful list, but we have found many specimens of a plant that agrees well with Peck's description so far as it goes except that he gives the stem as reticulated. In reality the scabrous dots are often arranged in lines and in the case of a dried specimen might easily give the appearance of reticulations. We feel sure that this is the plant so named by Peck. Some specimens resemble *scaber*, but that species has a more slender form, tubes *white when young*, stem with surface color whitish, grayish or pallid but never so yellow as in this species, and spores without an olive tint.

We have an authentic specimen of *B. rugosiceps* collected by Peck himself at Wading River, N. Y., which is identical with our smaller specimens. In his description he too mentions the fact that the species suggests *B. scaber*. Murrill puts this species under *B. subglabripes*, but that species has a much less scabrous stem, smaller spores, cap not rimose, and is more delicate in form.

ILLUSTRATIONS: Peck.   Bull. N. Y. St. Mus. **94**: pl. Q, figs. 6–10 (as *B. rugosiceps*).   1905.

NORTH CAROLINA.   Chapel Hill.   No. 504.   In woods, Oct. 5, 1912.   Spores fusiform, 4–5.5 x 12–16μ.   No. 1768.   Low, damp, shady place, Sept. 12, 1915.   No. 4615.   In dry mixed woods, Battle Park, July 13, 1920.   No. 10666.   On President Graham's lawn, Sept. 13, 1937.   No. 10776.   In woods east of Kenan Stadium, July 2, 1938.   Spores deep brown with little olive tint, fusiform, 4.2–5.5 x 14–18.5μ.

Highlands. No. 8978. July 26, 1931. Spores 4.2–5.5 x 12–16.6μ. No. 9021. Near Biological Laboratory, Aug. 2, 1931. No. 12527. On lawn back of Tricemont, Aug. 9, 1941. No. 12605. On Farnsworth lawn, Aug. 17, 1941. No. 12609. In grass on the dam at the laboratory, Aug. 17, 1941.

Boletus rubropunctus Peck. Rept. N. Y. St. Mus. **50**: 109. 1897.
   B. longicurvipes Snell and Smith. Journ. Elisha Mitch. Sci. Soc. **56**: 325. 1940.

Plate 30 and pl. 63, fig. 2

Cap 4–8 cm. broad, convex, more or less pitted, glabrous, viscid to glutinous, with a removable cuticle, chestnut brown, red-brown, or reddish orange, often lighter toward margin; cap of young plants often more yellow-orange and turning blackish when bruised. Flesh up to 12 mm. thick in the larger plants, white or pale yellow, unchanging or rarely bluish green when cut; taste mild or acid, odor none or slightly oily.

Tubes up to 10 mm. long, small, 2–3 to a mm., adnate to usually deeply depressed at stem, mouths round, surface often irregular, pallid cream to clear yellow or brownish yellow, sometimes with tint of greenish, darker brownish when bruised.

Stem 6–10 cm. long, tapering upward, rarely subequal, 8–12 mm. thick above, up to 2 cm. below, sometimes pinched below the swelling, usually bent near base, color like that of tubes above, slightly darker and at times with shade of cap color below except at base which is covered with pale yellow mycelium, conspicuously dotted all over with dry, reddish or pale flecks and squamules; flesh solid, firm, white above, pale reddish or with blackish streaks below; bruises on young stems sometimes blackish.

Spores (of No. 11093) dark olive brown in a good print, smooth, fusiform-elliptic, 4.5–5.8 x 12–15.2μ.

We have many good collections of this species, one of which we have compared with authentic material at Albany collected by Peck at Port Jefferson (Aug. 26–29, 1904) and found to be in full agreement. The spores of his plant are fusiform-elliptic, 4.8–6 x 13–17μ. In his original description Peck failed to mention the viscidity of the cap but does mention it later (Bull. N. Y. St. Mus. **94**: 47. 1905). The species is characterized by glabrous, distinctly viscid cap of brownish or reddish brown color, small yellow tubes, stem dotted all over with dry, reddish or pallid flecks over a yellow or yellowish ground color, and large spores. In the dried state the cap is usually quite dark, offering a distinct contrast with the stem, on which the lighter colors show up and the mycelium appears brighter yellow.

Murrill puts this species with a question under *B. inflexus* which we consider the same as *B. Curtisii*, but we think it differs from that species in absence of distinct inflexed free margin (the present species may show this to slight degree at times), absence of granules on the tubes, and in the *dry* stem with reddish flecks but without the distinct white boot at base, and in the darker and longer spores.

We have examined authentic specimens of *B. longicurvipes*, kindly sent us by Dr. Snell, and cannot find any important differences between them and our plants.

ILLUSTRATIONS: McIlvaine. Amer. Fungi, pl. 117, fig. 3.
Peck. Bull. N. Y. St. Mus. **94**: pl. 90. 1905.

NORTH CAROLINA. Chapel Hill. No. 11093. In deciduous woods, July 15, 1939.
Highlands. No. 11837. In mixed deciduous woods, Aug. 8, 1940. No. 11893. By road to Trillium Lodge, Aug. 9, 1940. Spores fusiform-elliptic, 5–6 x 13–16.6µ. No. 11997. In mixed woods, Sept. 5, 1940. No. 12390. In dense deciduous growth on Fodderstack Mt., July 17, 1941. No. 12681. In pine woods, Aug. 24, 1941. No. 12544. In grass in Farnsworth yard, Aug. 11, 1941. One group cespitose and one single plant. Also other collections from Highlands.

GEORGIA. Rabun County. No. 12621. Near top of Rabun Bald Mt., Aug. 20, 1941.

Boletus Curtisii Berk. *in* B. and C. Ann. & Mag. Nat. Hist. II, **12**: 429. 1853. Also in Grevillea **1**: 35. 1872.
B. inflexus Peck. Bull. Torr. Bot. Club **22**: 207. 1895.
B. fistulosus Peck. Bull. Torr. Bot. Club **24**: 144. 1897.
B. carolinensis Beards. Journ. Elisha Mitch. Sci. Soc. **31**: 147–148. 1915.

Frontispiece, fig. 1, and pl. 65, fig. 1

Gregarious or some cespitose; cap up to 8 cm. broad, hemispheric to more expanded, smooth, viscid to quite glutinous, bright lemon yellow to orange yellow or more reddish or brownish especially where the gluten has accumulated and dried, usually darker in the center, somewhat brown where bruised; thin sterile margin inflexed when young. Flesh whitish, unchanging, relatively thick in center, rapidly thinning to a membrane, cuticle acid to the tongue.

Tubes up to 1 cm. long, small to medium, usually 2 or 3 to a mm., light yellow when young, becoming fleshy straw yellow, adnate but depressed around the stem and easily separating from it, dotted with minute darker yellow or reddish droplets.

Stem rather slender, up to 12 cm. long and about 12 mm. thick, nearly equal, dotted in youth with viscid granules which usually run together to form a continuous viscid cuticle at maturity, the top part of the stem sometimes appearing somewhat scurfy under the gluten; color nearly that of cap but lighter; the long pointed base covered with a whitish layer resembling a volva, the texture of which is much like that of marshmallow, soft and gummy; flesh yellowish, typically hollow but sometimes not so.

Spores (of No. 10023) bright olive-yellow, smooth, elliptic or subventricose, thick-walled, 4.2–5.5 x 9.8–12.2µ.

The plant stains paper bright yellow. The white, volva-like tissue over the long pointed base is a conspicuous feature. In the dry state the plants are orange colored to deep reddish with a lacquered appearance on cap and stem.

Snell (Mycologia **26:** 356, 1934, and **28:** 13, 1936) has shown that *B. carolinensis* is the same as *B. Curtisii.* We have a specimen of *B. inflexus* from Trexlertown, Pa. (Herbst, coll.), probably from type collection and labelled by Peck, which is identical with our plants and with authentic material of *B. carolinensis* from Beardslee. The spores from this plant are rather variable in size and even somewhat in shape, some being more tapering at the ends than others, 4.2–5.5 x 11–14μ.

Boletus Curtisii was originally described from South Carolina, growing in pine woods.

NORTH CAROLINA. Chapel Hill. No. 468. In mixed woods, pine and oak, Oct. 1, 1912. No. 10023. In pine woods, Sept. 29, 1935. No. 11602. In pasture under pines, Aug. 25, 1940. Spores olive-yellow, elliptic, 4.3–5.4 x 9.3–12.2μ. No. 11611. In mixed woods near Morgan Creek, Aug. 30, 1940. Spores 4.2–5.5 x 9.5–12.5μ.

Asheville. Beardslee (as *B. carolinensis*).

Boletus Atkinsonianus (Murrill) n. comb.

Ceriomyces Atkinsonianus Murrill. N. Amer. Flora **9:** 144. 1910.

Plate 31 (above) and pl. 63, figs. 3, 4

Cap 7–10 cm. broad, glabrous, shining, quite viscid when damp, leather color or ochraceous tawny (Ridg.), much darker brown in age and with a slight vinaceous tint; decided free margin, inrolled in youth and with white underside. Flesh up to 2 cm. thick, soft, sweet, pallid white with tints of rose here and there (also turning bluish in places), old grub channels brown.

Tubes up to 1 cm. long, small, 2 or 3 to a mm., adnate but depressed around the stem, straw colored in youth, deepening through dull olivaceous to a final reddish brown on mouth edges.

Stem up to 10 cm., about 1.8 cm. thick in middle region, gradually tapering upward from a bulbous base, rarely subequal, often longitudinally ridged or with inherent lines of darker color, subconcolorous with cap but paler, staining reddish, quite glabrous except at base and *cartilaginous,* hard and solid but with a small fibrous central core which is channeled by grubs.

Spores (of No. 9536) strongly olivaceous when fresh, fusiform-elliptic, smooth, 3.8–4.8 x 11–13μ.

We have found this species with certainty only a few times. The viscid, quite glabrous, leather colored cap, distinct free margin, small, olive-straw tubes, and glabrous, cartilaginous stem which tapers upward are distinguishing features. We have compared our plants with Murrill's type and find them in agreement. His original description gives the tubes as 4–5 to a mm., but the tubes of the type, even in the dried state, are not that small.

ILLUSTRATIONS: Atkinson. Mushrooms, pl. 55, fig. 165; 2nd ed., pl. 61, fig. 170 (as *B. obsonium* and not in color).

NORTH CAROLINA. Highlands. No. 9511. Mixed woods at entrance to Salinas place, Aug. 20, 1932. Spores olive brown, elliptic-fusiform, 3.8–4.6 x 11–13.3μ. No. 9536. In mixed woods near Glen Falls, Aug. 23, 1932. Pink Bed Valley, Pisgah Forest. No. 10979. With moss on bank under rhododendrons, Aug. 23, 1938. Spores somewhat smaller than usual, 3.5–4 x 10–12.5μ, but this collection came from the type locality and agrees in all essentials with the species. Transylvania County. No. 12751. By trail along Horsepasture River, Sept. 3, 1941.

GEORGIA. Rabun County. No. 11922. In mixed pine woods on Walhalla road, Aug. 22, 1940.

Boletus badius Fr. Elenchus Fung. **1:** 126. 1828.

Plate 4, fig. 3; pl. 32; pl. 63, fig. 5

Cap 3.7–8.5 cm. broad, convex then expanded and nearly plane, minutely felted-tomentose with a granular appearance, distinctly viscid when young or when wet, color bay brown or darker wood brown, at times with an olivaceous tint. Flesh up to 1.5 cm. thick, soft, white with tints of pink or yellow, scarcely changing when cut; tasteless and odorless.

Tubes up to 1.5 cm. long, adnate or depressed at stem, pale yellow, then passing through olive yellow to dull yellow, mouths of medium size, changing to dull blue-green when wounded or only to sordid, old bruises sometimes reddish.

Stem up to 10 cm. long and 1.5 cm. thick above, equal or larger downward, then tapering at base, resembling the stem of *B. gracilis* but shorter, concolorous, often abruptly yellow at top, streaked with darker lines and minutely dotted, more so below, white with mycelium at base; flesh solid, fibrous, pale-concolorous, sometimes reddish, especially near base.

Spores (of No. 10222) olive when fresh, long-elliptic to subventricose, 3.8–4.8 x 10–14μ.

This is not a common species with us. It is rather dark colored, both when fresh and when dry, and prefers pine woods. The cap is distinctly viscid and also somewhat tomentose. In the dry state the tomentum is scarcely visible, probably because of the inherent viscidity, and the surface often appears shining. Both the tubes and spores of the American plant are slightly smaller than in the European.

This species differs from *B. Atkinsonianus*, another viscid plant of somewhat similar color in age, in more tomentose cap, distinctly darker, pruinate stem, larger tube mouths, and also in a greater preference for pine woods. We have, however, two collections from Chapel Hill (not entered below) which grew in deciduous woods and have distinctly smaller spores but otherwise seem identical with *badius*.

ILLUSTRATIONS: Bresadola. Icon. Mycol. **19:** pl. 910. 1931.
Farlow. Icones Farlowianae, pl. 76. 1929.
Fries. Sveriges Svampar, pl. 50.
Gillet. Champ. Fr., Hymén., pl. 49. Tubes apparently smaller than usual.

Michael. Führer f. Pilzfreunde **1**: No. 30. 1918.
Nees von Esenbeck. Syst. Pilze, pl. 31, figs. 1–4. 1837.
Richon and Roze. Atl. Champ., pl. 55, figs. 14–16.
Rolland. Bull. Soc. Myc. Fr. **8**: pl. 3, fig. 3. 1892. Also Atl. Champ. Fr.,
pl. 80, fig. 179. 1910.

NORTH CAROLINA. Chapel Hill. No. 1697. Under pines, Sept. 8, 1915.
Spores 3.7–4.5 x 9.4–11.5μ, some longer. No. 10644. Under pines by
roadside, Sept. 5, 1937. This collection also varies from the typical form
in having spores smaller, 3.7–4.2 x 8–11μ.
Highlands. No. 9623. Under white pines, Aug. 17, 1933. Spores 4–5.5 x
11.5–14μ. No. 10218. In Primeval Forest, Aug. 24, 1936. No. 10847.
In pine straw by road, Aug. 3, 1938. Spores 4–4.5 x 11–13.5μ. No 12018.
On rich bank under hemlock, rhododendron, etc., July 13, 1939. No.
12394. Under white pines, July 19, 1941. Spores olive brown, long-
elliptic, 3.7–4.5 x 10–13(–14.8)μ. No. 12427. Same spot as just above,
July 22, 1941. Also a number of other collections from Highlands.
Blowing Rock. Atkinson and Schrenk.

Boletus projectellus Murrill. Mycologia **30**: 524. 1938.

Plate 1, figs. 3, 4, and pl. 63, figs. 6, 7

Plants gregarious in large numbers; cap 3–10 cm. wide, strongly convex at
all ages or only slightly so at maturity, essentially dry, minutely felted but soon
shining, in old wet plants the superficial felt at times becoming finely cracked;
color in youth rather light gray-brown with a tint of rose, becoming darker,
red-brown (about mahogany red of Ridg.), in old age much darker, about bay;
margin free, projecting when young and fresh up to 2 mm. and hanging straight
down, then crenulated as if showing the remnants of a veil. Flesh thick, up
to 1.5 cm. near the stem, rather firm, pale rose color throughout, fading in
age to more yellowish; taste slight, faintly acid, odor none.

Tubes small, 1–2 to a mm. when mature, pale yellow when very young, then
greenish yellow, finally dark brownish olive, deeply depressed at stem, up to
2.5 cm. long (in large plant); flesh concolorous.

Stem long to very long, 10–15 cm., tapering upward from a more or less swollen
base which is covered with white flocculent mycelium, about 1–1.8 cm. thick
in center, surface concolorous with cap, minutely granular, strongly and hand-
somely reticulated with raised lines which form long meshes, the reticulations
fading out toward base. Flesh firm, solid, rosy above, fading to dull pale
yellowish below.

Spores (of No. 10299) strongly olivaceous brown in a heavy print, fusiform-
elliptic, smooth, thick-walled, 6.6–9 x 20–26μ. A few slender projecting cystidia
seen.

This is a very handsome plant which was described from Lynchburg, Virginia,
and has been collected only a few times. We have compared our specimens with
a part of the type, kindly sent us by Dr. Murrill, and find them to be the same.
The projecting sterile margin is more exaggerated in the type than in our plants,
but the very large spores, the rose colored flesh, growth in pine straw, and other

characters are decisive. It differs from *B. badius*, which it may resemble in age, in wide sterile margin, lack of viscidity, much larger spores, and somewhat different colors.

NORTH CAROLINA. Chapel Hill. No. 10299. Under pines, Oct. 17, 1936. Chatham County. No. 13193. In pine grove on Oldham farm, about five miles from Chapel Hill, Oct. 20, 1942. No. 13201. Same grove as above, Oct. 24, 1942. Spores strongly olive brown, large, 7.4–8.5 x 20–26μ. No. 13235. Same place as above, Oct. 31, 1942.

Boletus auriporus Peck. Rept. N. Y. St. Cab. **23**: 133. 1873.
B. innixus Frost. Bull. Buf. Soc. Nat. Sci. **2**: 103. 1874.
B. caespitosus Peck. Bull. Torr. Bot. Club **27**: 17. 1900.

Plate 4, fig. 4; pl. 31 (below); pl. 63, fig. 8

Cap 4–9 cm. broad, convex, sometimes with margin abruptly drooped, a fine leather brown or vinaceous brown (sometimes dull red) or darker, at times tinted with green, especially in the dry state, glabrous to minutely felted or dotted, often more or less areolated, the cracks being paler, usually dry but may be quite viscid in wet weather. Flesh up to 1.2 cm. thick, quite firm, pallid yellowish or with vinaceous tint, unchanging; taste quite mild, cuticle moderately acid to the tongue, odor none.

Tubes up to 10 mm. long, small to medium, adnate-depressed and slightly decurrent by lines, *brilliant chrome yellow*, not changing or slowly to reddish on rubbing and *retaining the bright yellow color on drying* if collected in good condition.

Stem about 3–6 cm. long, with or without a strong swelling below the middle where it may be up to 2.5 cm. thick, up to 1.5 cm. thick at top, tapering rapidly below to a pointed, inserted, deep brown (except for mycelium) base, furfurescent dotted above, nearly smooth below, rarely lightly reticulated; color brownish yellow above, brown below, quite viscid in wet weather; flesh very firm, palely concolorous with surface.

Spores (of No. 9769) smoky olive or stronger olive, smooth, subcylindrical, 3.7–4.2 x 8–11μ.

This is a distinct and beautiful species not easily confused with anything else. The brown cap and stem and brilliant yellow tubes which retain their color in age and when dried readily distinguish it.

ILLUSTRATIONS: Farlow. Icones Farlowianae, pl. 77.
Murrill. Mycologia **5**: pl. 80, fig. 2. 1913.

NORTH CAROLINA. Chapel Hill. No. 1412. By path in woods, mostly deciduous, Oct. 24, 1914. Spores 3.8–4.5 x 8–11μ. No. 9851. On a lawn, Sept. 20, 1934. Spores oblong-elliptic, 3.5–4 x 8.5–10μ. No. 10785. In deciduous woods, July 5, 1938. Spores olivaceous, 3.5–4 x 8–10μ. Highlands. No. 9769. In open hillside pasture, Aug. 12, 1934. No. 10613. In mixed woods, Aug. 29, 1937. Spores 3.7–4.4 x 8.4–10μ. No. 12492. In deciduous woods, Aug. 3, 1941.
Also other collections from Chapel Hill and Highlands.

Transylvania County. Lake Toxaway. No. 10836.
Linville Falls. No. 5742. In deciduous woods, Aug. 24, 1922.
McDowell County. No. 12836. In deciduous woods, July 16, 1942.
Macon County. Coweeta Expt. Forest. No. 11944. Aug. 26, 1934.
Blowing Rock. Atkinson and Schrenk.
Pink Bed Valley, Pisgah Forest. Murrill.

GEORGIA. Rabun County. No. 12622. At parking place on Rabun Bald
Mt., Aug. 20, 1941.

Boletus viridiflavus n. sp.

Plate 2, figs. 6–8; pl. 33; pl. 63, fig. 9

Cap 2–7.7 cm. wide, convex to plane or rarely with margin uplifted, tomentose-felted in youth but distinctly *viscid* at all ages, glabrous at maturity and with a removable cuticle, color a peculiar olivaceous gold with reddish areas or varying to alutaceous with olive tints especially toward the margin, which is free and incurved. Flesh up to 1.3 cm. thick, vinaceous under the cuticle, whitish or pale yellow below and with rosy areas, not changing to blue; taste of flesh itself mild or slightly acid but cuticle distinctly acid, odor none.

Tubes up to 1.7 cm. long, mouths varying from ½–1 mm. wide, angular, their surface irregular and usually ventricose and deeply depressed at stem, color bright greenish yellow (about wax yellow of Ridgway) at all ages and if properly dried *retaining this color* when dry; if bruised when fresh turning dull brick red.

Stem up to 7.5 cm. long, nearly equal or slightly enlarged downward, then narrowed at very base, up to 1.8 cm. thick but usually smaller, concolorous with tubes, but often brighter yellow above or nearly all over or concolorous with cap downward, glabrous and lined above (at times lightly reticulated there), minutely tomentose or scurfy below toward the white mycelium; bruised places becoming brick red.

Spores (of No. 11960) strongly olive brown, fusiform-elliptic, smooth, 4–5 x 11.5–15 (–16.6)μ.

This species closely resembles in various respects several other well established species, such as *subtomentosus, badius, auriporus,* and *Atkinsonianus.* From all these species (except in regard to tubes of *auriporus*) it differs in brighter colors and in the retention of the tube color in the dried state. From *subtomentosus* it differs also in distinct viscidity; from *badius,* in mainly glabrous stem and preference for deciduous woods or open places; from *auriporus,* in distinctly larger spores and in the longer, greenish yellow rather than golden yellow tubes; and from *Atkinsonianus,* in smaller size, presence of tomentum in young state and in the larger tube mouths. *Boletus dichrous* Ellis was described as having tubes "becoming at length permanently yellow," but plants in Washington (Path. and Myc. Coll.) collected by Ellis at Newfield, N. J., Aug. 1, 1887, do not bear out this statement. The plants do not appear at all like ours although the descriptions would indicate similarity.

NORTH CAROLINA. Chapel Hill. No. 9804. In humus in deciduous woods, Sept. 24, 1934. Spores 3.8–4.5 x 10.5–13(–14.8)μ. No. 9850. In mossy lawn, Sept. 20, 1934. Spores olivaceous, fusiform-elliptic, smooth, 4–5.5 x

11–14μ. No. 9863. In moss and grass, Sept. 26, 1934. No. 10021. Same spot as collection above, Sept. 27, 1935. No. 10661. Same spot as above, Sept. 11, 1937. Spores 4–5.2 x 11–14μ.

Highlands. No. 11007. In mixed woods, Aug. 28, 1938. Spores olivaceous, fusiform-elliptic, 4–5.2 x 10–14(–15)μ. No. 11910. By roadside, Aug. 21, 1940. No. 11960 (type). In mixed woods, Aug. 26, 1940. Also several other collections in our herbarium from the above places. Jackson County. No. 13078. By roadside in Horse Cove, Aug. 28, 1942.

Boletus subtomentosus L. Sp. Plant. **2:** 1178. 1753. Fuller descr. in Fl. Suec., p. 453. 1755.

Plate 34 (above) and pl. 63, fig. 15

Cap up to 9 cm. broad, convex, usually remaining so, dry, distinctly tomentose-felted, ochraceous tawny or golden brown with olive tint, rarely with vinaceous areas, or darker olive brown, sometimes areolated at maturity; narrow free margin inrolled in youth. Flesh up to 1.2 cm. thick at stem, whitish to pale yellow, often tinged with pinkish, not changing at all or slowly to dull flesh, the cuticle itself and grub channels more or less vinaceous; tasteless and odorless.

Tubes up to 1.2 cm. long, large, 1–2 mm., angular and irregular, adnate-depressed, yellow to greenish yellow and rarely changing to darker bluish green or dirty brown when wounded.

Stem up to 7 cm. long and 2 cm. thick, yellowish or yellow-brown and more or less lined and dotted with fine reddish particles; flesh solid in youth but often becoming hollow, especially below, colored as in cap.

Spores (of No. 12025) smoky olive in light print, dark olive brown in heavy print, subfusiform, 3.7–4.5 x 10–13μ.

This species is not common with us. It is characterized by dry, tomentose, golden brown or olive brown cap, large, irregular, angular tubes of greenish yellow color, and whitish to pale flesh which does not change to blue (the tube mouths may show this change to some extent). Some specimens of *B. Roxanae* resemble this species, but *Roxanae* has small tubes, whitish in youth, relatively longer stem which is enlarged below, and is a more delicate plant in general.

In one of our collections (No. 12025) there was apparently a mycorrhizal connection with the root of a sassafras tree. The fungus arose from an exposed root on an overhanging bank just where the root emerged from the ground and the mycelium extended on the root into the earth to where the root was cut and beyond. The stem base of the *Boletus* completely surrounded a small lateral root of the larger exposed root, the smaller one thus forming a central *core* for the stem, while the stem base made a little boot and from this the light yellow mycelium extended upward along the main root as a compact membrane covering half of the surface.

ILLUSTRATIONS: Bresadola. Icon. Mycol. **19:** pl. 914.
    Dufour. Atl. Champ., pl. 62, No. 136.
    Farlow. Icones Farlowianae, pl. 79.
    Michael. Führer f. Pilzfreunde **1:** No. 28. 1918.
    Murrill. Mycologia **2:** pl. 19, fig. 6. 1910.
    Rolland. Atl. Champ. Fr., pl. 80, No. 181.

NORTH CAROLINA. Chapel Hill. No. 214a. In mixed woods, Battle Park, Sept. 14, 1910.

Highlands. No. 9593. In rich mixed woods, Sept. 1, 1932. Spores 3.7–4.4 x 10–13μ. No. 11766. On bank by road near Mirror Lake, July 27, 1940. No. 11818. Under rhododendron, Aug. 6, 1940. Spores olive, 4–4.8 x 10–12μ. No. 11902. In open woods, Aug. 20, 1940. Spores olivaceous, subfusiform, 3.8–4.8 x 11–13μ. No. 12025. Growing from an exposed root on an overhanging bank, July 15, 1939. No. 12403. In deciduous woods on Little Bear Pen Mountain, July 20, 1941. Also other collections from Highlands.

Asheville. Beardslee.

Blowing Rock. Atkinson and Schrenk.

"Common. Earth in woods." Curtis.

Pink Bed Valley. Pisgah Forest. Murrill.

Boletus illudens Peck. Rept. N. Y. St. Mus. **50**: 108. 1897.

Plate 35 and pl. 63, fig. 16

Cap 6–19 cm. broad, convex, somewhat irregular, dry, felted to distinctly tomentose, at first buffy yellow, then yellow-brown blotched with darker chestnut or reddish brown and sometimes with a grayish overcast. Flesh up to 2 cm. thick, soft, white with pinkish areas, unchanging when cut but old grub channels reddish; tasteless and odorless.

Tubes about 7–16 mm. long, large, especially near stem, 1–2 mm. wide, angular and irregular, adnate to decurrent, brilliant clear yellow when young or mouths with faint vinaceous tint, becoming olivaceous brown, sometimes showing slight blue change when rubbed but later reddish.

Stem up to 9 cm. long and 2.5 cm. thick at top, tapering downward to a sharp point or more nearly equal above and tapered only near base, often bent, subglabrous, ground surface whitish to pale yellow but strongly reticulated with darker reddish brown lines in long meshes, all the way to the base in large specimens, about one-half way down in small ones; flesh solid, firm, colored as in cap.

Spores (of No. 12157) strongly olive brown, elliptic-subfusiform, smooth, 3.7–4.5 x 9.3–12μ.

This species varies so greatly in size that one may be doubtful of the identity of the various plants. Peck's original description gave the size as up to 3 in. (7.6 cm.), but there are examples in his herbarium considerably larger than this figure. Our specimen 6 cm. broad is exactly like the one 19 cm. in all respects except size. The species is very close to *B. subtomentosus*, the only differences being the peculiar, strongly reticulated stem, often larger size, and the more decurrent tubes which show a slight blue change. We find the spores of the type of *illudens* to be elliptic-fusiform, 3.7–4.8 x 9.3–12.2μ, just like those of our plants. The spores of some collections of *B. subtomentosus* are slightly larger but many are in close agreement.

ILLUSTRATIONS: McIlvaine. Amer. Fungi, pl. 118, fig. 3. Stem too red. Murrill. Mycologia **5**: pl. 92, fig. 7. 1913. This shows stem more red and not so pointed below as in our plants.

NORTH CAROLINA. Chapel Hill. No. 10428. In mixed woods, July 14, 1937. No. 11598. In a pasture with scattered pines, Aug. 24, 1940. Spores olivaceous, rather evenly elliptic, 3.8–4.4 x 9.5–11.5µ. Highlands. No. 10273. On west side of Horseshoe Mt., Aug. 31, 1936. Spores 3.7–4.8 x 9–12µ. No. 12157. In low place in woods, Aug. 13, 1939. No. 12523. By road in flat woods, Aug. 9, 1941. Spores 3.7–4.1 x 9–11µ. Also other collections from Highlands.

Boletus parasiticus Bull. Herb. Fr., pl. 451, fig. 1. 1789.

Plate 34 (below) and pl. 63, fig. 10

Cap up to 6.3 cm. broad in our specimens, rather evenly convex, dry, smooth and leathery or delicately felted, cuticle sometimes cracked into areas, yellow-brown or olivaceous or with a grayish tint over yellow, margin strongly inturned in youth. Flesh whitish, turning yellow when cut, old surface wounds reddish. Tubes yellow, then olivaceous, mouths large, radially elongated at stem, lightly stuffed in youth, more or less decurrent, sometimes strongly so. Stem 2.5–5 cm. long, up to 1.2 cm. thick, subequal, curved, about color of cap or more yellow, dotted and lined with darker fibrous flecks. Spores (of No. 11988) very dark in a heavy print, blackish olive, subventricose, smooth, 4–5.2 x 13.5–17µ.

This remarkable species has rarely been reported in this country, and only on species of *Scleroderma*. Berkeley (Outlines Brit. Fungol., p. 231) gives it on species of *Elaphomyces*). Its habitat alone will distinguish it, but its glabrous, yellow-brown or olivaceous cap, large, decurrent, yellow tubes, and large spores are also identifying characters.

ILLUSTRATIONS: Berkeley. Outl. Brit. Fungol., pl. 15, fig. 4. 1860.
Boudier. Icones Myc. **1:** pl. 145.
Bulliard. Herb. Fr., pl. 451, fig. 1.
Coker. Journ. Elisha Mitch. Sci. Soc. **42:** pl. 48. 1927. (Not in color.)
Gillet. Champ. Fr., Hymén., pl. 70.
Kallenbach. Die Pilze Mitteleuropas **1:** pl. 21.
Kavina. Mykologia **2:** 2nd pl. after p. 32. 1925.
Overholts. Mycologia **16:** pl. 17, fig. 1. 1924. (Not in color.)
Rolland. Atl. Champ. Fr., pl. 86, fig. 191. 1910.

NORTH CAROLINA. Blowing Rock. No. 5686. On *Scleroderma aurantium* in mossy humus in mixed woods near a hemlock tree, summer, 1922. Highlands. No. 9025. On *Scleroderma aurantium*, Aug. 1, 1931. Spores subelliptic with oblique mucro, 3.8–5 x 12–15.5µ. No. 11924. On *Scleroderma* on a stump near laboratory, Aug. 23, 1940. No. 11988. Same spot as above, Sept. 5, 1940. Also other collections from Highlands. Graham County. No. 12056. Joyce Kilmer Forest, July 28, 1939. We also have specimens from Long Island, Massachusetts, and France.

Boletus subglabripes Peck. Bull. N. Y. St. Mus. **2**, No. 8: 112. 1889.
B. flavipes Peck. Rept. N. Y. St. Mus. **39**: 42. 1886. Not *B. flavipes*
Berk.

Plate 36 and pl. 63, fig. 11

Cap 2.7–7 cm. broad, convex, glabrous, not viscid, but sometimes with a wet, soaked look, chestnut color to reddish brown or Sanford's brown (Ridg.), the margin sometimes more yellowish and more or less mottled; cuticle separable. Flesh up to 1 cm. thick in center, pale yellow, not changing when cut but old wounds reddish; slightly acid to taste (cuticle more so), odor none.

Tubes up to 1 cm. long, small, 2 or 3 to a mm., not stuffed when young, adnate to depressed, clear yellow, about empire yellow (Ridg.) when young, then through olive yellow to finally brownish olive.

Stem 6–8 cm. long, 8–16 mm. thick, subequal or somewhat smaller upward, the very base contracted, concolorous with tubes, but with reddish stains, often slightly ridged or lined longitudinally, dotted with small pale particles which may disappear in part; flesh yellowish, solid and firm.

Spores (of No. 4478) smoky olivaceous when fresh, elliptic-ventricose, smooth, 4–5.2 x 11–14.8μ, with rather thick wall.

Old injuries on tubes, flesh, or stem are distinctly reddish, about color of cap. The quite glabrous, dry, reddish brown cap, rather small yellow tubes, yellow stem with minute scurfy particles, and rather large olivaceous spores are distinguishing characters. *Boletus Atkinsonianus* resembles this species in many respects but averages much larger, has distinctly viscid cap and glabrous, cartilaginous stem. We compared our plants with Peck's at the Albany Herbarium and find them in agreement.

ILLUSTRATIONS: Murrill. Mycologia **5**: pl. 80, fig. 6. 1913.
Peck. Rept. N. Y. St. Mus. **51**: pl. 55, figs. 1–7. 1898. Also in Mem. N. Y. St. Mus. **3**, No. 4: pl. 64, figs. 1–7. 1900.

NORTH CAROLINA. Chapel Hill. No. 4478. Mixed woods by Battle Branch, July 20, 1920. No. 4481. As above, July 21, 1920. Spores olivaceous, elliptic-ventricose, 4–5.4 x 12–14μ. No. 4487. Near same spot as above, July 21, 1920. A slender form with spores 3.6–4 x 9.3–12.5(–14)μ. No. 4515. Damp mixed woods, July 25, 1920. Spores subventricose, 4–5.5 x 11.5–15μ, a few longer. No. 11101. In deciduous woods, Battle Park, July 19, 1939.

Boletus subglabripes var. **corrugis** Peck. Bull. N. Y. St. Mus. **2**, No. 8: 112. 1889.

Plate 36 (below)

This differs from the typical in strongly rugose-pitted cap, more thickened stem above the base (usually), and narrow sterile margin.

Peck's *B. dictyocephalus* (Bull. N. Y. St. Mus. **2**, No. 8: 111), described from North Carolina, is probably this, but the type has been lost.

ILLUSTRATIONS: Peck. Rept. N. Y. St. Mus. **51**: pl. 55, figs. 8–10. 1889.
Also in Mem. N. Y. St. Mus. **3**: No. 4: pl. 64, figs. 8–10. 1900.

NORTH CAROLINA. Chapel Hill. No. 4479. In deciduous woods, July 21,
1920. Spores 3.7–4.8 x 11–13μ. No. 10025. By path in Battle Park,
Oct. 5, 1935. Spores 3.7–4.5 x 11–14μ.
Chatham County. Near Falls of Haw River. No. 9871. In swampy
deciduous woods, Sept. 30, 1934.

Boletus pallidus Frost. Bull. Buf. Soc. Nat. Sci. **2**: 105. 1874.

Plate 5, figs. 4, 5; pl. 37; pl. 63, fig. 12

Cap convex, up to 14 cm. broad, rarely larger, dull to subshining, dry, minutely
felted (slight pruinose effect), smooth, pale dusky gray when quite young,
becoming light buffy gray with a tint of rose to distinctly rosy buff or a darker
buffy brown in age; margin thick, only narrowly extended into a crenated,
inturned membrane. Flesh soft, nearly white with a faint lemon tint especially
near the tubes, up to 2.5 cm. thick, not changing color or slightly to bluish but
old darker plants may show a lilac tint in the flesh of central region; taste mildly
pleasant or bitterish.
Tubes up to 1.5 cm. long, nearly white when young, turning through pallid
olive gray to bright clear olive, mouths of medium size, angular, lightly stuffed
when very young, adnate, more or less depressed around the stem, turning dull
smoky blue then brownish when wounded.
Stem often crooked, nearly equal or often enlarged downward, about 8–10
cm. long, 1.2–2.5 cm. thick in center, quite smooth or lightly reticulated above,
white when young, later becoming streaked with grayish brown downward or
all over, the very base white and sometimes tomentose with mycelium, apex
often lemon yellow; flesh white or slightly reddish within, firm, silky-fibrous,
not becoming hollow.
Spores (of No. 10237) olivaceous when fresh, smooth, subelliptic, typically
slightly broader toward the proximal end, 3.7–4.5 x 9–11.8μ.

This species is rather common in our mountains, less so at Chapel Hill. It is
well named, and the pale gray cap and whitish stem streaked with gray-brown
make it easily recognizable. If plants have not passed maturity when collected
they retain the pale gray color in the dried state. Our plants have been compared with specimens in Peck's Herbarium and found to agree.

ILLUSTRATIONS: McIlvaine. Amer. Fungi, pl. 117, fig. 4.
Murrill. Bull. Torr. Bot. Club **35**: pl. 38. 1908.
Peck. Bull. N. Y. St. Mus. **54**: pl. 81, figs. 1–5. (1901) 1902. Also in
Report **55**: same plate. 1903.

NORTH CAROLINA. Chapel Hill. No. 471. In mixed woods, Oct. 1, 1912.
Spores subelliptic, somewhat broader toward proximal end, smooth, 4–5 x
10–12μ. No. 9820. By a sugar maple tree, Sept. 25, 1934. No. 10657.
In deciduous woods, Sept. 13, 1937. Spores 3.7–4.4 x 9.5–11.2μ.

Highlands. No. 9514. Under deciduous trees, Aug. 20, 1932. No. 9725. In open old field, Aug. 6, 1934. Spores olivaceous, 3.6–4 x 9.3–11μ, rarely larger. No. 10237. In woods near Kalalanta, Aug. 26, 1936. No. 12606. In pine straw in Farnsworth yard, Aug. 17, 1941. Also many other collections from Highlands and Chapel Hill. Macon County. No. 12177. Deciduous woods in Horse Cove, Aug. 29, 1938. Jackson County. No. 12135. Whiteside Cove, Aug. 10, 1939. Polk County. Tryon. No. 11930. Pearson's Falls gorge, Aug. 24, 1940.

SOUTH CAROLINA. Hartsville. No. 11136. On dry hillside under wisteria vine, Oct. 12, 1939.

GEORGIA. Rabun County. No. 11918. In rich ravine by Big Creek, Aug. 22, 1940. No. 12421. By parking place near top of Rabun Bald Mountain, July 22, 1941. Spores very dark olive brown, subelliptic with proximal end slightly broader, 4–4.8 x 9.4–11.5μ.

Boletus subpallidus (Murrill) n. comb.

Ceriomyces subpallidus Murrill. N. Amer. Fl. **9**: 145. 1910.

We have not collected this species and we give below the original description.

Pileus hemispheric, only slightly expanding, 5 cm. broad, 2 cm. thick; surface dry, smooth, glabrous, feeling very much like soft kid, avellaneous-isabelline, not becoming white-spotted nor having a separable pellicle; margin entire, fertile, the tubes slightly projecting; context milk white, entirely unchanging, very light in weight, spongy-fleshy; tubes yellow or greenish-yellow within, equalling the thickness of the context, adnate, plane in mass, becoming somewhat depressed next to the stipe, mouths dark-melleous, becoming browner with age, slightly angular, of medium size; spores fusiform, smooth, pale-ochraceous under a microscope from dried specimens, 10–12 x 4–5μ; stipe cylindric, equal, curved at the base, white, delicately but distinctly reticulate nearly to the base, slightly pruinose, solid, white and unchanging within, about 5 cm. long and 1 cm. thick.

Type collected in Pink Bed Valley, North Carolina, 1000 meters, on the ground in oak-chestnut woods, July, 1908, W. A. Murrill and H. D. House 63.

Boletus Roxanae Frost. Bull. Buf. Soc. Nat. Sci. **2**: 104. 1874.

Plate 38 and pl. 63, figs. 13, 14

Cap up to 8 cm. broad but usually smaller, convex or with margin uplifted, bright chestnut brown or yellow-brown, dry, tomentose, the tomentum in fine fasciculate tufts which often resemble small warts; sterile margin about 2–3 mm. wide, involute. Flesh rather thin, up to 8 mm., firm, whitish then pale yellow, not changing when cut but staining paper bright yellow-green; no taste or odor.

Tubes small, 2 to a mm., up to 9 mm. long, deeply depressed at stem, mouths angular, whitish at first then light olive yellow, not changing color when cut but darker olive at maturity.

Stem up to 7 cm. long, about 6–9 mm. thick above, enlarging downward, gourd-shaped, base up to 2.9 cm. thick in one large specimen, abruptly smaller at very base, a beautiful yellow or orange yellow, usually streaked with darker lines above, glabrous or rarely tomentose-dotted, quite solid, flesh yellow.

Spores (of No. 12076) olive brown, subelliptic with oblique mucro, smooth, 3.8–4.4 x 9.5–12(–13)μ. When viewed directly a heavy print is drab with a buffy tint, but at an angle the olive becomes more apparent.

This is a well marked species. The dry, yellow-brown cap with distinct tufts of tomentum, medium size, sterile involute margin in youth, small depressed tubes with angular mouths, and the yellow stem enlarging downward are characteristic. We have compared our plants with those of Frost at Albany and find them identical.

NORTH CAROLINA. Highlands. No. 9532. In mixed woods, Aug. 23, 1932. Spores 3.5–4.2 x 9.3–11.5μ. No. 9848. In pasture by road, Aug. 29, 1934. No. 10555. In open chestnut woods, Aug. 18, 1937. Spores 3.6–4.8 x 9–11.5μ. No. 12076. By a road, Aug. 2, 1939. No. 12225. In a pasture, Aug. 25, 1939. No. 12233. By a woods road, Aug. 27, 1939. Spores olivaceous, elliptic-subventricose, 3.8–4.8 x 10–12.5μ. No. 12455. By Rhododendron Trail, July 28, 1941. Also several other collections from Highlands. Asheville. Beardslee (unpublished notes sent to W. C. C.). Polk County. No. 11934. Pearson's Falls gorge, Aug. 24, 1940. Spores 3.5–4.2 x 8.8–11.2μ. Transylvania County. No. 12715. By Horsepasture River, Aug. 28, 1941. Very small specimen.

Boletus fraternus Peck. Bull. Torr. Bot. Club **24:** 145. 1897.

Plate 3, fig. 1; pl. 39 (above); pl. 64, fig. 1

Gregarious and often cespitose; cap convex, becoming plane, up to 9 cm. broad, usually 4–6 cm. and often smaller; surface dry, velvety-tomentose, not rimose at first but later with many small or medium cracks, usually most conspicuous near the margin, which show the light yellow color of the exposed flesh; color a fine deep brownish red, about dragon's blood red (Ridg.) to chestnut, somewhat lighter on the margin and fading more or less in age; margin generally irregular and bent upward in places. Flesh yellow, turning more or less blue when cut, the blue fading back to yellow; taste mild, delicate or slightly acid.

Tubes about 5–13 mm. long, deeply depressed around the stem or nearly squarely attached, running down the stem in lines, the surface uneven and the mouths large, 1–2 mm. wide, angular and irregular, larger near stem, pure bright yellow when young, becoming deeper greenish yellow and finally yellow-brown, turning deep green-blue when bruised, then back again.

Stem about 4–6 cm. long, and 1 cm. or less thick, straight or bent, usually with longitudinal ridges at top, and with minute granulations, or at times nearly smooth above and scurfy below; color like that of cap but paler, and the top colored like the tubes; flesh solid, firm, light yellow, sometimes with tints of reddish below.

Spores (of No. 9823) distinctly olivaceous, elliptic to subfusiform, smooth, 4–5 x 9.3–12.2μ. Pointed yellow cystidia about 9.8μ thick and projecting as much as 27μ present in hymenium.

This species is characterized by rather small size, cespitose habit, dry, tomentose cap which is some shade of red and usually rimose, yellow flesh which turns blue when cut and is not red under the cuticle, and large irregular deeply depressed tubes which turn greenish blue when cut. In the dried state both cap and stem of *fraternus* become yellow-brown with almost no red color. The spores are quite variable in size even on the same spore print.

This is one of our common species. It seems to prefer lawns but occurs also on banks by roads, in woods, and even around the bases of pine stumps. It is very frequently attacked by a white mold. We have compared our plants with Peck's types and find them identical.

Murrill has placed this species and *B. chrysenteron* as synonyms of *B. communis*, but we consider each of these species distinct. *Boletus chrysenteron* differs from *B. fraternus* in the red surface layer which shows in the cracks, usually paler flesh, proportionately shorter tubes which are less depressed, and in somewhat different color both in fresh and in dry state. See *B. communis* for further discussion; see also *subfraternus*.

NORTH CAROLINA. Chapel Hill. No. 463. In grass on the campus, Sept. 30, 1912. Spores 4–5.5 x 11–13.5μ. No. 2170. In mossy soil in a yard, June 20, 1916. Spores 4–5.5 x 9.6–12μ. No. 4564. On and around the bases of pine stumps, July 26, 1920. Spores strongly olivaceous, elliptic-subventricose, 3.8–5 x 11–14μ. No. 9823. On lawn of "The Rocks," Sept. 26, 1934. No. 12811. In grass in a yard, June 10 and 13, 1942. Highlands. No. 10517. In grass on a lawn, Aug. 13, 1937. Spores smaller than usual, 3.5–4 x 9–11μ. No. 10549. In open chestnut woods, Aug. 18, 1937. Spores 3.7–5 x 10–14μ. Also many other collections from above places.

SOUTH CAROLINA. Hartsville. No. 10279. On a lawn, Sept. 16, 1936. No. 10778. On hillside under deciduous trees, Kalmia Gardens, July 1, 1938. No. 11035. In low mixed woods, Sept. 14, 1938. Spores 3.8–4.8 x 10–12.5μ.

Boletus subfraternus n. sp.

Plate 40 and pl. 63, fig. 17

Cap 2.4–6 cm. broad, convex, center sometimes flat or depressed, dull, dry, minutely granular-subtomentose, dull red, varying from cinnamon rufous to brick red, uniformly colored all over, not rimose. Flesh thick for size of plant, soft, pale yellow, turning blue when cut, then back to yellowish; tasteless and odorless.

Tubes long, up to 13 mm., often hanging below the cap margin, mouths large, irregular, 1–2 mm. or those near stem may be radially elongated to several mm., deeply depressed at stem and decurrent by a tooth, clear light yellow in youth, then through sordid yellowish to deep red-brown (about cinnamon rufous to hazel of Ridgway) throughout their whole length at maturity, turning dark greenish blue when bruised, then dark brown.

Stem 3.5–6 cm. long, crooked, 4–9 mm. thick, usually expanding into the cap above and marked there with descending lines, concolorous with cap or slightly paler, longitudinally streaked, minutely fibrous to granular; flesh solid, yellow or sometimes reddish yellow below, changing as in cap; mycelium apparently white.

Spores (of No. 12647) dark olive brown, smooth, subelliptic, often slightly broader toward proximal end, 3.8–4.5 x 11–12.5μ.

The small size, dull red cap which is not rimose, red stem, light yellow flesh turning blue when wounded, and yellow tubes which become brownish red at maturity are distinguishing characters. This species differs from *fraternus*, which is nearest, in the smooth, not areolated cap surface, reddish tube mouths and flesh after maturity, red stem throughout, and in the fact that both cap and stem retain the dull reddish color in the dried state, whereas *fraternus* becomes yellow-brown with little or no red. Both species are frequently attacked by mold.

Neither Peck for *rubinellus* nor Kauffman for *rubritubifer* states the color of the tubes when young, but Webster (Rhodora **2**: 175. 1900) says for *rubinellus*: "In its young state its coloring is most attractive, the comparatively large pores and often the upper part of the stem being of a peculiar red—almost Indian red in one instance." This is sufficient to separate *rubinellus* from our present plant, but other differences in *subfraternus* are larger tubes, thicker spores, and occurrence on sand-clay bank not associated with conifers.

NORTH CAROLINA. Highlands. No. 9828. On bank by road to Glen Falls, Aug. 26, 1934. Spores olive buff, 3.8–4.8 x 9–12μ. No. 10148. Same locality as above, July 19, 1936. No. 10516. On same roadside bank, Aug. 13, 1937. Spores subelliptic with slightly broader proximal end, 3.7–4.2 x 9.5–12 (–13)μ. No. 12647 (type). On sand-clay bank by road to Glen Falls, Aug. 22, 1941. Also Nos. 10462, 11006, 12537, and 12585 from same roadside.

Boletus communis Bull. Herb. Fr., pl. 393. 1788.

B. *chrysenteron* var. *albocarneus* Peck. Rept. of the State Botanist for 1900: 185–186. 1901. Also in Rept. N. Y. St. Mus. **54**: 185–186. 1902.

Plate 41 and pl. 64, fig. 2

Cap 5.5–12 cm. broad, convex, subtomentose or in places nearly smooth, rosy leather or rosy brown or reddish or sometimes grayish leather color, dry (slightly viscid in very wet weather), at times becoming rimose, especially in the center. Flesh usually thick, up to 2 cm. at stem, soft, whitish to light yellow (pallid apple-meat color), typically with a reddish layer just under the surface, sometimes reddish nearly or all the way through, usually changing to blue when cut, sometimes not changing, grub channels usually reddish; taste mild, scarcely acid.

Tubes about 9–15 mm. long, adnate, often depressed around the stem, rather dull greenish yellow, then brownish, turning to blue when wounded; mouths irregular, medium large, surface pitted, not stuffed when young.

Stem 4–10 cm. long, 9–17 mm. thick, equal or slightly enlarged just above the pinched base, nearly glabrous, minutely tomentose-dotted in places, not reticulated, varying from dull yellow with mottlings of reddish, the red sometimes in streaks, to rhubarb color all over, at times turning blue-green when rubbed; flesh solid, yellow, turning bluish, grub channels reddish.

Spores (of No. 11102) strongly olivaceous, elliptic to subventricose, smooth, 3.8–4.8 x 10–13μ.

Fries (Syst. Mycol. **1**: 389–390) included as synonyms under *B. subtomentosus* L. both *B. communis* Bull. and *B. chrysenteron* Bull. Later (Hymen. Eur., pp. 502–503) he recognized as distinct *B. chrysenteron* but still gave *communis* as a synonym of *subtomentosus*, saying concerning the latter (and by inference both) that the flesh under the cuticle was concolorous. Now this is a contradiction of both Bulliard's description and plate (see Plate 393, fig. C) which distinctly show that the flesh is red under the cuticle.

We are accepting Bulliard's name *communis* for our plants here described because they agree in all essential respects with his description and figures. Our interpretation of *subtomentosus* differs from the present species in smaller average size, distinctly more tomentose cap, absence of red layer under the cuticle, no change of cap flesh to blue, and essentially brown rather than reddish color.

The present species differs from what we consider *chrysenteron*, which we find in the mountains of this state but not in Chapel Hill, in larger average size, distinctly less tomentose cap and stem, somewhat different shape of spores (longer in proportion to their thickness), and in the fact that the cracks in the cap surface are not reddish. The red color in the cracks on the cap of *chrysenteron* apparently comes from the cuticle itself rather than from any rosy flesh beneath the cuticle.

ILLUSTRATIONS: Bulliard. Herb. Fr., pl. 393.

Peck. Rept. of the State Botanist (N. Y.) for 1900: pl. 76, figs. 21–25. 1901. Also in Rept. N. Y. St. Mus. **54** (1): pl. 76, figs. 21–25. 1902. (As *B. chrysenteron* var. *albocarneus*.)

Sowerby. Engl. Fungi, pl. 225 (tube mouths shown too large for our specimens).

NORTH CAROLINA. Chapel Hill. No. 3285. In grass in cemetery, June 3, 1919. No. 3313. In deciduous woods, June 7, 1919. No. 4570. Under a willow oak, July 29, 1920. Spores broadly and rather evenly elliptic, smooth, 4–5 x 9.5–12 (–13)μ. No. 4571. Under shrubs, July 29, 1920. No. 9842. In a grassy lawn, Sept. 6, 1934. Spores 4–5.5 x 10–12.5μ. No. 11046. On lawn at "The Rocks," Sept. 14, 1938. No. 11102. In grass by sidewalk, July 20, 1939. No. 11601. In grass by Gimghoul Road, Aug. 26, 1940. Spores elliptic, scarcely ventricose, 3.7–4.5 x 10–12μ. Also other collections from Chapel Hill.

Boletus bicolor Peck.   Rept. N. Y. St. Mus. **24**: 78.   1872.

B. rubeus Frost.   Bull. Buf. Soc. Nat. Sci. **2**: 102.   1874.

Plate 42 and pl. 64, fig. 3

Cap usually large, 8–15 cm. broad, sometimes larger, convex, dry, pruinose-felted when young, becoming glabrous and sometimes finely rivulose, deep rosy red or purplish red, becoming paler and mottled with yellowish.   Flesh thick, pale or distinctly yellow, later deep golden yellow on exposure and if properly dried retaining this color in the herbarium, old grub channels often red; odorless and tasteless or nearly so; very soft and friable in the dried state.

Tubes small to medium and usually very short, 5–8 mm. (in very large plants up to 15 mm.), adnate-depressed, angular and subcompound, lightly "stuffed" apparently when quite young but only closed by folding, bright yellow, then through greenish yellow to brownish olivaceous, rarely with reddish mouths when mature, becoming blue when wounded.

Stem typically subequal but variable, up to 10 cm. long and rarely 2.5 cm. thick, sometimes enlarged in center or below and then up to 4 cm. thick, straight or crooked, typically yellow at top and red below, the red distributed as a mottled velvety superficial layer, but occasionally yellow nearly all over with red punctations below, surface even or rarely with faint reticulating lines at top; flesh solid, firm, yellow, changing to blue when wounded, old wounds tending to reddish brown.

Spores (of No. 11765) strongly olive when fresh, smooth, oblong-elliptic, 3.7–4.2 x 8.5–11μ.

This is a common and variable species.   It belongs in the group of closely related species including *Peckii*, *speciosus*, and *miniato-olivaceus*.   We tried for a number of years to make out consistent differences between *bicolor* and *rubeus*, but have come to the conclusion that they cannot be separated.   As originally described, *rubeus* seemed to have a thinner cap, tubes "sometimes with red mouths," stem more slender, and to occur "in deep woods."   These differences do not seem to be important and are not correlated.   For instance, the heavier plant of more open places may have tubes mouths which become reddish at least in areas at maturity.   Furthermore the species is variable in several characters.   The flesh may or may not change color in the same collection, and the spores vary in size.   For example, Nos. 10467 and 10470 came from the same spot only three days apart, and the spores of No. 10467 are noticeably larger than those of No. 10470.

The distinguishing characters of *B. bicolor*, as we are treating it, are: cap red in youth, fading to yellowish or mottled with yellow; tubes yellow at first, and always relatively *short* in comparison with thickness of cap flesh; flesh yellow, becoming deeper yellow on exposure and, if well dried, retaining this bright yellow in the herbarium; stem yellow at apex and red below or mottled with red, and *smooth* or at most delicately reticulated at top.   In this and all other species in this group, the flesh is very soft and friable in the dried state.

We have examined numerous collections of *bicolor* made and determined by Peck and find that they are identical with ours.

Boletus miniato-olivaceus, which seems nearest this species, differs in having stem yellow all over, or practically so, cap somewhat different color (more pink with a bloom) when mature, tubes tending to be decurrent, and in the more prompt and extensive change of the flesh to blue. There is also usually a difference in the proportions of the plant, that is, the stem of *miniato-olivaceus* is apt to be longer in proportion to the width of the cap than in *bicolor*.

Boletus Peckii differs in average smaller size, more strongly reticulated stem, cap rose red with a distinct bloom, fading to brownish, flesh paler in color and bitter in taste.

Boletus speciosus differs in yellow stem usually reticulated all over (our No. 9610 shows variations), more brilliant colors, and in the *very narrow* cylindrical spores.

Kallenbach (Die Pilze Mitteleuropas **1**: 123. 1937) reduces *bicolor* to synonymy with *B. sanguineus* With., which it certainly strongly resembles. However, its generally larger size, shorter tubes in proportion to thickness of flesh, and smaller spores cause us to retain it as a separate species.

ILLUSTRATIONS: McIlvaine. Amer. Fungi, pl. 117, figs. 1, 2.

Murrill. Mycologia **5**: pl. 80, fig. 7. 1913.

Peck. Rept. N. Y. St. Mus. **24**: pl. 2, figs. 5–8, 1872; ibid. **55**: pl. 81, figs. 6–11, 1903; Bull. N. Y. St. Mus. **54**: pl. 81, figs. 6–11, 1902 (same as above).

NORTH CAROLINA. Chapel Hill. No. 238. By the Schizomeris pool, Oct. 1, 1909. Spores 4–4.5 x 9.5–11.5μ. No. 519. In mixed woods south of campus, Oct. 7, 1912. No. 4340. In mixed woods, June 26, 1920. No. 10022. In mixed woods, Sept. 29, 1935. Spores strongly olivaceous, 4–5.2 x 10–13.5μ.

Highlands. No. 9554. On a road bank, oak-chestnut woods, Aug. 25, 1932. Spores oblong-elliptic, 3.6–4.4 x 9.3–11.2μ. No. 10467. By roadside south of Harbison Lake, Aug. 3, 1937. Spores ventricose-elliptic, 4.4–5.2 x 11–13 (–15)μ. No. 10470. Same spot as above, Aug. 6, 1937. Spores smaller in this collection. No. 11713. By roadside below Country Club, July 12, 1940. No. 12079. On bank on side of Bear Pen Mt., Aug. 4, 1939.

Haywood County. No. 8030. Mixed woods, Aug. 5, 1926. Spores 3.4–4 x 10–12μ. No. 8061. Mountain woods, Aug. 6, 1926. Spores 4–4.5 x 10–13μ.

Also numerous other collections from Chapel Hill and Macon County.

Asheville. Beardslee.

Blowing Rock. Atkinson.

Pink Bed Valley, Pisgah Forest. Murrill.

GEORGIA. Rabun County. No. 11961. On Big Creek by Walhalla road, Aug. 27, 1940. No. 12408. Same locality, July 20, 1941.

Boletus miniato-olivaceus Frost. Bull. Buf. Soc. Nat. Sci. **2**: 101. 1874.

B. sensibilis Peck. Rept. N. Y. St. Mus. **32**: 33. 1879.

B. tennesseensis Snell and Smith. Journ. Elisha Mitch. Sci. Soc. **56**: 327. 1940.

Plate 43 and pl. 64, fig. 4

Cap up to 11.5 cm. broad, convex, glabrous, dry, deep red in extreme youth, later onion skin pink or Japan rose (Ridg.) with a bloom, or in age some shade of rosy tan with greenish yellow areas and tints, usually paler on the margin, which is free and at first incurved. Flesh about 2 cm. thick, soft but toughish, dull white to pale yellow, turning instantly blue, then back to the original color after a few minutes or in some cases scarcely turning; taste none, odor distinctly of licorice, maple syrup or fenugreek.

Tubes about 7–11 mm. long, *small*, 2 or rarely 3 to a mm., lightly stuffed in youth, adnate to slightly decurrent, surface even, bright lemon yellow, turning quickly blue, then brown, duller gold or more pallid yellow at maturity, mouths sometimes tinted reddish in age.

Stem 8–10 cm. long, rarely longer, about 1.7–2 cm. thick in center, subequal or somewhat enlarged above and smaller to distinctly pinched at base, yellow all over or with reddish stains below, turning blue, smooth or minutely furfuraceous, not reticulated or lightly so at very top; flesh solid, like that of cap or more yellow, mycelium whitish (but see below).

Spores (of No. 11731) dark olive in a heavy print, smooth, oblong-elliptic, 3.6–4.2 x 9.8–12.2μ.

If plants are quickly dried they retain very well the colors of the fresh state. On standing over night, cut flesh becomes a clear deep yellow and the tubes become a clear brownish olive.

This species is very close to *B. bicolor*, and for many years we were unable to convince ourselves that it was anything but a form of that variable species. However, we are listing under this species plants which differ from *bicolor* in having the stem yellow all over or practically so, cap somewhat different color (more pink with a bloom), tubes tending to be decurrent, and usually more distinct sterile margin and more change of the flesh to blue. The form of this species which changes instantly to blue was first named *B. sensibilis* by Peck (Rept. N. Y. St. Mus. **32**: 33. 1879), but later reduced by him to a variety of *miniato-olivaceus* (Boleti of the United States, p. 107). This is the common form with us, but we have found one colony (represented by No. 12361 entered below, collected in exceedingly wet weather) in which there was very little change to blue, and the plants differed also in having yellow mycelium and the stem tending to be swollen in places.

We have also studied specimens at Albany determined by Peck as *miniato-olivaceus*, and so far as can be seen from the dry state they are the same as ours.

This is the only species of *Boletus* we have that is known to be dangerously poisonous. Dr. F. S. Collins (Rhodora **1**: 21. 1899) relates his own experience from eating it. He was misled by the Palmer picture cited below.

We have examined Snell and Smith's *B. tennesseensis* (Journ. E. M. Sci. Soc. **56**: 327. 1940) and think it is only a short-spored form of this species. Our No. 11603 has been compared side by side with it and found identical.

ILLUSTRATION: Palmer. Mushrooms of America, pl. 7, fig. 4 (as *B. subtomentosus*).

NORTH CAROLINA. Chapel Hill. No. 11603. In mixed woods, Aug. 29, 1940. Spores 4–4.8 x 7.4–9.3μ, shorter than usual.

Highlands. No. 9521. In mixed woods, Aug. 21, 1932. Spores 3.8–4.8 x 10–13μ. No. 11731. In deciduous woods by trail to Black Rock, July 19, 1940. No. 12186. Mixed woods by same trail as above, Aug. 20, 1939.

Spores deep olive, rather evenly elliptic, 3.7–4.3 x 9.3–12.2μ. No. 12361. On rhododendron bank by Rhododendron Trail, July 11, 1941. Spores 3.6–4.2 x 10–12.5μ.
Also other collections from Chapel Hill and Highlands.
McDowell County. No. 12835. In deciduous woods about one mile from the fish hatchery, July 16, 1942.

South Carolina. Hartsville. No. 12266. On a bluff under kalmia, Kalmia Gardens, July 1, 1941.

Boletus speciosus Frost. Bull. Buf. Soc. Nat. Sci. **2**: 101. 1874.

Plate 44 (above) and pl. 64, fig. 5

Cap about 7–12 cm. broad, rarely larger, convex, inherently felted, a beautiful grayish or purplish rose, about Corinthian red or varying to vinaceous russet (Ridg.) with some yellowish areas at maturity, slightly glaucous. Flesh up to 2 cm. thick, moderately firm, light yellow, turning quickly blue when cut then back to deep yellow; mild in taste, odor none.
Tubes up to 10 mm. long, small, 2 to 3 to a mm., lightly stuffed when young, adnate but varying to slightly depressed or decurrent, bright yellow, turning immediately blue then darker blue-brown when bruised, mouths often dull reddish at maturity.
Stem up to 3 cm. thick, some pinched at very base, bright yellow all over or reddish at base, finely reticulated usually all over, sometimes only above; flesh yellow, firm, turning blue.
Spores (of No. 10520) distinctly olive brown, smooth, almost cylindrical, 2.8–3.5 x 9.3–11.2μ.

This is a beautiful species with its brilliant colors of rose and bright yellow. The change of the flesh to blue is almost as intense as in *B. cyanescens*. Old wounds and grub channels are deep yellow on standing. The size of the plant seems to average smaller in the south than in the north, though it is otherwise identical. The narrow, cylindrical spores are characteristic.

Illustrations: Farlow. Icones Farlowianae, pls. 81 and 82. (The latter plate looks more like our *B. Peckii.*)

North Carolina. Chapel Hill. No. 11112. In deciduous woods, Battle Park, July 20, 1939. This was a very young specimen and may possibly not belong here, though so far as could be ascertained it seemed to agree. Highlands. No. 9610. In mixed woods, Aug. 15, 1933. Spores rod-elliptic, 3–3.8 x 9.3–11.5μ. No. 10520. By road to Trillium Lodge, Aug. 14, 1937. No. 11802. In road at top of Little Bear Pen, Aug. 2, 1940. No. 11892. By road to Trillium Lodge, Aug. 19, 1940.
Macon County. No. 10918. In rich deciduous woods in Coweeta Expt. Forest, Aug. 12, 1938. Spores 2.8–3.7 x 9.3–12.8μ.
Blowing Rock. Atkinson and Schrenk.
Pink Bed Valley, Pisgah Forest. Murrill.

Boletus Peckii Frost *in* Peck.   Rept. N. Y. St. Mus. **29**: 45.   1878.

B. roseotinctus Peck.   Bull. Torr. Bot. Club **27**: 612.   1900.

Plate 45 and pl. 64, fig. 6

Cap 4.5–9.5 cm. broad, rarely larger, convex to nearly plane, finely tomentose, dry, rose colored to a greater or less degree, sometimes a pretty ashes of roses color, fading to a yellowish brown in older plants or brownish rose even in young ones, with a distinct bloom like a peach; narrow free margin. Flesh nearly white, turning more or less blue, soft at maturity, about 1.2 cm. thick; taste strongly bitter or at least acid-bitter. Old wounds clear rose red and sometimes stained with red when freshly cut.

Tubes about 4–10 mm. long, small, about 2 or 3 to a mm., adnate or slightly decurrent, rarely depressed, round, lightly stuffed when young, pallid yellowish or grayish cream when young, turning dull bluish when wounded, later becoming dull drab yellow or brownish with reddish mouths.

Stem 4–6.5 cm. long, subequal or somewhat bulbous, about 1.2–1.5 cm. thick, rosy red or deep blood red, very top usually color of tubes, base dull yellowish as is the mycelium; surface reticulated nearly all over or only above (in two collections some stems practically smooth); flesh solid and firm, colored as in cap or (in No. 10453) deep wine red throughout.

Spores (of No. 9013) smoky olivaceous, elliptic or slightly broader near mucro end, 3.6–4 x 9–11μ.

Although intermediates occur, the typical form of this species differs from its close relatives, *B. bicolor* and *speciosus*, as follows. From *bicolor* in average smaller size, distinct bloom on cap, flesh bitter in taste and less yellow in color, not golden on standing, longer tubes, and stem more reticulated. From *B. speciosus* it differs in much less brilliant colors of tubes and stem, flesh bitter and less yellow, and spores distinctly broader. The reticulations on the stem in this group vary so much that it should not be made a major basis of distinction. In this connection it is well to note that Peck himself described a var. *laevipes* of *B. Peckii* (Bull. N. Y. St. Mus. **2**, No. 8: 125. 1889). As Frost remarked in the original description of *B. Peckii*, the stem retains its color better than does the cap, but not rarely the lower part of the stem fades to brownish, leaving a distinct red band at the top.

NORTH CAROLINA. Chapel Hill. No. 1867. On high mossy bank, Sept. 22, 1915. No. 10779. In woods near Meeting of Waters, July 4, 1938. Spores nearly rod-elliptic, 3.7–4.2 x 8–11μ. No. 11091. In deciduous woods, July 15, 1939.

Highlands. No. 9013. On side of Mt. Satulah, July 31, 1931. No. 9515. On lawn of the Salinas place, Aug. 20, 1932. Spores rather evenly elliptic but a few slightly broader toward proximal end, 3.6–4.5 x 8.5–12μ. No. 10453. By trail to Kalalanta, July 26, 1937. Spores smoky olive, 3.4–4 x 9.3–11.2μ. No. 10879. On roadside bank north of Mirror Lake, Aug. 7, 1938. No. 12589. Deciduous woods, Aug. 16, 1941. Tubes lightly stuffed when very young.

Macon County. No. 10902. In deciduous woods, Aug. 11, 1938. Spores 3.6–4.2 x 9–11μ. No. 10962. In deciduous woods by trail to Standing Indian, Aug. 20, 1938.

Jackson County. No. 12137. Mixed woods in Whiteside Cove, Aug. 10, 1939.

Pisgah Forest. No. 10982. In woods near Big Bear Pen Creek, Aug. 23, 1938.

Transylvania County. No. 12760. By trail along Horsepasture River near falls, Sept. 3, 1941.

Also other collections from Chapel Hill and Macon County.

Asheville. Beardslee.

Blue Ridge. (Atkinson) Peck (as *B. roseotinctus*).

GEORGIA. Rabun County. No. 12419. In mixed woods near parking place on Rabun Bald Mt., July 22, 1941. No. 12619. Same place as above, Aug. 20, 1941.

Boletus subclavatosporus Snell. Mycologia **28**: 474. 1936.

This species was described from material collected in North Carolina, and we give below the original description. We have not seen the type.

Pileus convex to plano-convex, 5–10 cm. broad. Surface dry, glabrous to subpruinose, rarely minutely and obscurely subtomentose, in places minutely rimose-areolate, dingy warm buff. Flesh dingy white, turning King's blue when cut, sometimes deeper blue, fading again, 15 mm. thick; taste bitter. Tubes convex, adnate to slightly subdecurrent, more or less depressed, at first white or very pale yellowish-white, becoming at maturity light yellowish-olive, brownish-olive where bruised, 5–9 mm. long; mouths rotund to subangular, 2–3 a mm. when young, 1–2 when older. Stipe medium slender, equal or nearly so, even, glabrous or obscurely scurfy-dotted except at apex where it is slightly reticulate from decurrent walls of tubes, slightly paler than pileus; within dingy white above, dingy reddish in lower half, unchanging; 6–12 cm. long, 8–15 mm. thick. Spores probably brownish-olivaceous in mass, broadly clavate or sub-clavate, with one end narrowed, few somewhat narrowly diamond-shaped, few subcylindric, pale olivaceous or slightly olivaceous-yellow tinged, 11–14 x 4–5μ. Cystidia abundant, often clustered, fusiform, hyaline, 40–60 x 4–8μ.

Subcespitose or gregarious along river. Hot Springs, North Carolina. Coll. C. H. Kauffman. No. 556 in Mich. Herb.; 488 in Herb. WHS.

Boletus parvulus n. sp.

Plate 46 and pl. 64, fig. 7

Cap 1.9–2.3 cm. broad, convex, dry, dull, velvety-pubescent, terra cotta red all over. Flesh rather firm, pale yellow, turning blue then light rosy red on standing; no taste or odor.

Tubes small, angular, up to 6 mm. long, deeply and widely depressed at stem, almost free but with lines running down the top of the stem, pale, then strongly olive, turning blue then reddish or brown when rubbed.

Stem 1.9–2.5 cm. long, nearly equal or somewhat larger downward, up to 5 mm. thick in center, firm, color of cap (but paler) all over except at very apex or base where it may be yellowish, granular above, base pinched to a point.

Spores (of No. 11855) smoky olive, elliptic to slightly ventricose, 3.8–4.6 x 8.5–11μ.

This is the smallest *Boletus* we know. *Boletus rubinellus* and *piperatus* some-times approach this small size, but are in several ways quite different, such as adnate to decurrent tubes which are differently colored, and in the case of the latter the peppery taste.

NORTH CAROLINA. Polk County. No. 11928. Pearson's Falls gorge, Aug. 24, 1940.

SOUTH CAROLINA. Pickens County. No. 11855 (type). In rich deciduous woods on bank of Eastatoe River, Aug. 11, 1940.

Boletus chrysenteron Bull.   Herb. Fr., pl. 490, fig. 3.   1790.

Plate 44 (below) and pl. 64, fig. 8

Cap up to 7 cm. broad, convex, dry, dull, subtomentose to distinctly tomen-tose, dark drab brown when young, a fine chestnut brown at maturity, or whole surface with more or less strong tint of vinaceous red, soon delicately areolated with the cracks reddish; margin a thin, nearly white membrane.   Flesh whitish to light yellow with thin surface layer (cuticle) rosy and showing rosy stains here and there, changing to blue-green when cut or sometimes not changing; nearly tasteless and odorless.

Tubes up to 8 mm. long, more or less depressed at stem, mouths rather large, irregular, clear light yellow (Pinard yellow of Ridg.) when young, through dull olive yellow to darker brownish olive with the mouths stained reddish, turning blue when rubbed at all ages.

Stem up to 6 cm. long, about 6–8 mm. thick, nearly equal, slightly swollen below, crooked, surface more or less granular dotted all over, pale yellow or buffy above, rosy vinaceous (about rhubarb) in great part, color of cap or golden brown or buffy brown at base except for the inserted white part.

Spores (of No. 12395) dark olive brown in a good print, elliptic to slightly broader toward proximal end, and with a truncated distal tip in many cases, 3.8–5 x 9.5–12.5μ.

Our interpretation of this species is in agreement with that of later work by Peck and reports by Snell.   The cracks in the cap surface show a red color, while in *communis*, although there is a rosy layer of flesh under the cuticle, the cracks show yellowish.   See treatment of *B. communis* for further discussion.

In his Boleti of the United States, p. 116, in discussing this species, Peck says: "In one strongly marked form the tubes are decidedly depressed around the stem, in another the flesh is whitish tinged with red.   It may be doubted whether these are varieties or distinct species."   In his Report for 1900 (pp. 185–186, 1901; also in Rept. N. Y. St. Mus. **54** (1): 185. 1902), he describes the white-fleshed form as *B. chrysenteron albocarneus*.   This latter description agrees in all respects with what we are now calling *B. communis* except that his specimens are slightly smaller than ours.   In the meantime (Bull. Torr. Bot. Club **24**: 145. 1897) he had described as *B. fraternus* a plant which is undoubtedly a member of the group often included in and described under *B. chrysenteron*. The commonest form we have in this group agrees perfectly with his description of *B. fraternus* and with his plants at Albany.

The spores of *B. chrysenteron* show a remarkable peculiarity. In many of the spores the distal tip is distinctly truncate, and even under moderately high magnification shows a pore (see drawing). However, spores from the same print may fail to show it even under the highest powers and with water or oil immersion.

ILLUSTRATIONS: Bulliard. Herb. Fr., pl. 490, fig. 3.
Güssow and Odell. Mushrooms and Toadstools, pl. 90 (not in color).
Massee. Brit. Fungi and Lich., pl. 27, fig. 3.
Michael. Führer f. Pilzfreunde **1**: No. 29.
Rolland. Atl. Champ. Fr., pl. 80, No. 180.

NORTH CAROLINA. Highlands. No. 11878. On bank by road west of Mirror Lake, Aug. 16, 1940. Spores olivaceous, elliptic-subventricose, and with distal end often appearing truncate, 4.2–5.4 x 9.5–12μ. No. 12014. Deep mixed woods, Primeval Forest, July 13, 1939. No. 12368. In a cespitose cluster in pine grove, July 13, 1941. No. 12391. In same place as above, July 17, 1941. Spores olive brown, subelliptic, 4–4.8 x 11–12.2μ, often with a truncated tip. No. 12395. Same pine grove as above, July 19, 1941. Also other collections from Highlands.
Graham County. No. 12055. On path to Joyce Kilmer Memorial Forest, July 28, 1939.
Haywood County. No. 8133. In low woods, Aug 9, 1926.
Pisgah Forest. No. 10983. Near Fish Hatchery, Aug. 23, 1938.
Transylvania County. No. 11936. In open grove, Aug. 24, 1940.
Asheville. Beardslee.

Boletus sordidus Frost. Bull. Buf. Soc. Nat. Sci. **2**: 105. 1874.
B. fumosipes Peck. Rept. N. Y. St. Mus. **50**: 108. 1897.

Plate 39 (below) and pl. 64, figs. 9, 10

Cap 4.5–8.5 cm., rarely 13 cm. broad, convex, finely tomentose, the tomentum sometimes fasciculate, scarcely at all viscid, dull, becoming delicately areolated or more coarsely so near the margin; color light brownish drab when young, becoming darker brown and less drab at or after maturity, with a slight tint of blue-green near the margin. Flesh whitish (pallid apple meat), soft but not cottony, about 7–10 mm. thick near stem, when cut showing tints of rose and also blue-green, and staining paper deep blue-green; tasteless and with a slight nitrous odor.

Tubes small to medium, varying somewhat according to the size of the cap, about 7–8 mm. long, deeply depressed around the stem, not decurrent but with lines due to receding, round, when young nearly white, pallid straw or fleshy, becoming darker brownish straw with a faint reddish sheen at certain angles; mouths dotted at all ages with fine particles which may be dark smoky brown, not stuffed when young; when bruised turning deep blue-green, then very soon deep brownish red.

Stem 4.5–6 cm. long, 7–10 mm. thick near center, crooked, nearly equal or tapering slightly upward, the base pinched to a point; surface finely dotted, often somewhat streaked, about the color of the cap below and tubes above, with dilute or distinct greenish or bluish green tint at top; flesh very firm with a less firm center, turning faintly rosy when cut.

Spores (of No. 10234) rich brown with tint of reddish, subelliptic, slightly broader toward proximal end and tapering distally, not striate, smooth, 4.5–5.5 x 11–13.5μ.

This species is common in the mountains of North Carolina, less so at Chapel Hill. It is found on banks, often in bare clay, and in open woods, both coniferous and deciduous. The dark brown color of cap and stem, greenish area at the top of the stem, large spores, and staining of paper blue-green are distinguishing characters.

We have studied good specimens of B. sordidus collected and determined by Frost himself and are satisfied that they are the same as ours. We have also examined a number of Peck's collections of B. fumosipes, and can find no real difference between the two species. Peck (Boleti of the United States, p. 146) describes as B. sordidus plants from Ohio with tube mouths large and angular, whereas in our plants they are prevailingly small to medium and rounded. However, in our collections in which the plants themselves are large the tubes also vary to large and irregular, and the plants are otherwise identical. The caps in our plants are often rimose-areolated, but we have some which are not so. The spores of Frost's plants are subventricose-elliptic, often slightly broader toward proximal end, smooth, 5.5–7 x 10.5–13μ, according to our measurements.

ILLUSTRATIONS: Murrill. Mycologia **5**: pl. 92, fig. 5. 1913. (As B. fumosipes.)

NORTH CAROLINA. Chapel Hill. No. 9806. By path beside the arboretum, Sept. 24, 1934. Spores dark rosy brown, smooth, 4.5–5.5 x 10–13μ. No. 10647. On a lawn under white pines, Sept. 8, 1937.

Highlands. No. 9034. Under white pines, Aug. 3, 1931. Spores rosy brown, 4.2–5.6 x 9.5–12μ. No. 10234. By road to Black Rock, Aug. 26, 1936. No. 10877. On roadside bank, Aug. 7, 1938. Spores 4.6–5.8 x 10–13.5μ, slightly broader near proximal end and tapering distally. No. 12569. On bank at base of Sunset Rock, Aug. 14, 1941. No. 12586. On bank by road, Aug. 15, 1941.

Also other collections from Chapel Hill and Highlands.

Blowing Rock. No. 5582. On a roadside bank, Aug. 19, 1922. Also reported by Atkinson.

Cashiers. No. 9578. In open woods, Aug. 28, 1932.

Haywood County. No. 10980. On bank in deciduous woods, Pisgah Forest, Aug. 23, 1938. Also reported from Pink Bed Valley, Pisgah Forest, by Murrill.

Polk County. No. 11937. Pearson's Falls gorge, Aug. 24, 1940.

Transylvania County. No. 10833. On clay bank by road, July 30, 1938.

Boletus chrysenteroides Snell. Mycologia **28**: 468–471. 1936.

Plate 47 and pl. 64, fig. 12

Cap 4–5 cm. broad (larger in Snell's specimens), convex, minutely tomentose, the fibers aggregating into inherent squamules, often areolated, about mummy brown (Ridg.), with or without a faint chestnut tint, rarely slightly viscid. Flesh

3–6 mm. thick near stem, thinning to a membrane, pale yellow, soft, turning blue when wounded, then dull reddish, old gnawed places deep red; nearly tasteless and odorless.

Tubes up to 10 mm. long, 1–2 to a mm., round, uneven on the edges, deeply depressed at stem, bright greenish yellow when young, later dull olivaceous, turning blue then reddish when cut.

Stem 4–7 cm. long, slender, 5–8 mm. thick, subequal, crooked, color of cap below, more reddish above, somewhat longitudinally striate, not reticulated but tomentose above and punctate-squamulose below; flesh solid and tough, nearly concolorous with surface.

Spores (of No. 10941) dark brown with an olive tint, elliptic with mucro tip bent, distinctly *longitudinally striate*, 5.5–6.8 x 11–14.5μ.

This species is not common but we have collections from both Chapel Hill and the mountains. It seems to prefer deciduous woods. In outward appearance it is much like *B. sordidus* but differs in color of tubes in youth and at maturity, absence of greenish or bluish band at top of stem, and especially in the spores. It also resembles *B. chrysenteron* but it is duller in color and without the reddish cracks, and has entirely different spores.

We have one collection of this species (No. 4459) which grew on a rotting oak log. It is not typical, the cap being nearly black in youth and very dark brown at maturity, smooth, and the spores are shorter. However, the spores have the peculiar and characteristic longitudinal striations and are very dark in color, and other characters agree.

NORTH CAROLINA. Chapel Hill. No. 1132. On mossy ridge above a marsh, July 12, 1914. No. 2198. In woods, June 22, 1916. Spores longitudinally striate, 5–6.8 x 11–13.6μ. No. 4459. On an oak log, July 20, 1920. Spores striate, 5–6.5 x 9–10μ. No. 4526. By an oak log and on mound of earth from upturned roots, July 26, 1920. Spores striate, 5–7 x 10.5–13.5μ. Nos. 4578 and 4580. On damp sandy and mossy soil by Bowlin Creek, July 28, 1920. No. 13157. On rotten deciduous stump, Sept. 13, 1942. Highlands. No. 9836. In rich woods in Primeval Forest, Aug. 28, 1934. Spores very dark, almost blackish in heavy print, with olive tint when fresh, striate, 5.5–6.2 x 10–12.5μ. Jackson County. No. 1639. At Balsam, July 22, 1915. No. 10941. In open deciduous woods, Whiteside Cove, Aug. 17, 1938. No. 12925. On bank by Chattooga River, Aug. 7, 1942.

GEORGIA. Rabun County. No. 12475. In low deciduous woods by Big Creek, Aug. 1, 1941.

Boletus Ananas M. A. Curtis. Amer. Jour. Sci., ser. 2, **6**: 351. 1848. Also in Hooker's Jour. Bot. & Kew Gard. Misc. **1**: 101. 1849.

Plate 64, fig. 11

Cap up to 10 cm. broad, nearly hemispherical at first, finally expanded, pale tan to dull buff with rosy stains, covered with coarse imbricated fibrous scales; margin extended into a fimbriate-lacerate membrane, the remnant of a delicate ephemeral veil. Flesh moderately soft, whitish, turning more or less blue when cut; taste mild and pleasant, odor none.

Tubes up to 1.5 cm. long, deeply depressed around the stem, mouths medium to rather large, reddish brown in our mature plants, deep blue when rubbed.

Stem up to 8 cm. long and about 1.5 cm. thick, nearly equal, enlarged at base with mycelium, smooth to delicately fibrous above, pale flesh color, solid and firm.

Spores (of No. 5847) rather evenly elliptic with proximal end somewhat narrowed, longitudinally striate, 6–8 x 14–18.5μ; described as "ferruginous" (Curtis) and "dark brown" (Murrill) but we have no spore print.

This is a rare and remarkable species. It was first described from South Carolina, and is known only from the South Atlantic and Gulf states. It approaches the habit of *Strobilomyces strobilaceus* in its rough cap and lacerated margin, but is quite different in its smooth stem without annulus, very different spores, and less tough flesh (see also under the genus *Strobilomyces*). The markings of the spores are very peculiar. The longitudinal lines which are conspicuous under oil immersion seem to be narrow grooves on the inside of the spore wall, which at the ends of the spores appear as fine pits in the wall, resembling those in the spores of some species of *Lycoperdon*. In addition to these lines, there are other much finer ones, visible under apochromatic water immersion lens, which run at right angles to the more conspicuous ones, but we do not feel sure of the nature of these.

This species, so far as we know, is always found under or near pines. Murrill (Mycologia **1**: 10. 1909) quotes Prof. F. S. Earle as saying that "it always occurs either as a wound parasite on pine trunks or about the base of living pine trees." We have not been able to verify the parasitism of the species. Murrill (l.c., p. 9) erected a new genus *Boletellus* for this species, and gave its growth on wood as a generic character. Snell (Mycologia **33**: 422. 1941) accepts this genus and places in it four other species, *Betula, Russellii, chrysenteroides*, and *subflavidus. Boletus chrysenteroides* has spores similar in markings to *Ananas*, but any other resemblance is obscure to us. *Boletus Betula* and *subflavidus* have spores minutely warted, and *Russellii* has them longitudinally ridged like a cantaloupe. Other characters in all these cases are so different that to attempt to segregate them as a unified group would seem to us inadvisable.

NORTH CAROLINA. Brevard. "One specimen of this striking species was found growing on the roadside near Brevard, N. C. I have never seen it near Asheville." Beardslee.

Low district. Under pine logs. Curtis.

SOUTH CAROLINA. Hartsville. No. 5847. In mixed woods near pines, Aug. 31, 1922. No. 9429. By Prestwood Lake, Sept. 22, 1933. Spores striate, 5–7 x 10.5–18.5μ.

FLORIDA. Gainesville. Under pines, Aug. 4, 1937. Collection sent us by Dr. Murrill.

Boletus Russellii Frost. Bull. Buf. Soc. Nat. Sci. **2**: 104. 1874.

Plate 48 and pl. 64, fig. 14

Cap 2.5–4.5 cm. broad (original description gives up to 4 inches), convex, dry, felted-tomentose with the tomentum pinched and separated into areas and squamules, color brownish yellow with the cracks more yellow or brownish red all over. Flesh thin, mild, yellowish, unchanging.

Tubes rather long, about 8 mm. in center, adnate or depressed around the stem, mouths large, angular, walls thin, cream colored at first, then greenish yellow.

Stem long, up to 11 cm. in our specimens, slender, tapering upward, strongly bent at base, covered with wide lacerated plates which absorb moisture and swell when wet, bright flesh color or red all over; flesh yellow, firm, solid.

Spores (of No. 2418) dark brown in heavy print with faint tint of olive, elliptic, strongly ridged longitudinally like a cantaloupe, 7–9.3 x 13.5–17μ.

This remarkable plant is rare in Chapel Hill and we have found it only a few times. It is distinguished from *B. Betula*, which it strongly resembles, in the dry, fasciculate-tomentose cap and ridged spores.

ILLUSTRATIONS: Farlow. Icones Farlowianae, pl. 80. 1929. McIlvaine. Amer. Fungi, pl. 118, fig. 2.

NORTH CAROLINA. Chapel Hill. No. 1960. In moldy soil in oak woods April 12, 1915. Spores longitudinally ridged, 7.5–9.5 x 14–19μ. No. 2418. In deciduous upland woods, July 22, 1916. No. 9417. In mixed upland woods, Aug. 9, 1933.

Jackson County. No. 10916. In gorge above Tuckaseigee Falls, Aug. 14, 1938.

Asheville. "Common in thick woods." Beardslee.

Boletus Betula Schw. Syn. Fung. Car., No. 860. 1822. *B. Morgani* Peck. Bull. Torr. Bot. Club **10**: 73. 1883.

Plate 2, figs. 4, 5; pl. 49; pl. 64, fig. 13

Cap 3–4.5 cm. broad, small for the height of the plant, convex, often pitted or reticulated, glabrous, quite viscid, bright or egg yellow, with or without a brownish or red center, in age usually orange all over. Flesh yellow with more or less red in center, the red extending down the stem.

Tubes long and rather large, deeply depressed around the stem, at first light yellow, becoming greenish yellow, later much darker olive brown.

Stem up to 15 cm. long, slender, tapering upward or equal, usually crooked and sometimes twisted like a corkscrew, covered with prominent yellow reticulated lacerations, in age the reticulations becoming reddish brown, as the depressions usually are from the first (sometimes lighter, more orange); flesh solid, brittle, reddish.

Spores (of No. 768) about olive-brown (Ridg.) but more smoky, the olive more apparent in light prints (heavy prints very dark brown with almost no trace of olive), subelliptic, usually flattened at the distal end, minutely warted, 7–9.3 x 15–19.5μ.

This is a fairly common species which was originally described from North Carolina. Beardslee (in Lloyd, Myc. Notes, p. 97. 1902) considered *B. Russellii* Frost the same as *B. Betula*, but the spores are entirely different, those of *Russellii* being strongly ridged longitudinally, and also the cap of *Russellii* is tomentose and normally dry.

ILLUSTRATIONS: Hard. Mushrooms, fig. 305. 1908. (As *B. Morgani* and not in color.)

Peck. Bull. Torr. Bot. Club 10: pl. 35. 1883. (As *B. Morgani* and not in color.)

NORTH CAROLINA. Chapel Hill. No. 234. In deep leaf mold, Oct. 1, 1909. No. 248b. In rocky mixed woods, Sept. 28, 1910. No. 768. Battle Park, Sept. 14, 1913. No. 1659. Among leaves in a low place, July 27, 1915. Spores warted, 7.4–9.2 x 13–21μ. No. 10677. In rich woods near University Lake, Sept. 19, 1937. Spores elliptic, warted, 7.5–9.3 x 14.8–22μ, with a pore at the distal end. Also numerous other collections from Chapel Hill.

Pink Bed Valley, Pisgah Forest. Murrill.

Middle district. Ligneous earth. Curtis.

SOUTH CAROLINA. Oconee County. No. 12126. About five miles from Walhalla, Aug. 9, 1939. No. 12193. In humus in Oconee State Park, Aug. 21, 1939.

GEORGIA. Rabun County. No. 11020. Mixed pine woods near Big Creek on Walhalla road, Aug. 22, 1940.

Boletus granulatus L. Sp. Plant. 2: 1177. 1753.

B. circinans Pers. Neues Mag. Bot. 1: 107. 1794.

Plate 50 and pl. 65, fig. 10

Cap 4–15 cm. broad, convex, smooth, glutinous with an easily removable translucent pellicle, color when young bay red to dull reddish tan, becoming more buffy yellow, especially on the margin, and often with splotches and streaks of gluten; margin extending beyond the tubes and incurved, whitish and fibrous-felted when young, this extension often not conspicuous at maturity. Flesh thick in center, up to 1.2 cm., elastic, pure white to pale yellow, the yellow most obvious above the tubes, unchanging but old grub channels pink; odor none, taste mild, cuticle not acid.

Tubes small, about 2 to a mm., short, 2–5 mm., adnate, angular, color pale cream with dots of reddish gluten when young, then yellowish and finally dull reddish or olivaceous brown.

Stem up to 7 cm. long but usually shorter, about 1 cm. or more thick, subequal, crooked, ground color nearly white to pale yellow, especially above, brownish when rubbed, dotted all over (usually) or only above with small glutinous droplets which are pinkish in youth, drying to much darker reddish brown or blackish.

Spores (of No. 10914) rich yellow-brown (between Dresden and buckthorn,

Ridg.) in good print, elliptic, smooth, 2.5–3.4 x 6–8.2μ.

This well known species is common in open woods, especially near pines. It is distinguished from others in this group by darker cap, usually with shades of brown, thick, pale flesh, and whitish to light yellow, usually strongly dotted stem.

ILLUSTRATIONS: Bresadola. Funghi Mang., pl. 87.
Dufour. Atl. Champ., pl. 64, No. 139. 1891.
Farlow. Icones Farlowianae, pl. 75.
Fries. Sveriges Svampar, pl. 23. 1861.
Gillet. Champ. Fr., Hymén., pl. 61.
Güssow and Odell. Mushrooms and Toadstools, pl. 93 (not in color).
Krieger. Mushroom Handbook, pl. 9. 1936.
Murrill. Mycologia 5: pl. 80, fig. 3. 1913.
Peck. Rept. N. Y. St. Mus. 48: pl. 34, figs. 1–5. (1894) 1895.
Richon and Roze. Atl. Champ., fasc. 7: pl. 56, figs. 6–10.
Rolland. Atl. Champ. Fr., pl. 78, fig. 175. 1910.

NORTH CAROLINA. Chapel Hill. No. 77. In mixed woods, Oct. 25, 1911. Spores elliptic, smooth, 2.5–3.5 x 6–8.5μ. No. 481. In mixed woods with pines, Oct. 3, 1912. Spores rich yellow-brown, 2.6–3.6 x 7–8.5μ. No. 3739. On the wood of a hollow oak stump, Nov. 12, 1919. Spores 2.6–3.5 x 7.4–9.2μ. This seems typical except for its habitat. Highlands. No. 9541. In mixed woods, Aug. 23, 1932. Spores 2.8–3.4 x 6–8.5μ. No. 10864. Under hemlock and rhododendron, Aug. 6, 1938. Spores buckthorn brown (Ridg.), 2.5–3 x 5.5–7.4μ. No. 10914. Under white pines, Aug. 14, 1938. No. 11024. In mixed mountain woods, Sept. 2, 1938. Spores 2.8–3.7 x 7.8–9.3μ, a few slightly longer. No. 12701. Under pines, Aug. 25, 1941.
Jackson County. No. 12133. In mixed woods, Whiteside Cove, Aug. 10, 1939.
Also many other collections from Chapel Hill and Macon County.
Asheville. Common. Beardslee.
Blowing Rock. Atkinson and Schrenk.
Pink Bed Valley, Pisgah Forest. "Common, preferring open places in woods, and found more abundantly near pines." Murrill.

Boletus placidus Bon. Bot. Zeit. **19**: 204–205. 1861.
B. albus Peck. Rept. N. Y. St. Cab. **23**: 130. 1873.

Plate 51 and pl. 65, fig. 12

Cap 3–6 cm. broad in our plants, convex, smooth, glutinous, pale yellowish white to pure milk white. Flesh white, rather thin.

Tubes medium to small, quite short, adnate to decurrent, white at first, becoming yellow to ochraceous, dotted with viscid droplets.

Stem up to 7.5 cm. long and 1 cm. thick, white or nearly so, dotted with viscid pinkish droplets which darken in age.

Spores (of No. 8970) rather evenly elliptic, smooth, 2.5–3.4 x 6.5–8.5μ.

We have only three collections of this species and our notes are incomplete. It is very close to *granulatus*, apparently differing mainly in its white color and average longer stem. The stem and sometimes the cap become almost black in drying.

Konrad (Bull. Soc. Myc. Fr. **43:** 199–204. 1927) discusses this species in detail and gives a number of synonyms. As Snell has pointed out (Mycologia **25:** 231. 1933), it seems rather generally agreed that Peck's *B. albus* is the same as the European *B. placidus*.

ILLUSTRATIONS: Bresadola. Icon. Mycol. **19:** pl. 944 (as *Gyrodon*).
Kallenbach. Die Pilze Mitteleuropas **1:** pl. 37.
Konrad and Maublanc. Icon. Selectae Fung. **5:** pl. 415.
Murrill. Mycologia **5:** pl. 80, fig. 4 (as white form of *granulatus*). 1913.
Peck. Bull. N. Y. St. Mus. **150:** pl. 121 (as *B. albus*). 1911.

NORTH CAROLINA. Highlands. No. 8970. Under white pines, July 29, 1931.
No. 11739. In woods, mostly white pines, by Ravenel Lake, July 20, 1940.
No. 12707. Under white pines, Aug. 26, 1941.

Boletus brevipes Peck. Rept. N. Y. St. Mus. **38:** 110. 1885.
B. viscosus Frost. Bull. Buf. Soc. Nat. Sci. **2:** 101. 1874.

Plate 52 and pl. 65, fig. 11

Cap 4.5–10 cm. broad, usually of medium size, broadly convex, reddish chestnut to purplish with blackish or sometimes olive stains and covered with a thick glutinous tough pellicle; a narrow sterile margin present. Flesh white to light yellow, especially near the tubes, not changing or rarely so (see form mentioned below); taste very pleasant.

Tubes small, 2 or 3 to a mm., about 3.5–8 mm. long, adnate, slightly decurrent, creamy white when young, changing through pallid yellow to cinnamon buff and finally brownish (but see Alabama plants entered below).

Stem short, 1.5–3.5 cm. long, 1–2 cm. thick at top, tapering downward or subequal, color when young pure white all over or yellow above, becoming yellow all over and with brownish red stains, especially below, not dotted or with a few dark granules near the top; flesh solid, white to yellowish, and sometimes reddish (see form below).

Spores (of No. 241) cinnamon buff (Ridg.), subcylindric, smooth, 2.4–3 x 6.5–8μ.

This is an edible species that appears late in the season, usually under pines. It is reduced to *R. granulatus* L. by Murrill, and Atkinson considers it only a variety of that species, but we think it distinct enough to retain the specific name. However we have two collections (Nos. 1021 and 10052), one made with typical *B. brevipes*, that seem to be intermediate, but these show pinkish or rhubarb colors in the flesh especially of the stem, a character not noted for either of the species.

ILLUSTRATIONS: Peck. Mem. N. Y. St. Mus. **3**, No. 4: pl. 66, figs. 1–6. 1900.

NORTH CAROLINA. Chapel Hill. No. 76. By branch in mixed woods, Oct. 20, 1911. Spores honey yellow, subelliptic with sides nearly parallel, 2.2–3 x 6.8–8.5μ. No. 241. Battle Park, mixed woods, Oct. 28, 1910. No. 416. Mixed woods, Nov. 10, 1911. No. 586. Near branch in mixed woods, Oct. 17, 1912. No. 971. In poor hillside pasture under pines, Nov. 11, 1913. When this collection was made the weather was freezing and many of the plants were frozen through. They were in all stages of development and so plentiful that a peck of them was obtained. No. 1021. Under cedars and pines, Nov. 28, 1913. This is an intermediate form with rhubarb colored flesh. Spores like the typical form, 2.5–3.2 x 6.5–8μ. No. 10052. Under pines near University Lake, Nov. 17, 1935. In this colony were both the typical form and an intermediate with longer stem and rhubarb colored flesh. The spores were alike in all. No. 12261. Under pines by Price's Creek, May 12, 1940. Also other collections from Chapel Hill.

SOUTH CAROLINA. Pickens County. In a deep gorge, Oct. 9, 1938.

ALABAMA. Sealy Springs, Dec. 28, 1941. No. 12797. The tubes in this collection were somewhat depressed but of the usual brownish buff color. No. 12798. The tubes in these plants which grew only a foot or two away from the others, were somewhat decurrent but light sulphur colored, otherwise typical.

Boletus luteus L. Sp. Plant. **2**: 1177. 1753.
B. subluteus Peck. Bull. N. Y. St. Mus. **1**, No. 2: 62. 1887.

Plate 5, figs. 2, 3; pl. 53; pl. 55 (below); pl. 65, fig. 13

Cap convex to expanded, 4–10 cm. broad, glutinous, brownish or reddish yellow to dark smoky tan with fibrous lines and patches of darker color giving it a mottled appearance, rarely almost egg yellow, smooth, pellicle removable. Flesh up to 1.4 cm. thick, cream colored, becoming tinted with flesh at maturity, sometimes faintly greenish at top of stem, tough and elastic, faintly acid but pellicle very acid.

Tubes short, 5–8 mm. long, small, about 2 to a mm., rarely up to 1 mm. wide, angular and irregular, pallid yellowish when young, later dull ochraceous or quite dark, not changing color, mouths dotted with viscid particles.

Stem up to 8 cm. long, about 7–10 mm. thick, subequal, yellowish or darker above, whitish toward base, dotted and splotched with brownish or blackish gluten both above and below the annulus, rarely faintly reticulated above. Veil a pale glutinous membrane which remains as a collapsed annulus about 1 cm. or less from the top of the stem.

Spores (of No. 11050) rich golden brown in a heavy print, rather evenly elliptic, smooth, 3.2–3.7 x 7.4–9.5μ.

This species seems to prefer pine woods but grows also in mixed woods. From other members of the glutinous, *granulatus* group it is distinguished by the presence of an annulus on the stem. In rare cases this may disappear, but, if so, remnants of the distinct veil may almost always be found on the cap margin. This form or condition may represent the plant referred to *B. collinitus* Fr. by

Peck in his Boleti of the United States, p. 98 (not the one so referred in his 23rd Report, p. 129). We are unable to separate consistently Peck's *subluteus* from the European *luteus* and think they are the same thing. Some European illustrations show a distinctly heavier plant with the dots only above the annulus (Rolland, Atl. Champ. Fr., pl. 78, fig. 174), while others show plants just like ours (Kallenbach, cited below). The latter author also gives *subluteus* as a synonym of *luteus*. The explanation seems to be that the presence or absence of a volval sheath on the lower part of the stem at maturity depends on whether or not it breaks at the bottom and is pulled up by the expanding cap. If not, there are of course no glandular dots visible below the veil, but in all our collections they are present when the volval sheath has pulled up or shredded off below. The distinctions that Peck sets forth are not upheld by Fries's own figures (see below).

ILLUSTRATIONS: Boudier. Bull. Soc. Myc. Fr. **3**: pl. 18.   1887.
    Dufour. Atl. Champ., pl. 54, fig. 124.
    Farlow. Icones Farlowianae, pl. 71.
    Fries. Sveriges Svampar, pl. 22.   1861.
    Güssow and Odell. Mushrooms and Toadstools, pl. 94 (not in color).
    Gillet. Champ. Fr., Hymén., pl. 66.
    Kallenbach. Die Pilze Mitteleuropas **1**: pl. 19.
    Murrill. Mycologia **12**: pl. 2, fig. 1.   1920.
    Peck. Rept. N. Y. St. Mus. **48**: pl. 33.   (1894) 1895.
    Richon and Roze. Atl. Champ., fasc. **7**: pl. 56, figs. 1–5.
    Schaeffer. Fung. Bavar., pl. 114.

NORTH CAROLINA. Chapel Hill. No. 238. Under a pine tree, Nov. 9, 1909. Spores subventricose-elliptic, 3.4–3.7 x 7.5–10μ. No. 397. In mixed woods, Oct. 25, 1911. No. 474. Mixed woods, Oct. 2, 1912. No. 11050. Mixed woods, Oct. 4, 1938.
    Highlands. No. 9545. In pine woods, Aug. 24, 1932. Spores ochraceous in a good print, subelliptic, 3.4–3.8 x 8–10μ. No. 10225. In pine woods, Aug. 25, 1936. In this collection the spores are larger than usual, 3.7–4.8 x 9.3–13μ, but otherwise the plants agree. No. 12226. Under rhododendron and pines, Aug. 25, 1939. No. 12745. Low mixed woods, Sept. 2, 1941.
    Cashiers. No. 12295. Under pines, Sept. 7, 1940.
    Also many other collections from Chapel Hill and Highlands.

SOUTH CAROLINA. Hartsville. No. 11036. In low mixed woods, Sept. 14, 1938.

Boletus hirtellus Peck. Bull. N. Y. St. Mus. **2**, No. 8: 94–95. 1889.
    B. subaureus Peck (in part). Rept. N. Y. St. Mus. **39**: 42; and Bull. **1**, No. 2: 63.

Plate 65, figs. 8, 9

Cap up to 11 cm. wide, usually about 5–8 cm., convex to nearly plane, viscid, light ochraceous orange, about Capucine yellow (Ridg.) when young, later pallid yellow or yellow-brown, *dotted all over with tufts of brownish fibrils*. Flesh moderately thick for size of cap, pale yellow, unchanging when cut but more yellow on exposure; tasteless, cuticle not acid, odor faintly fragrant when fresh, not so pleasant when dry.

Tubes 3–8 mm. long, small, 1½–2 to a mm., adnate, angular, pale yellow, then dull yellow to brownish.

Stem up to 7 cm. long, 7–12 mm. thick, equal, subcespitose, often crooked, pale yellow, usually more orange yellow at apex, rarely nearly white, punctate all over with reddish brown viscid granules, rarely stained vinaceous on lower half; expanding below into plates of white mycelium.

Spores (of No. 11599) distinctly olive brown when fresh, elliptic, some narrowly so, smooth, 3–3.6 x 7–9.3μ.

Peck originally assigned to *subaureus* the plants he later called *hirtellus*, and they do resemble *subaureus* in the medium to small size of the tubes and not very bright color, especially in the dried condition. The species is distinguished mainly by the tufts of fibrils on the cap and the dark olive brown spore mass. The olivaceous tint may be somewhat lost in drying, but the spores are never the rusty color of those of *americanus* and *subaureus*. The cap fibrils are in the dried state usually so stuck down by the dried gluten as not to be very obvious. The cut flesh stains paper greenish yellow.

NORTH CAROLINA. Chapel Hill. No. 11105. Under pines in mixed woods, July 20, 1939. Spores 3.2–3.6 x 8–9.5μ. No. 11599. In pasture under pines, Aug. 25, 1940. No. 13178. In pine duff and bark, Oct. 31, 1942. No. 13189. In mixed woods. Oct. 18, 1942. Spores distinctly olive brown, subelliptic with sides nearly flat, 3–3.6 x 7.4–9.3μ. No. 13211. On clay bank at edge of pine woods, Oct. 25, 1942. No. 13224. In pine woods, Oct. 29, 1942. No. 13249. In pine woods, Nov. 7, 1942.

Chatham County. No. 13195. In pine woods about five miles from Chapel Hill, Oct. 20, 1942. No. 13229. Same place as above, Oct. 31, 1942.

Boletus americanus Peck. Bull. N. Y. St. Mus. **1**, No. 2: **62–63**. 1887.

Plate 54 (above) and pl. 65, fig. 4

Cap 4–8 cm. (rarely 10 cm.) broad, convex, often umbonate, to nearly plane, very viscid when moist, bright chrome yellow with tinge or splotches of red here and there, and when young somewhat squamulose with reddish flecks especially on the more or less inturned margin, which when fresh is fringed by a soft pendent tissue that later shrinks and turns red. Flesh *thin*, toughish and elastic, yellowish, turning dull pinkish brown when cut, then later back to deep yellow or in places, especially near top of stem, drying bright red; staining paper orange; taste of flesh mild but cuticle quite acid.

Tubes about 6–8 mm. long but of irregular lengths, mouths large, 1–2 mm. wide, often in radiating rows as in *Boletinus* and somewhat subdivided, adnate or slightly decurrent, dull yellow when young and delicately pruinose with minute sticky particles, both tubes and particles becoming brownish in age.

Stem *slender*, rarely up to 10 mm. thick, up to 6 cm. long, crooked, yellow, dotted with viscid droplets which become reddish brown and run together in places, white-mycelioid at base; solid but often badly worm-eaten. There is no annulus but a thin flocculent extension of the margin covers the pores in very young plants, and its pendent remains may be noticed later on the cap margin.

Spores (of No. 10922) rusty ochraceous, evenly elliptic or a few slightly broader toward proximal end, smooth, 3.7–4.2 x 8–10μ.

This species is common under pines in our mountains, but so far we have never found it at Chapel Hill. The very viscid, bright chrome yellow cap tinged with red in places, the large irregular tube mouths, and slender stem are distinguishing characters. In the dried state the cap is often rather bright yellow, while the tubes and stem are dark brown to almost black. From *granulatus* it differs in thinner cap of different color, more slender stem, larger tubes and spores; from *subaureus* in thinner and more yellow cap, more slender stem, larger tubes and somewhat larger spores; from *punctipes* in color of the young hymenium and of the spores, and in the size and appearance of the stem. Intermediate forms occur in this group and are often hard to place. This group seems to connect *Boletus* and *Boletinus*, as shown by the irregular, radiating tube mouths, and the fact that the tubes while separable are not easily so.

ILLUSTRATIONS: Farlow. Icones Farlowianae, pl. 73.

Murrill. Mycologia **5**: pl. 80, fig. 5 (as *B. subaureus*). 1913.

NORTH CAROLINA. Highlands. No. 9508. Under hemlock, Aug. 19, 1932. No. 10922. Under white pines, Aug. 14, 1938. Spores 3.7–4.2 x 8–9.8μ. No. 10953. On a lawn near pines, Aug. 19, 1938. Spores 3.8–4.8 x 9.8–12.2μ. No. 11873. In white pine needles, Aug. 16, 1940. Spores rusty ochraceous, 3.5–3.8 x 8–10.5μ. No. 12705. In pine woods, Aug. 26, 1941. Also many other collections from Highlands.

Jackson County. No. 12134. Under pines, Aug. 10, 1939.

Cashiers. No. 12296. Sept. 7, 1940.

Toxaway. No. 12094. Near pines and dogwood, Aug. 5, 1939.

Blowing Rock. Atkinson.

Boletus americanus var. **reticulipes** n. var.

Plate 54 (below) and pl. 65, fig. 5

This variety agrees with *americanus* in all respects, such as slender stem, large tubes, and yellow viscid cap, except that the stem is reticulated all over with soft surface tissue which is *not viscid*. The dried plant has the light brown color of *subaureus* rather than the more yellow color of well dried *americanus*.

One might ask if it is not possible that this be the same as the plant described as *B. subaureus* var. *siccipes*. Both have, for this group, the very peculiar character of soft, fibrous, *nonviscid* dots on the stem, arranged in a reticulum in one case, in the other not so. While it may be true that they are variants of the same thing, the plants as studied by us show other differences. Moreover, one grew in deciduous woods, the other under conifers. Possibly this is a mycorrhiza-forming species of *Boletus* and that, as Peyronel thought he found in another case, the fruit body may have a different appearance on one host from that on another.

NORTH CAROLINA. Highlands. No. 11746. Under pines and hemlock, July 22, 1940.

Boletus subaureus Peck. Rept. N. Y. St. Mus. **39**: 42. 1886 (in part).
Bull. N. Y. St. Mus. **2**, No. 8: 94. 1889.

Plate 55 (above) and pl. 65, fig. 6

Cap up to 10 cm. broad, convex to nearly plane, pale yellow, often with darker reddish brown spots, very viscid when moist. Flesh yellowish, rather tough, up to 1.5 cm. thick in our plants, turning pinkish brown when cut; taste mild, cuticle acid.

Tubes up to 13 mm. long, small to medium, somewhat angular, usually adnate but may be subdecurrent or rarely depressed, yellow, becoming ochraceous brown, dotted with sticky droplets which soon darken.

Stem up to 8 cm. long and 15 mm. thick, equal or nearly so, yellow, dotted with reddish brown sticky droplets which soon turn blackish, not reticulated, white-mycelioid at base; flesh solid, yellow.

Spores (of No. 9513) *rusty cinnamon*, rather evenly elliptic, a few slightly tapering distally, 3.2–3.7 x 7–9μ.

This species is distinguished from *B. americanus*, which it strongly resembles, in typically paler yellow, thicker cap, distinctly *stouter stem*, smaller tubes and somewhat smaller spores. The dried plants have a dull brown color, less yellow than well dried plants of *americanus*.

ILLUSTRATIONS: Güssow and Odell. Mushrooms and Toadstool, pl. 97 (not in color).

Peck. Mem. N. Y. St. Mus. **3**, No. 4: pl. 61, figs. 6–13. 1900.

NORTH CAROLINA. Chapel Hill. No. 347. In mixed woods, Oct. 4, 1911
Spores "dirty brown," elliptic, 2.6–3.5 x 6.5–8.5μ. No. 578. In ravine east of Tenney's, Oct. 17, 1912. Spores 3–3.5 x 7.4–9μ. No. 765. In mixed woods but near pines, Sept. 14, 1913. Spores 2.6–3.5 x 7.4–9.3μ.
Highlands. No. 9513. Under pines, Aug. 20, 1932. No. 12908. In hemlock leaf humus, Aug. 4, 1942.
Macon County. No. 10900. On road to gold mine off Route 64, Aug. 11, 1938.

Boletus subaureus var. **siccipes** n. var.

Plate 56 and pl. 65, fig. 7

Cap up to 11 cm. broad, convex then expanded, very viscid, pale clear yellow with a few reddish brown stains; margin when young a thick white roll of cottony fibers, when mature a thin, free, inturned membrane. Flesh light yellow, reddish brown when bruised; taste of flesh mild but cuticle acid, odor oily.

Tubes short, 3–6 mm. long, mouths small, up to 1 mm., radially elongated, irregular, yellow, dull reddish brown when cut or bruised, usually free of droplets and not viscid (with droplets in one of our collections).

Stem rather stout, short, 3–6 cm. long above surface of substratum, rather deeply inserted in humus and diffusing into obvious mycelial plates and strands, equal or slightly enlarged upward, yellow all over, *fibrous-warted*, not with secreted droplets and *not viscid*.

Spores (of No. 11906) ochraceous brown, about the color of the bruised flesh, narrowly elliptic, 3–3.5 x 7.6–9.5μ.

This is another puzzling form in the *americanus* group. It differs from *subaureus* in the fibrous-warted, dry stem and usually in non-viscid tubes. In the dry state it has the dull grayish clay color of *subaureus* rather than the brighter yellow color of *americanus*. Our plants grew in open deciduous woods, but apparently *subaureus* is not so much confined to pine-hemlock woods as is *B. americanus*.

NORTH CAROLINA. Highlands. No. 11720. In deciduous woods, July 17, 1940. Spores ochraceous, 2.6–3.2 x 7.5–9.3μ. No. 11906. Same place as above, Aug. 20, 1940. No. 12379. Under kalmia and oak, July 15, 1941. No. 12613. In humus by a branch, Aug. 18, 1941. Also several other collections from Highlands.

Boletus punctipes Peck. Rept. N. Y. St. Mus. **32:** 32–33. 1879.

Plate 57 and pl. 65, fig. 14

Cap 4.5–10.5 cm. wide, convex, glutinous with a removable cuticle, felted-fibrous in youth, at maturity usually showing only granules and irregular roughenings; color dull light yellow, sometimes with reddish or brownish splotches; margin paler to nearly white, very edge white-tomentose in youth and inturned. Flesh 5–18 mm. thick, pale yellow, unchanging when cut; tasteless but odor distinctly sweetish oily, rather peculiar when dry.

Tubes short, 3.5–8 mm., small, 2 to a mm., adnate, mouths quite irregular and tube surface pitted, color a peculiar *muddy yellow-brown* (about Isabella color to Saccardo's umber, Ridg.) *at all ages* but more yellow tinted in age, dotted in youth with minute whitish specks which darken later.

Stem up to 8.5 cm. long and 1.8 cm. thick, decidedly swollen at base and tapering upward, often pinched into a lateral point at the side of the blunt base, irregularly flattened and grooved; color like that of cap except for the dense peppering of brownish red, glutinous droplets from top to base; flesh yellowish, solid above, softer and more stringy in the more or less fistulose base which rapidly decays, all becoming color of the surface in age; base of stem white with mycelium which extends out into the pine needles in thick strands.

Spores (of No. 11751) distinctly dark olive brown in a good print, rather evenly elliptic, a few slightly tapering toward the distal end, smooth, 2.6–3.6 x 7.8–10μ.

This agrees well with Peck's description and with his specimens at Albany. The color of the stem is not truly rhubarb, although the dull red dots have a faint purplish tint and largely contribute to the stem color.

The species is distinguished from its relatives mainly by the brownish color of the young hymenium, the color of the stem, which is enlarged below, and the darker olive brown color of the spore mass. Taken generally the plant is nearly the same color throughout. If soaked when collected the stem dries black.

ILLUSTRATIONS: Atkinson. Mushrooms, p. 180, fig. 167 (not in color). Farlow. Icones Farlowianae, pl. 74.

NORTH CAROLINA. Chapel Hill. No. 845. In woods, Sept. 26, 1913. No. 11099. In mixed woods, July 19, 1939. No. 11105. In mixed woods, July 20, 1939. No. 11121. In mixed woods, Aug. 3, 1939. Spores dark, strongly olive, 3.2–3.6 x 7–9.3μ.
Highlands. No. 8938. By Dillard road, July 28, 1931. Spores 3.2–4 x 8.5–11μ. No. 9547. In pine woods, Aug. 24, 1932. Spores olivaceous, 3.2–3.8 x 8–9.5μ. No. 11751. Damp dense woods south of Farnsworth place, July 23, 1940. No. 11999. Same spot as above, Sept. 7, 1940. Spores strongly olive in a heavy print, 3.4–3.8 x 7.8–9.5μ. No. 12070. In pine-kalmia woods near Trillium Lodge, Aug. 1, 1939. No. 12180. Same spot as above, Aug. 19, 1939. No. 12721. In dense pine needles on the Farnsworth place, Aug. 29, 1941. Also other collections from Highlands. Blue Ridge Mountains. Atkinson. Common "at an elevation of between 4000 and 5000 feet."

THE GENUS BOLETINUS

Plants much like *Boletus*, but lower surface of cap flesh uneven and descending in small points among the tubes. Tubes large, angular, of unequal length, arranged in more or less radiating rows separated by higher lamella-like plates; tubes rather toughish and not easily separating from each other or from the flesh of the cap. Spores smooth.

Key to the Species

Stem central to excentric
    Cap red or reddish, scaly-fibrous.....................................*B. pictus*
    Cap tawny to deep brown
        Plants small; tubes adnate to slightly decurrent.................*B. castanellus*
        Plants of medium size; tubes very strongly decurrent...........*B. squarrosoides*

Stem excentric to lateral
    Cap tomentose to tufted; tubes light brown, large.................*B. squarrosoides*
    Cap glabrous or nearly so; tubes greenish yellow, small to medium....*B. merulioides*

Boletinus castanellus Peck. Bull. Torr. Bot. Club **27**: 613. 1900.

Plate 65, fig. 15

Cap about 2 cm. broad, convex, tawny brown, finely tomentose.

Tubes short but large for the size of the plant, $\frac{1}{2}$–1 mm. in diameter, adnate or slightly decurrent.

Stem central, about 3.5–4 cm. long, tapering upward, glabrous, concolorous with cap.

Spores (of No. 84) yellow ochraceous, rather broadly elliptic, some slightly broader toward proximal end, smooth, 4–5 x 7.4–10μ, usually with one shining globule.

This little plant is quite rare with us. We have found it only once, and our notes are incomplete, but we have no doubt that this is true *B. castanellus*. North American Flora reports it southward only to Virginia, but in an unpublished manuscript by E. R. Memminger in our files it is reported from Flat Rock, Henderson County, N. C.

North Carolina. Chapel Hill. No. 84. In Battle Park near a branch, Oct. 2, 1911.

Boletinus squarrosoides Snell and Dick. Mycologia **28**: 468. 1936.

Plate 59 (right, above) and pl. 65, fig. 16

Cap up to 8.5 cm. broad, convex to plane or with slightly depressed center, tomentose to strongly tufted-tomentose but somewhat viscid when moist, deep brown, nearly chestnut; usually with narrow inturned margin. Flesh up to 1.9 cm. thick, pale, turning pale cap color when cut; taste and odor slight or none.

Tubes medium to quite large, especially near the stem where they may be elongated, 5–8 mm. long, radiating, angular and subdivided, tan to light brown in our plants, decurrent into the reticulated stem apex.

Stem central to excentric but not truly lateral, enlarged upward or nearly equal, pinched at base, 3.5–6.5 cm. long, 1–1.5 cm. thick, color of tubes above and of cap below, reticulated above or nearly all over with lines which are often darker than the surface between.

Spores (of No. 11782) about honey-yellow, between mustard yellow and old gold in good print, short-elliptic to elliptic, 3.8–4.8 x 8.5–10.5μ.

This species seems nearest *B. castanellus* but differs in larger size, more decurrent tubes, more tufted-tomentose cap, and perhaps somewhat in color of tubes and stem, though our plants do not show such differences as indicated in the original description. Possibly this should be treated as only a variety of *B. castanellus*. From *B. merulioides* this species differs distinctly in spore shape, strongly tomentose cap, more nearly central stem, and larger tubes of different color.

NORTH CAROLINA. Highlands. No. 8947. By Dillard road, July 28, 1931. Spores 4–5 x 8–10μ. No. 11782. In open place near old school house on Dillard road, July 29, 1940. No. 12138. Same place as above, Aug. 10, 1939. Spores 4–4.8 x 8–11μ. No. 12224. Same place as above, Aug. 25, 1939. Spores 3.8–5 x 8–10μ. No. 12462. On grassy lawn at Kettle Rock, July 30, 1941.

GEORGIA. Rabun County. No. 11912. In rich ravine, Aug. 22, 1940. No. 11954. Same place as above, Aug. 27, 1940. No. 12477. Same place as above, Aug. 1, 1941.

Boletinus merulioides (Schw.) n. comb.
Daedalea merulioides Schw. Trans. Amer. Phil. Soc. II, **4**: 160. 1832.
Paxillus porosus Berk. *in* Lea. Catl. Plants of Cincinnati, p. 54. 1849.
Boletus lateralis Bundy *in* Chamberlain. Geol. of Wisc. **1**: 398. 1883.
Boletinus porosus (Berk.) Peck. Bull. N. Y. St. Mus. **2**, No. 8: 79. 1889.

Plate 58 and pl. 65, fig. 17

Single or cespitose; caps up to 10 cm. broad, flabelliform with inturned margin, which is usually indented and lobed, or sometimes with margin upturned, depressed in center, surface glabrous or with a fine tomentum which may collapse and form a shining layer, color a deep rich brown, about Brussels brown or raw umber (Ridg.) or with more olive in it, but turning a darker, more reddish color when strongly rubbed. Flesh up to 1 cm. thick near stem, thinning gradually toward margin, soft but tough, pale greenish yellow, faintly pinkish toward the surface, usually not changing when cut but at times turning blue-green, especially near stem; tasteless, odor not agreeable (raw white potato).

Tubes decurrent, small to medium, about 3–5 mm. deep, arranged in more or less radiating rows, the pore surface very uneven, cut by higher anastomosing ridges into areas which in turn are subdivided into shallower pores, color when quite fresh light yellow with tint of green, later becoming dull ochraceous with or without greenish tints; when young, bruises are dark olivaceous, later dull brown with reddish tint.

Stem excentric to lateral, 2–3 cm. long, about 6–10 mm. thick near base and expanding upward into the cap, the base firmly inserted with fibers or plates, color of cap below, of tubes above, at times with reddish brown stains, reticulated at top; flesh solid, color of cap flesh, blackish at base.

Spores (of No. 1803) dull olive brown, blunt-elliptic, smooth, 4.8–6.6 x 7.2–9.3μ, mucro rarely visible under ordinary powers. Basidia (of No. 11079) 4-spored, clavate, 7.5–9.3μ thick near top.

ILLUSTRATIONS: Farlow. Icones Farlowianae, pl. 91 (as *B. porosus*).
Güssow and Odell. Mushrooms and Toadstools, pl. 99 (as *B. porosus* and not in color).
Murrill. Mycologia 2: pl. 19, fig. 7 (as *Boletinellus*). 1910.

NORTH CAROLINA. Chapel Hill. No. 320. In Strowd's pasture, Sept. 30, 1911. Spores olive brown, short-elliptic with very blunt ends, 4.8–6 x 7–9.3μ. No. 1803. In edge of pine woods by branch, Sept. 17, 1915. No. 2454. On damp ground, Bowlin's Creek swamp. Oct. 1, 1916. Spores 4.8–6.3 x 8–10.5μ. No. 3580. Same locality, Nov. 2, 1919. No. 7026. On rotting deciduous wood, on moss, and on bare earth, Aug. 3, 1923. Spores oval to blunt-elliptic, 4.5–5.5 x 6.5–8.8μ. No. 8314. Under *Abelia* in Coker Arboretum, June 15, 1928. No. 9318. In marsh below old Emerson mill, Oct. 4, 1932. No. 11079. On damp mossy soil under box elder, June 17, 1939.

Boletinus pictus Peck. Bull. N. Y. St. Mus. **2**, No. 8: 77. 1889.
Boletus pictus Peck. Rept. N. Y. St. Cab. **23**: 128. 1872. (Bot. ed.)
B. Spraguei B. & C. Grevillea **1**: 35. 1872. Not *B. Spraguei* Frost.
Bull Buf. Soc. Nat. Sci. **2**: 102. 1874.

Plate 59 (below and left, above) and pl. 65, fig. 18

Cap 3–12 cm. broad, convex, dry or slightly viscid, dark red when fresh, between brick red and dragon's blood red (Ridg.), strongly fibrous-squamulose, later the tips of the squamules becoming more elevated, especially toward the margin, making the cap more yellow by exposure of surface between the squamules, drying fawn with patches of red or brown hairs. Flesh up to 1.3 cm. thick, creamy yellow, becoming slowly reddish when cut or bruised, drying fawn with tint of pinkish.

Tubes adnate to slightly decurrent, dull yellow when fresh, drying light brown, up to 5 mm. long, large, 0.5–2 mm. wide, mouths angular, compound.

Stem 4.5–7 cm. long, 1–2 cm. thick, slightly swollen at base, concolorous with cap, flocculent-scaly like cap. Veil whitish, drying mouse color, pubescent, persisting as a flocculent roll on the top of the stem.

Spores (of No. 5613) ochraceous brown, elliptic or with proximal end slightly broader, smooth, 3.5–4 x 7.5–10μ.

This is a beautiful plant common in the mountains of our state and preferring groves of white pine. We have only one collection from Chapel Hill, and that was found in mixed woods.

ILLUSTRATIONS. Farlow. Icones Farlowianae, pl. 90.
Marshall. Mushroom Book, pl. opposite p. 103. 1913.
Peck. Bull. N. Y. St. Mus. **5**, No. 25 (Rept. 52): pl. 61, figs. 1–5. 1899.
Also in Mem. N. Y. St. Mus. **3**, No. 4: pl. 61, figs. 1–5. 1900.

NORTH CAROLINA. Chapel Hill. No. 5381. In mixed woods, July 22, 1922. Spores elliptic, smooth, 3.5–4 x 7.5–10μ.
Blowing Rock. No. 5613. In humus under a log, Aug. 20, 1922. No. 7512. Under pines, Sept. 1924.
Highlands. No. 8792. In mixed woods, July 20, 1931. No. 8990a. Under pines, Aug. 23, 1933. Spores 3.4–4 x 8–10μ. No. 10602. Mixed woods, Aug. 26, 1937. Spores rich ochraceous brown, smooth, subelliptic, distal end often slightly more tapering, 3.4–3.8 x 8.5–10μ. No. 12456. Deciduous woods, July 29, 1941. Also other collections from Highlands.
Asheville. "Very common." Beardslee.

THE GENUS STROBILOMYCES

Plants much like *Boletus*, but tubes not easily separating from the cap flesh, which becomes tough. Cap and stem strongly scaly-warted and becoming blackish. Spores globose, warted.

We have found only one species in North Carolina, but Wolf found in Alabama a plant with entirely different spores (7 x 20μ, finely striated) that Lloyd referred to *S. pallescens* Cke. and Massee (Myc. Notes, p. 538). Lloyd actually says *S. pallidus*, but this is obviously a slip. We think it very probable that the plant from Alabama was really *Boletus Ananas* Curtis.

Strobilomyces strobilaceus (Scop.) Berk. Outl. Brit. Fungol., p. 236. 1860.
Boletus strobilaceus Scop. Anni Hist. Nat. **4**: 148. 1770.

Plate 60 and pl. 65, fig. 19

Cap 7–13.5 cm. broad, convex then plane to rarely concave, dry, covered with rather large dark brown to blackish flocculent-fibrous warts and scales, color between scales near margin paler to grayish white, the broad sterile margin jagged and irregular with appendiculate scales and fragments of the veil. Flesh white when quite fresh but changing through brick red to almost black when cut; taste mild.

Tubes whitish when young but becoming nearly black at maturity, rather long, especially toward stem then suddenly depressed at stem, mouths large, angular, covered in youth with a floccose whitish veil.

Stem up to 11 cm. long, nearly equal, solid and firm, sulcate-reticulate above or nearly all over, covered with fibrous scales and colored like the cap, somewhat paler above, with or without a cottony roll near top left from the veil.

Spores (of No. 834) black in mass but deep brown under microscope, subspherical with a distinct mucro, tuberculate and also appearing reticulated, 7.4–9.2 x 9–10μ.

ILLUSTRATIONS: Atkinson. Mushrooms, figs. 172–174. 1900 (figs. 177–179 of 1901 ed.). (Not in color but good.)
Dufour. Atlas Champ., pl. 52. 1891.
Gibson. Our Edible Toadstools and Mushrooms, pl. 23.
Hard. Mushrooms, fig. 312 (not in color but good).
Palmer. Mushrooms of America, pl. 7, fig. 6.
Peck. Bull. N. Y. St. Mus. **94**: pl. 92. 1905.
Richon and Roze. Atlas Champ., pl. 53.
Scopoli. Anni Hist. Nat. **4**: pl. 1, fig. 1.

NORTH CAROLINA. Chapel Hill. No. 242. Battle Park, Sept. 16, 1908. No. 834. Battle Park, Sept. 19, 1913. No. 867. In woods, Oct. 2, 1913. No. 2073. In cultivated soil in a yard, June 12, 1916. No. 10286. In a cellar, Oct. 2, 1936. Spores black in print, subspherical to oval, warted, 6.8–8.5 x 7.5–10μ.
Roanoke Island. Sept. 17, 1927. Spores reticulate-warted, 7–8.5 x 8.5–11μ.

Highlands. No. 10512. On roadside bank, Aug. 12, 1937. Spores nearly black, subspherical, warted-reticulate, 7.4–9 x 8–10μ. No. 12047. On blank by road, July 26, 1939. No. 12072. On Little Bearpen Mt., Aug. 2, 1939.

Also other collections from Chapel Hill and Highlands.

Blowing Rock. Atkinson.

Curtis. "Common."

Pink Bed Valley, Pisgah Forest, July, 1907. Murrill.

LITERATURE LIST

ATKINSON, G. F.

1900   Studies of American Fungi; Mushrooms, Edible, Poisonous, etc., pp. 172–185. 2nd ed., 1901.

——— AND HERMAN SCHRENK

1892   Some Fungi of Blowing Rock, N. C.   Journ. Elisha Mitchell Sci. Soc. 9: 95–107.

BEARDSLEE, H. C.

1901   Notes on the Boleti of West Virginia.   Torreya 1: 37–39.

1915   Notes on New and Rare Species of Fungi found at Asheville, N. C.   Journ. Elisha Mitchell Sci. Soc. 31: 145–149.

BERKELEY, M. J.

1860   Outlines of British Fungology, pp. 229–236.

BRESADOLA, J.

1931   Iconographia Mycologica 19: 901–944.

COLLINS, F. S.

1899   A Case of *Boletus* Poisoning.   Rhodora 1: 21–23.

ELROD, R. P., AND DOROTHY L. BLANCHARD

1939   Histological Studies of the Boletaceae and Related Genera.   Mycologia 31: 693–708.

ELROD, R. P., AND W. H. SNELL

1940   Development of the Carpophores of Certain Boletaceae.   Mycologia 32: 493–504.

FRIES, ELIAS

1821   Systema Mycologicum 1: 385–395.

1836–38   Epicrisis Systematis Mycologici, pp. 408–427.

1874   Hymenomycetes Europaei, pp. 495–521.

FROST, C. C.

1874   Catalogue of Boleti of New England, with Descriptions of New Species.   Bull. Buffalo Soc. Nat. Sci. 2: 100–105.

GILBERT, E. J.

1931   Les Bolets.   Librairie E. Le Francois, Paris.

HARD, M. E.

1908   The Mushrooms, Edible and Otherwise, pp. 350–383.

HERBST, WILLIAM

1899   Fungal Flora of the Lehigh Valley, Pa., pp. 117–130.

KALLENBACH, FRANZ

1926–   Die Pilze Mitteleuropas, Band I (Boletaceae).

KAUFFMAN, C. H.

1906   *Cortinarius* as a Mycorhiza-Producing Fungus.   Bot. Gaz. 42: 208–214.

KONRAD, P., AND A. MAUBLANC

1924–35   Icones Selectae Fungorum, pls. 393–420.

LEVINE, MICHAEL

1913   Studies in the Cytology of the Hymenomycetes, especially the Boleti.   Bull. Torrey Bot. Club 40: 137–181.

MCILVAINE, CHARLES, AND R. K. MACADAM

1902   One Thousand American Fungi, pp. 398–476 (2nd ed.)

MELIN, ELIAS

1925   Untersuchungen über die Bedeutung der Baummycorrhiza, eine ökologisch-physiologische Studie.   Jena.

MORGAN, A. P.

1884   The Mycologic Flora of the Miami Valley, Ohio.   Journ. Cincinnati Soc. Nat. Hist. 7: 5–10.

MURRILL, W. A.

1908   Collecting and Studying Boleti.   Torreya 8: 50–55.

Boleti from Western North Carolina.   Torreya 8: 209–217.

The Boleti of the Frost Herbarium.   Bull. Torrey Bot. Club 35: 517–526.

1909   The Boletaceae of North America—I and II. Mycologia 1: 4–18, 140–160.
       Boletaceae from Kentucky. Mycologia 1: 275.
1910   Boletaceae. North American Flora 9: 133–161.
       Poisonous Mushrooms. Mycologia 2: 258–259.
1913   Illustrations of Fungi—XIII. Mycologia 5: 1–5.
1938   New Boletes. Mycologia 30: 520–525.
1940   Additions to Florida Fungi—II. Bull. Torrey Bot. Club 67: 57–66.
NOACK, FRITZ.
1889   Ueber mykorhizenbildende Pilze. Bot. Zeit. 47, 389–397.
PECK, CHARLES H.
1872   Genus *Boletus* Fr. Rept. N. Y. St. Cab. 23: 127–133.
1887   New York Species of Viscid Boleti. Bull. N. Y. St. Mus. 1, No. 2: 57–66.
       Notes on the Boleti of the United States. Journ. Mycol. 3: 53–55.
1889   Boleti of the United States. Bull. N. Y. St. Mus. 2, No. 8: 73–166. See notes on
       this by Anderson and Kelsey in Journ. Mycol. 5: 220–221. 1889.
       Note: Many other references to Peck are given throughout this work.
PERSOON, C. H.
1801   Synopsis Methodica Fungorum, pp. 503–513.
1825   Mycologia Europaea, vol. 2, pp. 123–148.
PEYRONEL, B.
1921   Nouveaux cas de rapports mycorhiziques entre Phanérogames et Basidiomycètes.
       Bull. Soc. Myc. France 37: 143–146.
RAYNER, M. C.
1926–1927   Mycorrhiza. New Phytologist 25: 1–50, 65–108, 171–190, 248–263, 338–372
       (section on *Boletus*); 26: 22–45, 85–114.
REA, CARLETON
1922   British Basidiomycetes, pp. 553–573.
REESS, VON M.
1880   Ueber den Parasitismus von *Elaphomyces granulatus*. Bot. Zeit. 38: 729–733.
SMITH, W. G.
1908   British Basidiomycetes, pp. 317–332.
SACCARDO, P. A.
1888   *Boletus* Dill. Sylloge Fungorum 6: 2–51.
SNELL, WALTER H.
1932–1936   Notes on Boletes I-V. Mycologia 24: 334–341; 25: 221–232; 26: 348–359;
       28: 13–23, 463–475.
       Tentative Keys to the Boletaceae of the United States and Canada. Publ. No. 1
       of the Rhode Island Bot. Club.
1941   The Genera of the Boletaceae. Mycologia 33: 415–423.
——— AND ESTHER A. DICK
1941   Notes on Boletes VI. Mycologia 33: 23–37.
———, ALEXANDER H. SMITH, AND L. R. HESLER
1940   New Species of Boleti from Cades Cove in the Great Smokies. Journ. Elisha
       Mitchell Sci. Soc. 56: 325–328.
SUMSTINE, D. R.
1904   The Boletaceae of Pennsylvania. Torreya 4: 184–185.
UNDERWOOD, L. M.
1901   Suggestions for the Study of the North American Boletaceae. Contr. Dept.
       Bot. Columbia Univ., No. 176.
WEBSTER, H.
1900–1901   Boleti Collected at Alstead, N. H. Rhodora 2: 173–179; 3: 226–228.
WILLIAMS, M. E.
1897   Edible Boleti. Asa Gray Bull. 5: 75–76.

INDEX

96   INDEX

BLACK AND WHITE PLATES

PLATE 6

Boletus cyanescens. No. 12877 (above). A young plant, slightly reduced
Boletus castaneus. No. 8099 (below). Nat. size

PLATE 7

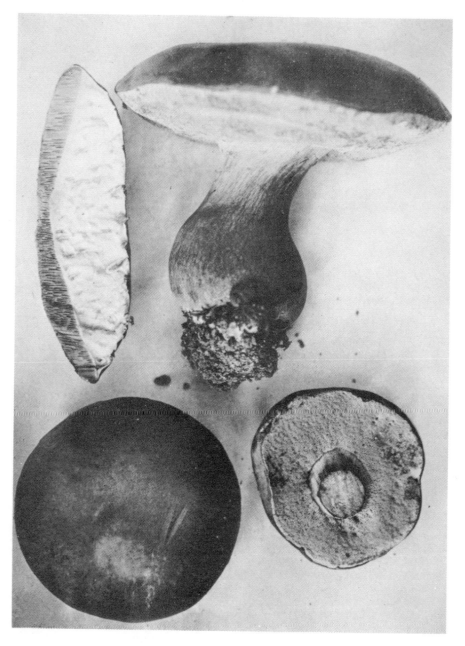

Boletus felleus.　No. 716.　Nat. size

PLATE 8

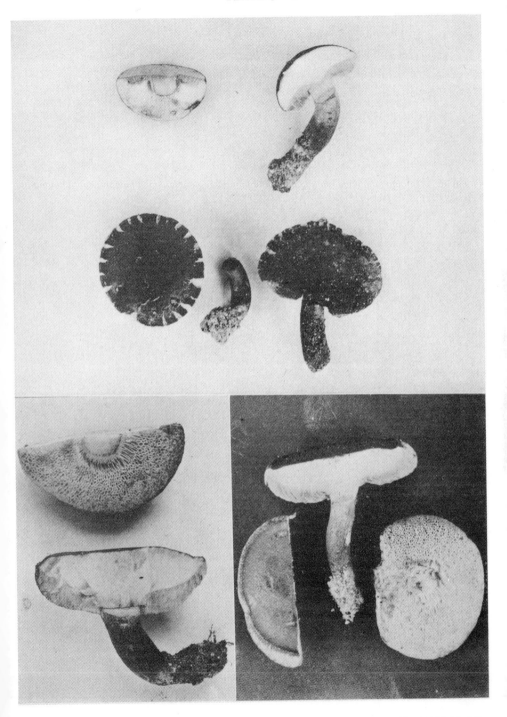

Boletus felleus var. minor. No. 12033 (above); No. 10824 (lower left); No. 10845 (right)
Nat. size

PLATE 9

Boletus indecisus.   No. 12227 (left, above); No. 9869 (right, above); No. 12019 (left, below);
No. 11840 (right, below).   Slightly reduced

PLATE 10

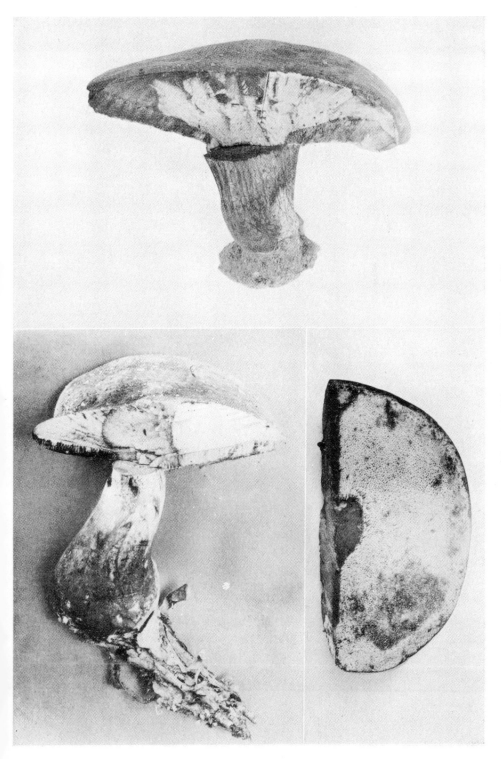

Boletus alboater. No. 10964 (above and lower right); No. 4538 (lower left). Reduced

PLATE 11

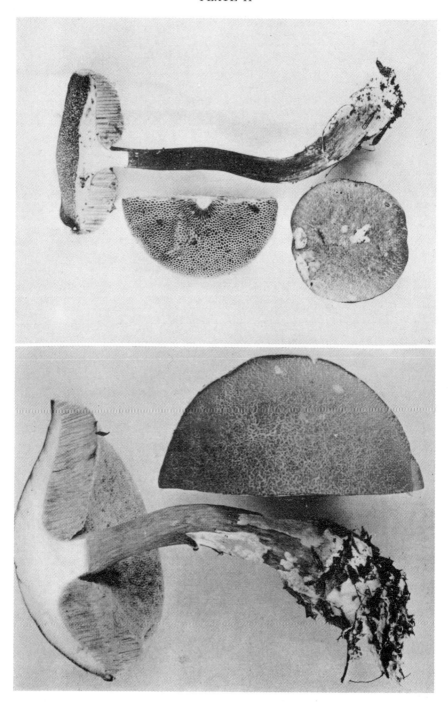

Boletus gracilis.   No. 12218 (left); No. 12011 (right).   Nat. size

PLATE 12

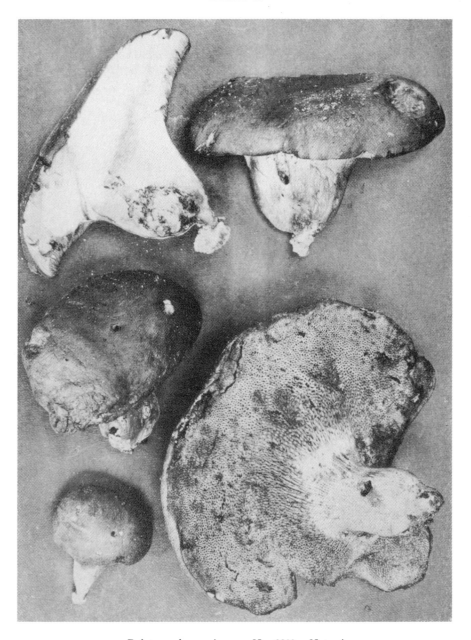

Boletus subsanguineus. No. 2289. Nat. size

PLATE 13

Boletus subsanguineus. No. 10026. Nat. size

PLATE 14

Boletus scaber. No. 12409 (above, left); No. 12096 (above, right); No. 10545 (below).
Lower figure reduced about one-third

PLATE 15

Boletus niveus.   No. 4456.   Nat. size

PLATE 16

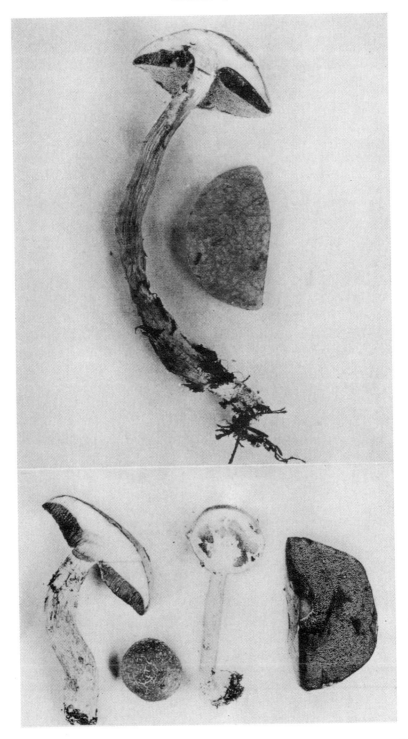

Boletus Ravenelii. No. 12077 (above); No. 10906 (below). Three-fifths natural size
The plant above has an unusually long stem, on which only a fragment of the
veil is left

PLATE 17

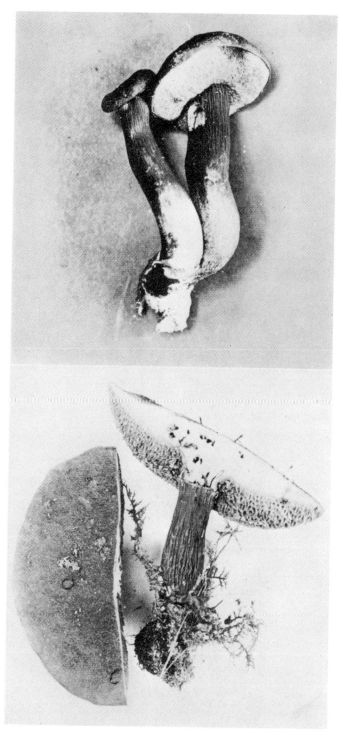

Boletus auriflammeus.   No. 1242 (above); No. 10868 (below).   Nat. size

PLATE 18

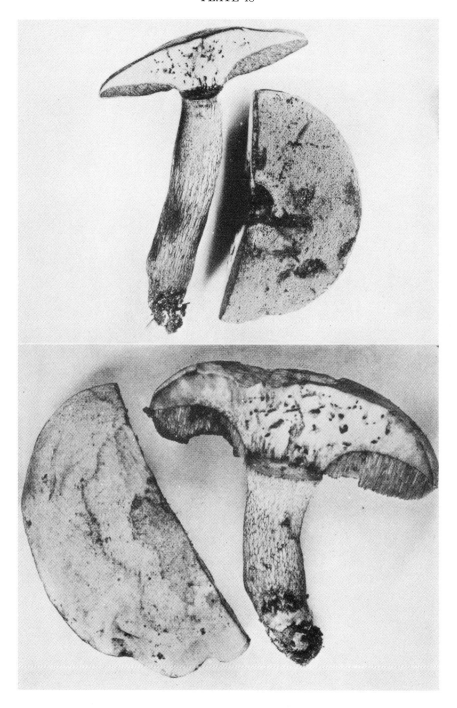

Boletus griseus. No. 10816 (above); No. 11772 (below). Nat. size

PLATE 19

Boletus retipes. No. 1644. Slightly reduced

PLATE 20

Boletus affinis. No. 12046 (left, above); No. 12434 (right, above and below)
Boletus affinis var. maculosus. No. 11899 (left, below). All slightly reduced

PLATE 21

Boletus edulis. No. 737. Slightly reduced

PLATE 22

Boletus separans. No. 11895 (above)
Boletus luridus. No. 12476 (below). Both figures about three-fourths natural size

PLATE 23

Boletus variipes. No. 10500 (above); No. 11885 (below). Lower left figure only slightly reduced; others about one-half

PLATE 24

Boletus eximius. No. 10192 (above); No. 10812 (below). Slightly reduced

PLATE 25

Boletus piperatus. No. 8140 (above); No. 8004 (below). Nat. size

PLATE 26

Boletus vermiculosus. No. 503 (left); No. 11794 (right). Nearly natural size

PLATE 27

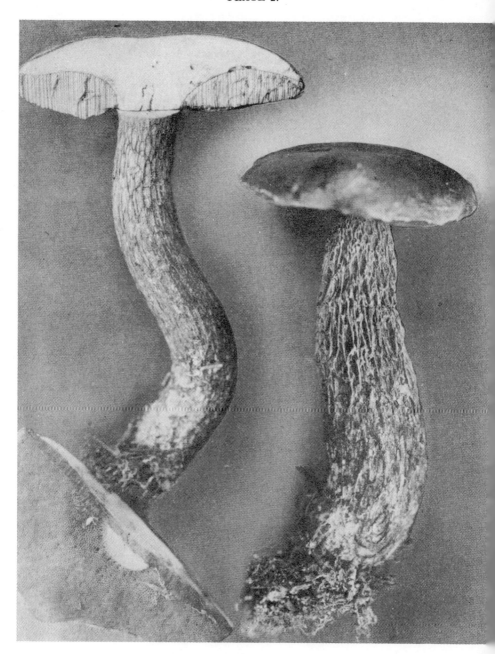

Boletus Frostii. No. 1114. Nat. size.

PLATE 28

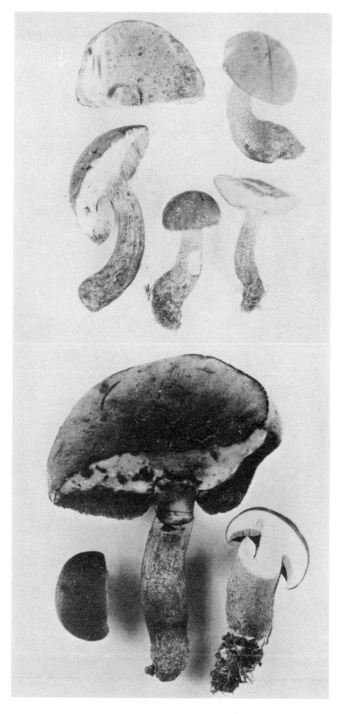

Boletus Morrisii. No. 10910 (above); No. 12693 (below). Nat. size

PLATE 29

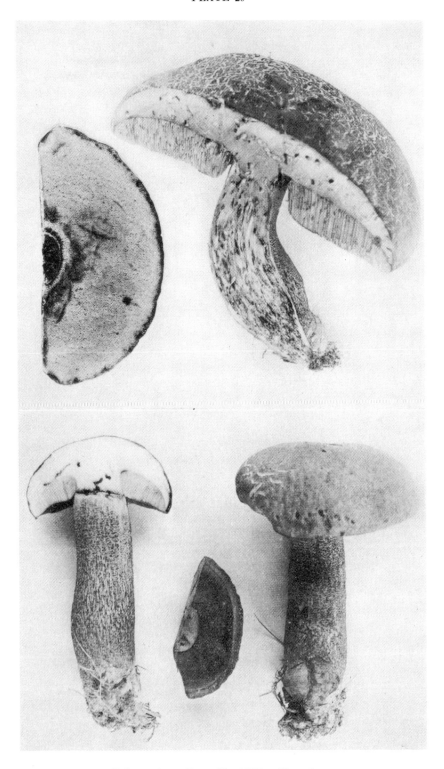

Boletus rimosellus.   No. 12609.   Nat. size

PLATE 30

Boletus rubropunctus. No. 11837 (above); No. 12292 (below). Slightly reduced

PLATE 31

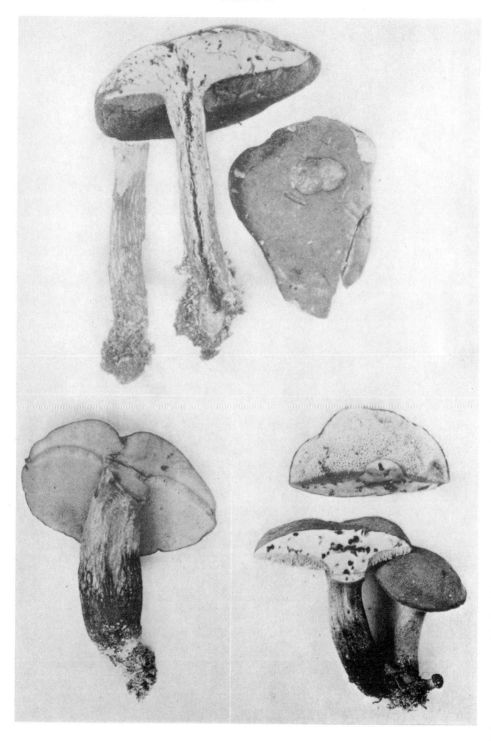

Boletus Atkinsonianus. No. 10979 (above)
Boletus auriporus. No. 11886 (right, below); No. 11839 (left, below). Nat. size

PLATE 32

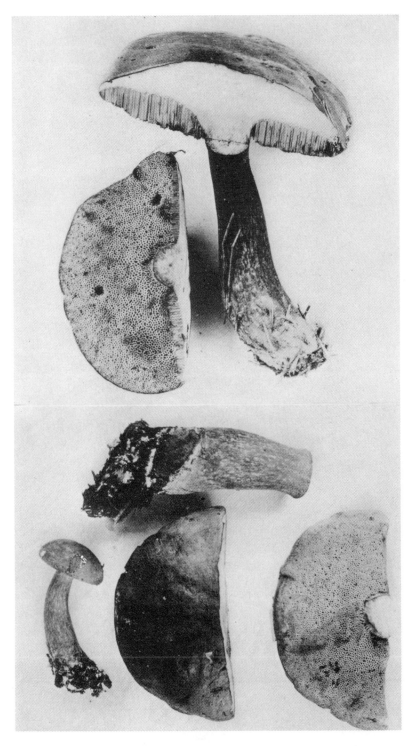

Boletus badius. No. 12394 (above); No. 12018 (below). Nat. size

PLATE 33

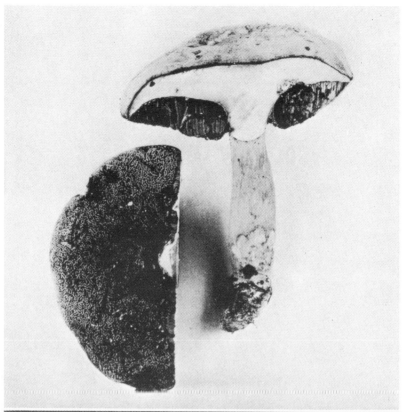

Boletus viridiflavus. No. 11960 (above); No. 9863 (below). Nat. size

PLATE 34

Boletus subtomentosus. No. 12025 (left, above); No. 11902 (right, above)
Boletus parasiticus. No. 11988 (below). All figures slightly reduced

PLATE 35

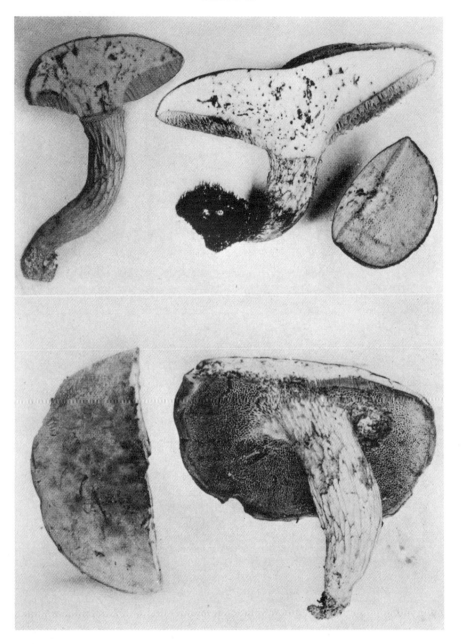

Boletus illudens. No. 10273 (left, above); No. 12523 (right, above); No. 12111 (below). Reduced

PLATE 36

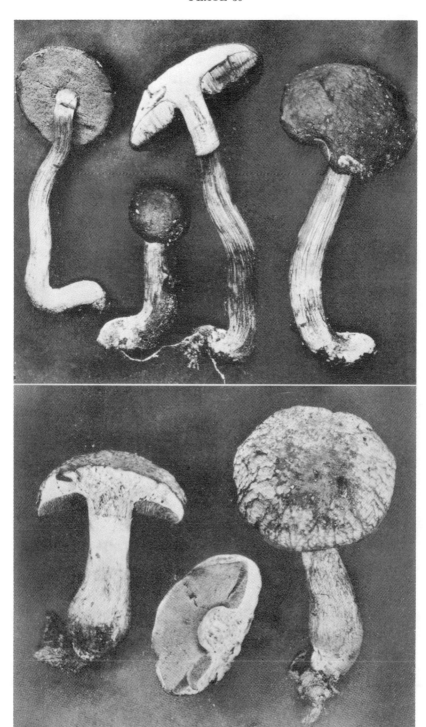

Boletus subglabripes. No. 4487 (above)
Boletus subglabripes var. corrugis. No. 4479 (below). Slightly reduced

PLATE 37

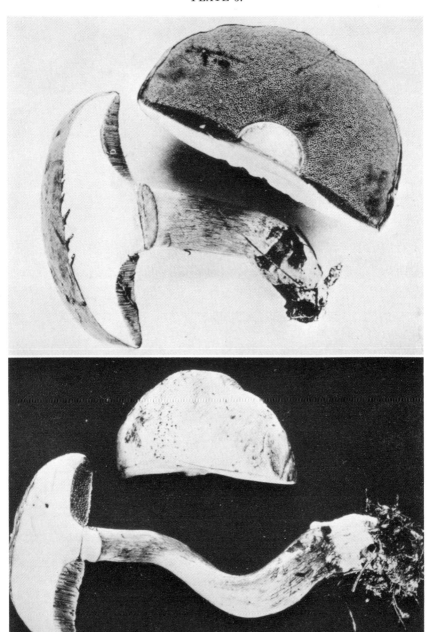

Boletus pallidus. No. 12177 (left); No. 11918 (right). Slightly reduced

PLATE 38

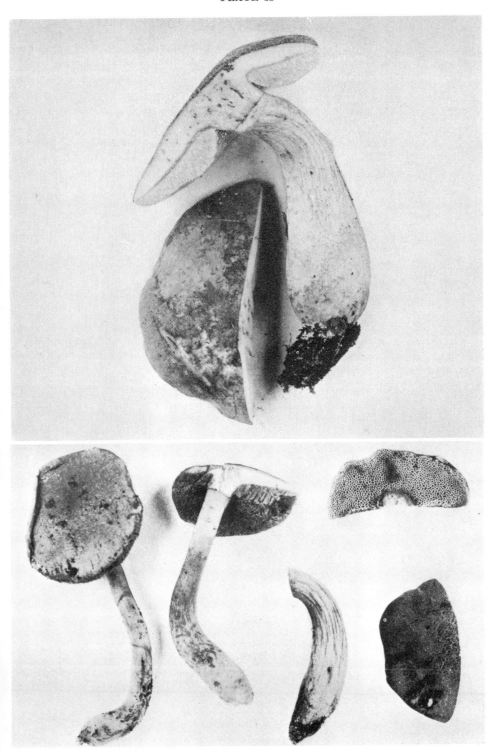

Boletus Roxanae.   No. 10821 (above); No. 11934 (left, below); No. 11773 (right, below).
Slightly reduced

PLATE 39

Boletus fraternus. No. 9823 (above)
Boletus sordidus. No. 12569 (left, below); No. 12586 (right, below). Reduced

PLATE 40

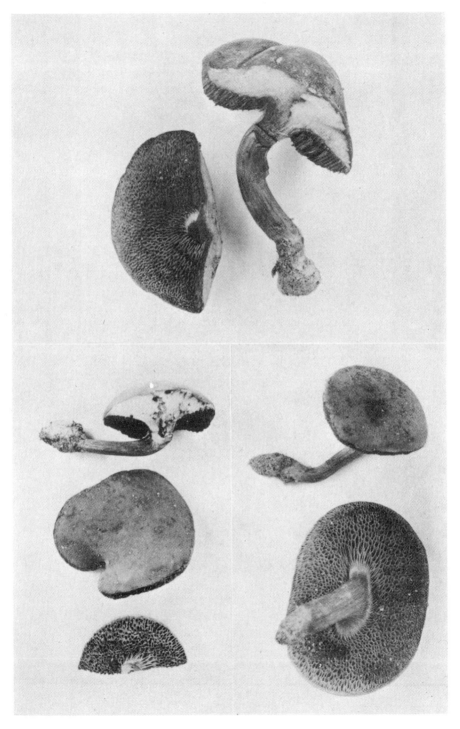

Boletus subfraternus.   No. 12647 (above and right, below); No. 12537 (left, below).
Nat. size

PLATE 41

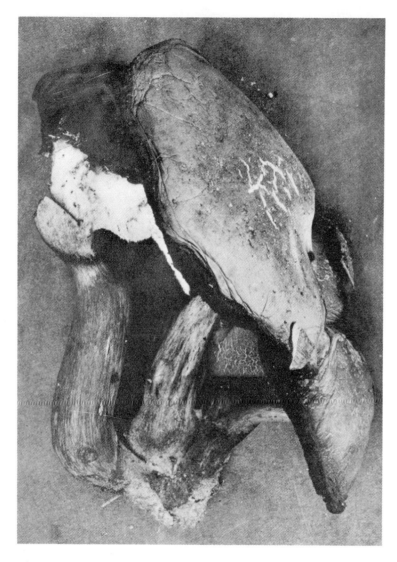

Boletus communis. No. 4570. Nat. size

PLATE 42

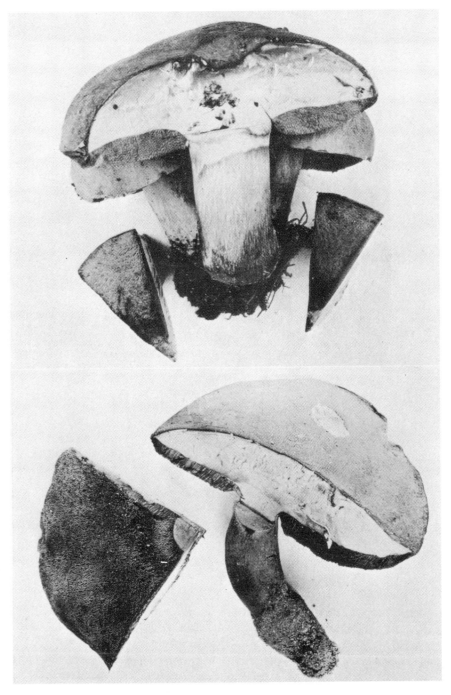

Boletus bicolor. Whiteside Cove (above); No. 12079 (below). Nat. size

PLATE 43

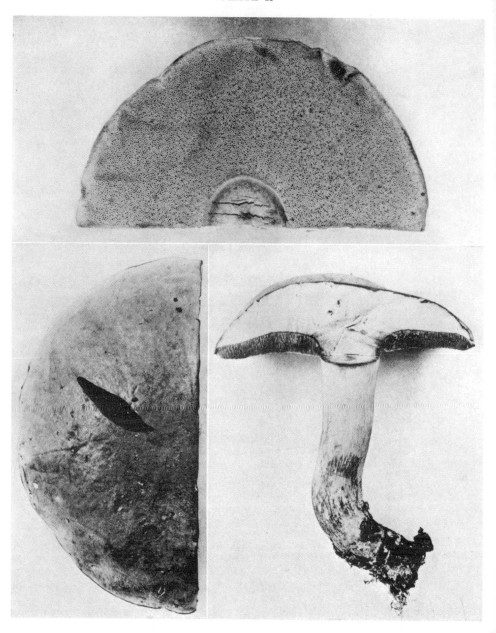

Boletus miniato-olivaceus.   No. 11731.   Nearly natural size

PLATE 44

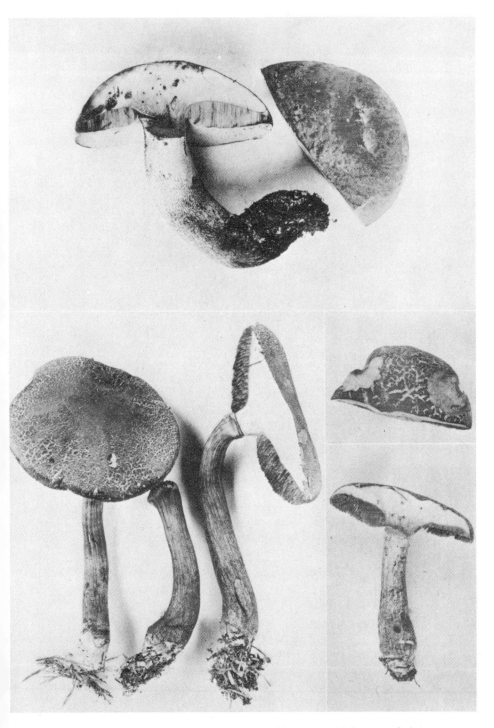

Boletus speciosus. No. 11892 (above). About two-thirds natural size
Boletus chrysenteron. No. 12395 (left, below); No. 12014 (right, below).
Slightly reduced

PLATE 45

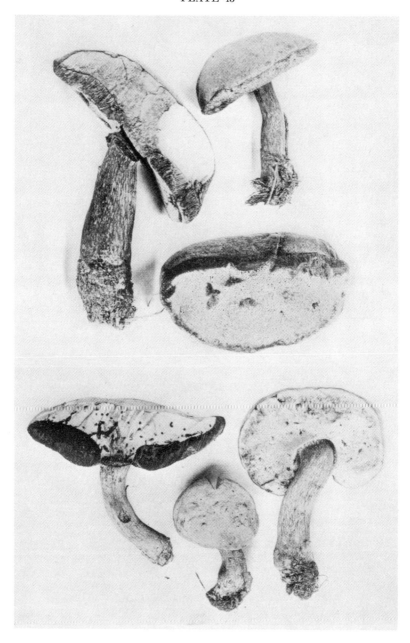

Boletus Peckii. No. 10879 (above); No. 10962 (below). Slightly reduced

PLATE 46

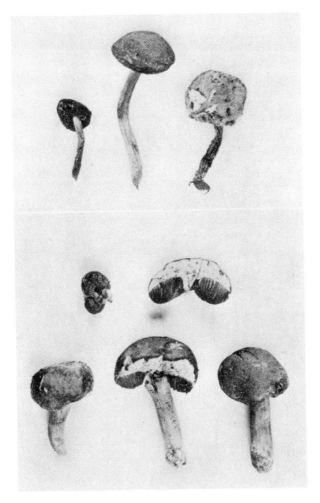

Boletus parvulus.   No. 11928 (above); No. 11855, type (below).   Nat. size

PLATE 47

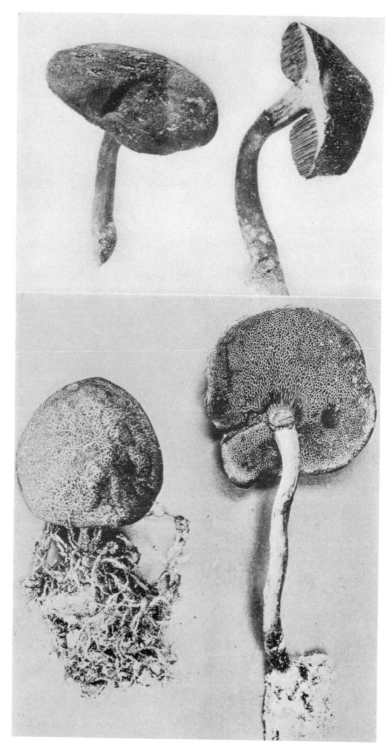

Boletus chrysenteroides. No. 4526 (above); Nos. 4578 and 4580 (below). Nat. size

PLATE 48

Boletus Russellii. No. 2418. Nat. size

PLATE 49

Boletus Betula.   No. 432.   Nat. size

PLATE 50

Boletus granulatus.   No. 481 (above); No. 11724 (below).   Nat. size

PLATE 51

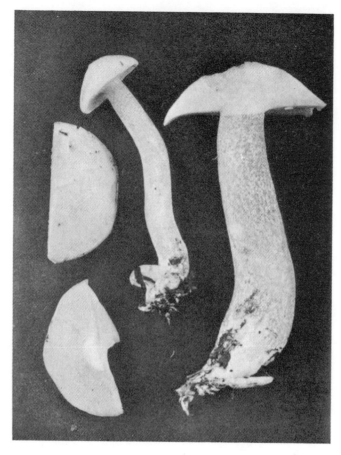

Boletus placidus.   No. 11739.   Nat. size

PLATE 52

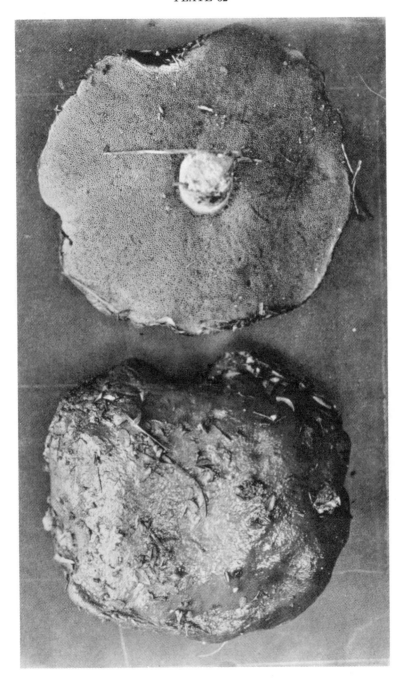

Boletus brevipes. No. 971. Nat. size

PLATE 53

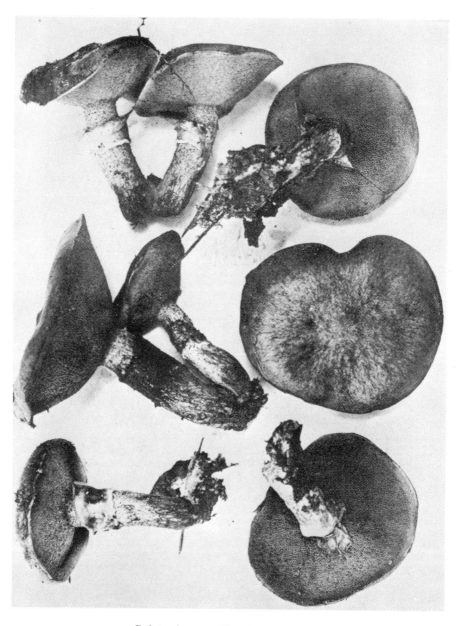

Boletus luteus. No. 474. Nat. size

PLATE 54

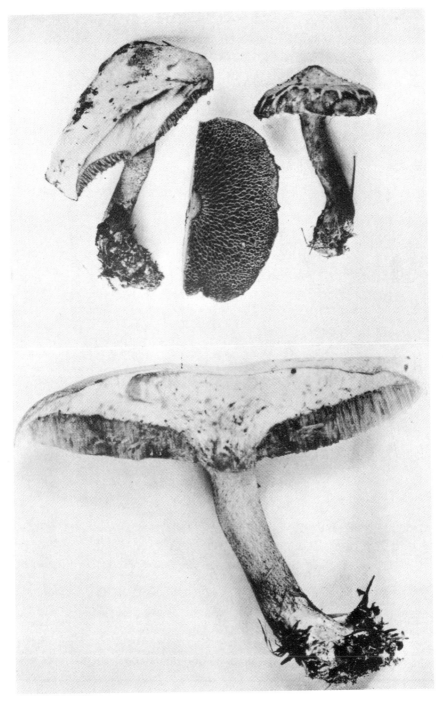

Boletus americanus.   No. 11873 (above)
Boletus americanus var. reticulipes.   No. 11746 (below).   Nat. size

PLATE 55

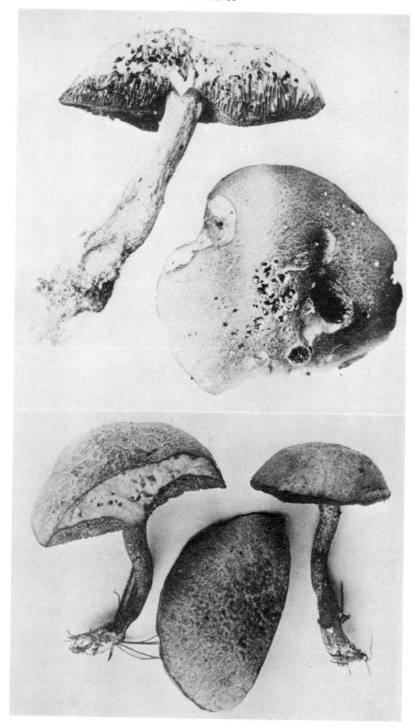

Boletus subaureus. No. 765 (above)
Boletus luteus. No. 12693 (below). The veil has been lost except for remnant on right
hand side. Nat. size

PLATE 56

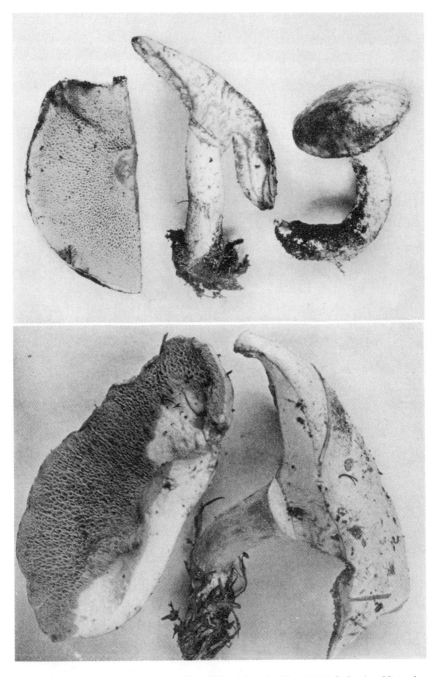

Boletus subaureus var. siccipes.　No. 11720 (above); No. 11906 (below).　Nat. size

PLATE 57

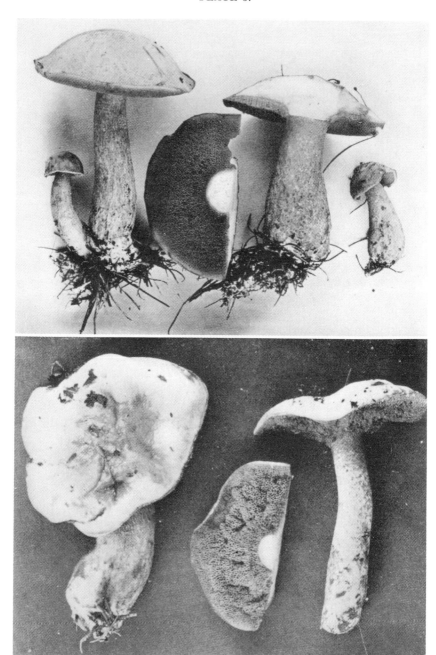

Boletus punctipes. No. 11999 (above); No. 12180 (below). Reduced one-fourth and one-third respectively

PLATE 58

Boletinus merulioides. No. 3580. Nat. size

PLATE 59

Boletinus pictus.   No. 12456 (left, above); No. 5613 (below)
Boletinus squarrosoides.   No. 11782 (right, above).   Slightly reduced

PLATE 60

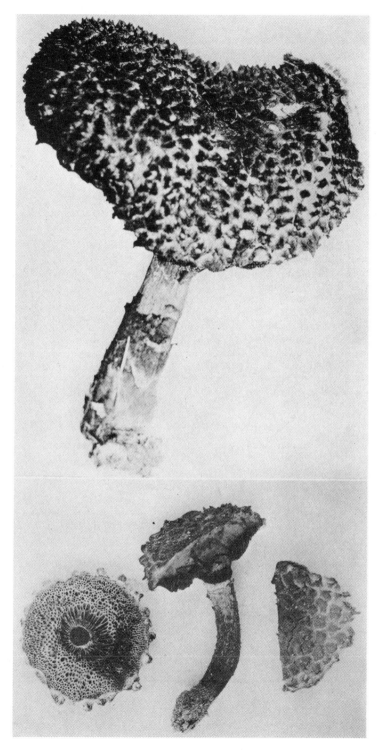

Strobilomyces strobilaceus.　No. 867 (above); No. 12047 (below).　Reduced

PLATE 61

(All figs. × 1620)

Fig. 1. Boletus castaneus. No. 10191.
Fig. 2. B. cyanescens. No. 9520.
Fig. 3. B. felleus. No. 10554.
Fig. 4. B. felleus var. minor. No. 10550.
Fig. 5. B. indecisus. No. 12142.
Fig. 6. B. indecisus. Menands, N. Y. (Peck Herb.).
Fig. 7. B. alboater. No. 9592.
Fig. 8. B. gracilis. No. 9635.
Fig. 9. B. Vanderbiltianus. Pink Bed Valley, N. C. (Peck Herb.).
Fig. 10. B. chromapes. No. 3072.
Fig. 11. B. subsanguineus. No. 2289.
Fig. 12. B. Housei. Type.
Fig. 13. B. rimosellus. No. 12605.
Fig. 14. B. scaber. No. 9609.
Fig. 15. B. niveus. No. 12468.
Fig. 16. B. Ravenelii. No. 9606.
Fig. 17. B. hemichrysus. Green Cove Springs, Fla. (U. N. C. Herb.).
Fig. 18. B. auriflammeus. No. 10507.

PLATE 61

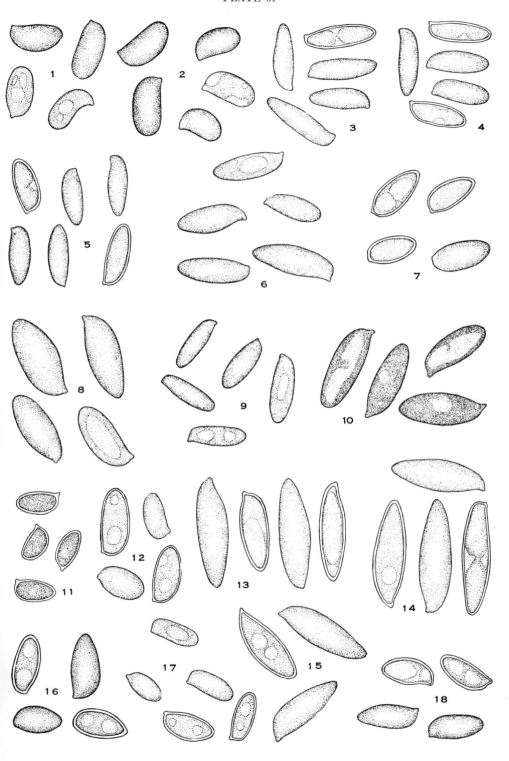

PLATE 62

(All figs. × 1620)

Fig. 1. Boletus griseus. No. 8912.
Fig. 2. B. retipes. No. 10515.
Fig. 3. B. auripes. No. 9805.
Fig. 4. B. affinis. No. 10196.
Fig. 5. B. affinis var. maculatus. No. 8826.
Fig. 6. B. edulis. No. 737.
Fig. 7. B. variipes. No. 10141.
Fig. 8. B. variipes. Menands, N. Y. (Peck Herb.).
Fig. 9. B. separans. No. 9826.
Fig. 10. B. eximius. No. 10192.
Fig. 11. B. piperatus. No. 8140.
Fig. 12. B. piperatus. Bethlehem, N. Y. (Peck Herb.).
Fig. 13. B. rubinellus. No. 9858.
Fig. 14. B. rubinellus. Friendship, N. Y., Aug. 1911 (Peck Herb.).
Fig. 15. B. parvus. No. 11967.
Fig. 16. B. vermiculosus. No. 8942.
Fig. 17. B. luridus. No. 9772.
Fig. 18. B. Frostii. No. 1114.

PLATE 62

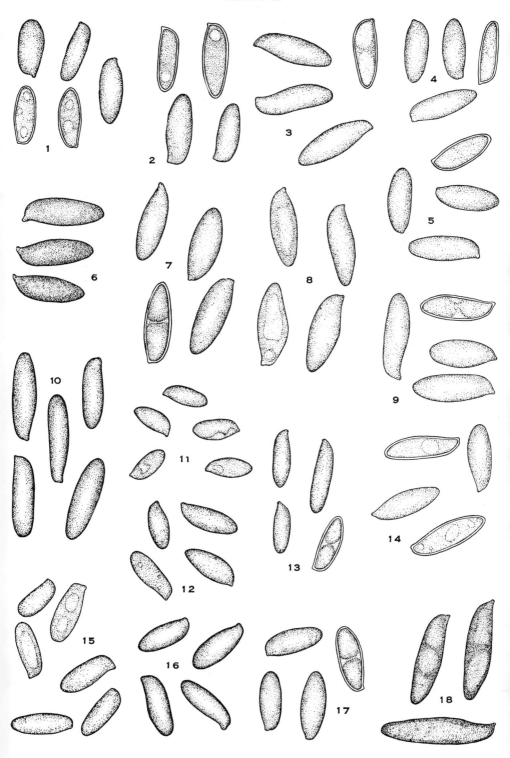

PLATE 63

(All figs. × 1620 except fig. 6 × 810)

Fig. 1. Boletus Morrisii. No. 10910.

Fig. 2. B. rubropunctus. No. 11093.

Fig. 3. B. Atkinsonianus. No. 10979.

Fig. 4. B. Atkinsonianus. Type.

Fig. 5. B. badius. No. 12394.

Figs. 6, 7. B. projectellus, cystidium and spores. No. 10299.

Fig. 8. B. auriporus. No. 9769.

Fig. 9. B. viridiflavus. No. 11960 (type).

Fig. 10. B. parasiticus. No. 11988.

Fig. 11. B. subglabripes. No. 4478.

Fig. 12. B. pallidus. No. 10237.

Fig. 13. B. Roxanae. No. 12076.

Fig. 14. B. Roxanae. Frost, No. 20. (Peck Herb.).

Fig. 15. B. subtomentosus. No. 12025.

Fig. 16. B. illudens. No. 12157.

Fig. 17. B. subfraternus. No. 12647.

PLATE 63

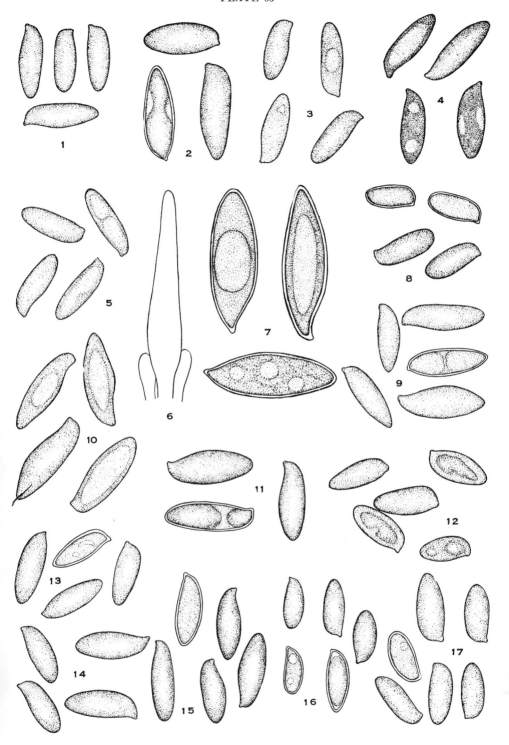

PLATE 64

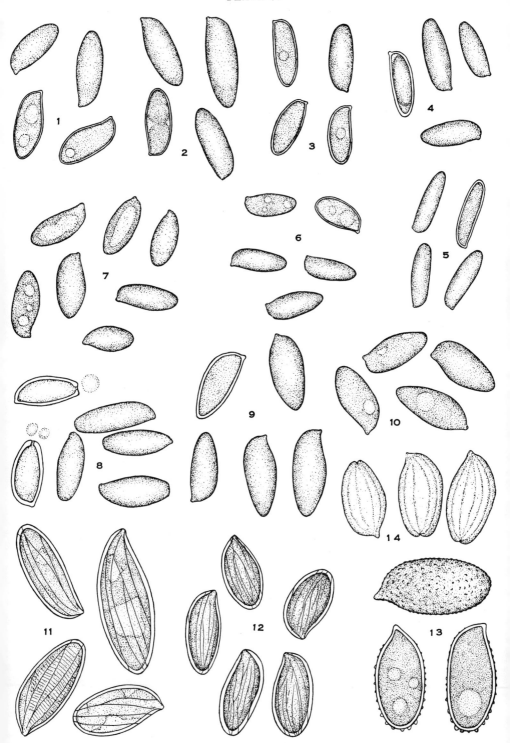

PLATE 65

(All figs. × 1620)

Fig. 1. Boletus Curtisii. No. 468.
Fig. 2. B. fistulosus. Type.
Fig. 3. B. inflexus. Trexlertown, Pa., Sept.; Wm. Herbst, coll. (Peck Herb).
Fig. 4. B. americanus. No. 10922.
Fig. 5. B. americanus var. reticulipes. No. 11746.
Fig. 6. B. subaureus. No. 9513.
Fig. 7. B. subaureus var. siccipes. No. 11906.
Fig. 8. B. hirtellus. Rensslaer Lake, N. Y. (Peck Herb.).
Fig. 9. B. hirtellus. No. 11599.
Fig. 10. B. granulatus. No. 10914.
Fig. 11. B. brevipes. No. 241.
Fig. 12. B. placidus. No. 8970.
Fig. 13. B. luteus. No. 240.
Fig. 14. B. punctipes. No. 12070.
Fig. 15. Boletinus castanellus. No. 84.
Fig. 16. Boletinus squarrosoides. No. 11782.
Fig. 17. Boletinus merulioides. No. 8314.
Fig. 18. Boletinus pictus. No. 5613.
Fig. 19. Strobilomyces strobilaceus. No. 834.

PLATE 65

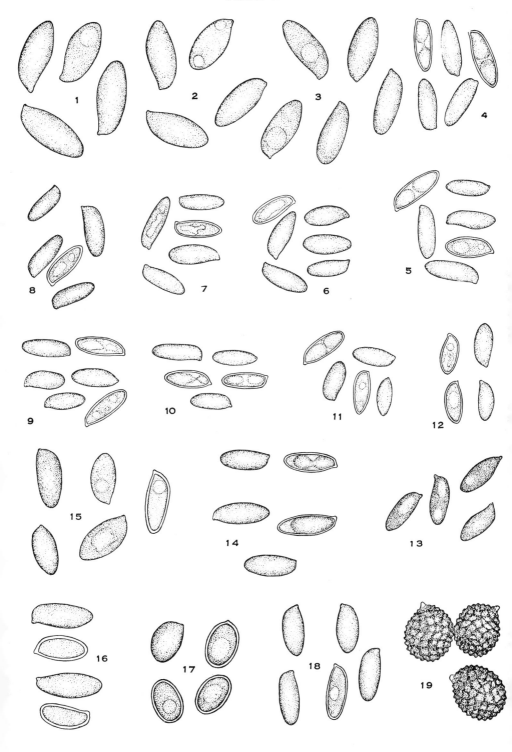

A CATALOGUE OF SELECTED DOVER BOOKS
IN ALL FIELDS OF INTEREST

A CATALOGUE OF SELECTED DOVER BOOKS
IN ALL FIELDS OF INTEREST

AMERICA'S OLD MASTERS, James T. Flexner. Four men emerged unexpectedly from provincial 18th century America to leadership in European art: Benjamin West, J. S. Copley, C. R. Peale, Gilbert Stuart. Brilliant coverage of lives and contributions. Revised, 1967 edition. 69 plates. 365pp. of text.
21806-6 Paperbound $3.00

FIRST FLOWERS OF OUR WILDERNESS: AMERICAN PAINTING, THE COLONIAL PERIOD, James T. Flexner. Painters, and regional painting traditions from earliest Colonial times up to the emergence of Copley, West and Peale Sr., Foster, Gustavus Hesselius, Feke, John Smibert and many anonymous painters in the primitive manner. Engaging presentation, with 162 illustrations. xxii + 368pp.
22180-6 Paperbound $3.50

THE LIGHT OF DISTANT SKIES: AMERICAN PAINTING, 1760-1835, James T. Flexner. The great generation of early American painters goes to Europe to learn and to teach: West, Copley, Gilbert Stuart and others. Allston, Trumbull, Morse; also contemporary American painters—primitives, derivatives, academics—who remained in America. 102 illustrations. xiii + 306pp.
22179-2 Paperbound $3.00

A HISTORY OF THE RISE AND PROGRESS OF THE ARTS OF DESIGN IN THE UNITED STATES, William Dunlap. Much the richest mine of information on early American painters, sculptors, architects, engravers, miniaturists, etc. The only source of information for scores of artists, the major primary source for many others. Unabridged reprint of rare original 1834 edition, with new introduction by James T. Flexner, and 394 new illustrations. Edited by Rita Weiss. 6⅝ x 9⅝.
21695-0, 21696-9, 21697-7 Three volumes, Paperbound $13.50

EPOCHS OF CHINESE AND JAPANESE ART, Ernest F. Fenollosa. From primitive Chinese art to the 20th century, thorough history, explanation of every important art period and form, including Japanese woodcuts; main stress on China and Japan, but Tibet, Korea also included. Still unexcelled for its detailed, rich coverage of cultural background, aesthetic elements, diffusion studies, particularly of the historical period. 2nd, 1913 edition. 242 illustrations. lii + 439pp. of text.
20364-6, 20365-4 Two volumes, Paperbound $6.00

THE GENTLE ART OF MAKING ENEMIES, James A. M. Whistler. Greatest wit of his day deflates Oscar Wilde, Ruskin, Swinburne; strikes back at inane critics, exhibitions, art journalism; aesthetics of impressionist revolution in most striking form. Highly readable classic by great painter. Reproduction of edition designed by Whistler. Introduction by Alfred Werner. xxxvi + 334pp.
21875-9 Paperbound $2.50

ADVENTURES OF AN AFRICAN SLAVER, Theodore Canot. Edited by Brantz Mayer. A detailed portrayal of slavery and the slave trade, 1820-1840. Canot, an established trader along the African coast, describes the slave economy of the African kingdoms, the treatment of captured negroes, the extensive journeys in the interior to gather slaves, slave revolts and their suppression, harems, bribes, and much more. Full and unabridged republication of 1854 edition. Introduction by Malcom Cowley. 16 illustrations. xvii + 448pp. 22456-2 Paperbound $3.50

MY BONDAGE AND MY FREEDOM, Frederick Douglass. Born and brought up in slavery, Douglass witnessed its horrors and experienced its cruelties, but went on to become one of the most outspoken forces in the American anti-slavery movement. Considered the best of his autobiographies, this book graphically describes the inhuman treatment of slaves, its effects on slave owners and slave families, and how Douglass's determination led him to a new life. Unaltered reprint of 1st (1855) edition. xxxii + 464pp. 22457-0 Paperbound $2.50

THE INDIANS' BOOK, recorded and edited by Natalie Curtis. Lore, music, narratives, dozens of drawings by Indians themselves from an authoritative and important survey of native culture among Plains, Southwestern, Lake and Pueblo Indians. Standard work in popular ethnomusicology. 149 songs in full notation. 23 drawings, 23 photos. xxxi + 584pp. 6⅝ x 9⅜. 21939-9 Paperbound $4.50

DICTIONARY OF AMERICAN PORTRAITS, edited by Hayward and Blanche Cirker. 4024 portraits of 4000 most important Americans, colonial days to 1905 (with a few important categories, like Presidents, to present). Pioneers, explorers, colonial figures, U. S. officials, politicians, writers, military and naval men, scientists, inventors, manufacturers, jurists, actors, historians, educators, notorious figures, Indian chiefs, etc. All authentic contemporary likenesses. The only work of its kind in existence; supplements all biographical sources for libraries. Indispensable to anyone working with American history. 8,000-item classified index, finding lists, other aids. xiv + 756pp. 9¼ x 12¾. 21823-6 Clothbound $30.00

TRITTON'S GUIDE TO BETTER WINE AND BEER MAKING FOR BEGINNERS, S. M. Tritton. All you need to know to make family-sized quantities of over 100 types of grape, fruit, herb and vegetable wines; as well as beers, mead, cider, etc. Complete recipes, advice as to equipment, procedures such as fermenting, bottling, and storing wines. Recipes given in British, U. S., and metric measures. Accompanying booklet lists sources in U. S. A. where ingredients may be bought, and additional information. 11 illustrations. 157pp. 5⅝ x 8⅛.
(USO) 22090-7 Clothbound $3.50

GARDENING WITH HERBS FOR FLAVOR AND FRAGRANCE, Helen M. Fox. How to grow herbs in your own garden, how to use them in your cooking (over 55 recipes included), legends and myths associated with each species, uses in medicine, perfumes, etc.—these are elements of one of the few books written especially for American herb fanciers. Guides you step-by-step from soil preparation to harvesting and storage for each type of herb. 12 drawings by Louise Mansfield. xiv + 334pp.
22540-2 Paperbound $2.50

AMERICAN FOOD AND GAME FISHES, David S. Jordan and Barton W. Evermann. Definitive source of information, detailed and accurate enough to enable the sportsman and nature lover to identify conclusively some 1,000 species and sub-species of North American fish, sought for food or sport. Coverage of range, physiology, habits, life history, food value. Best methods of capture, interest to the angler, advice on bait, fly-fishing, etc. 338 drawings and photographs. 1 + 574pp. 6⅝ x 9⅜.
22383-1 Paperbound $4.50

THE FROG BOOK, Mary C. Dickerson. Complete with extensive finding keys, over 300 photographs, and an introduction to the general biology of frogs and toads, this is the classic non-technical study of Northeastern and Central species. 58 species; 290 photographs and 16 color plates. xvii + 253pp.
21973-9 Paperbound $4.00

THE MOTH BOOK: A GUIDE TO THE MOTHS OF NORTH AMERICA, William J. Holland. Classical study, eagerly sought after and used for the past 60 years. Clear identification manual to more than 2,000 different moths, largest manual in existence. General information about moths, capturing, mounting, classifying, etc., followed by species by species descriptions. 263 illustrations plus 48 color plates show almost every species, full size. 1968 edition, preface, nomenclature changes by A. E. Brower. xxiv + 479pp. of text. 6½ x 9¼.
21948-8 Paperbound $5.00

THE SEA-BEACH AT EBB-TIDE, Augusta Foote Arnold. Interested amateur can identify hundreds of marine plants and animals on coasts of North America; marine algae; seaweeds; squids; hermit crabs; horse shoe crabs; shrimps; corals; sea anemones; etc. Species descriptions cover: structure; food; reproductive cycle; size; shape; color; habitat; etc. Over 600 drawings. 85 plates. xii + 490pp.
21949-6 Paperbound $3.50

COMMON BIRD SONGS, Donald J. Borror. 33⅓ 12-inch record presents songs of 60 important birds of the eastern United States. A thorough, serious record which provides several examples for each bird, showing different types of song, individual variations, etc. Inestimable identification aid for birdwatcher. 32-page booklet gives text about birds and songs, with illustration for each bird.
21829-5 Record, book, album. Monaural. $2.75

FADS AND FALLACIES IN THE NAME OF SCIENCE, Martin Gardner. Fair, witty appraisal of cranks and quacks of science: Atlantis, Lemuria, hollow earth, flat earth, Velikovsky, orgone energy, Dianetics, flying saucers, Bridey Murphy, food fads, medical fads, perpetual motion, etc. Formerly "In the Name of Science." x + 363pp.
20394-8 Paperbound $2.00

HOAXES, Curtis D. MacDougall. Exhaustive, unbelievably rich account of great hoaxes: Locke's moon hoax, Shakespearean forgeries, sea serpents, Loch Ness monster, Cardiff giant, John Wilkes Booth's mummy, Disumbrationist school of art, dozens more; also journalism, psychology of hoaxing. 54 illustrations. xi + 338pp.
20465-0 Paperbound $2.75

AGAINST THE GRAIN (A REBOURS), Joris K. Huysmans. Filled with weird images, evidences of a bizarre imagination, exotic experiments with hallucinatory drugs, rich tastes and smells and the diversions of its sybarite hero Duc Jean des Esseintes, this classic novel pushed 19th-century literary decadence to its limits. Full unabridged edition. Do not confuse this with abridged editions generally sold. Introduction by Havelock Ellis. xlix + 206pp. 22190-3 Paperbound $2.00

VARIORUM SHAKESPEARE: HAMLET. Edited by Horace H. Furness; a landmark of American scholarship. Exhaustive footnotes and appendices treat all doubtful words and phrases, as well as suggested critical emendations throughout the play's history. First volume contains editor's own text, collated with all Quartos and Folios. Second volume contains full first Quarto, translations of Shakespeare's sources (Belleforest, and Saxo Grammaticus), Der Bestrafte Brudermord, and many essays on critical and historical points of interest by major authorities of past and present. Includes details of staging and costuming over the years. By far the best edition available for serious students of Shakespeare. Total of xx + 905pp. 21004-9, 21005-7, 2 volumes, Paperbound $7.00

A LIFE OF WILLIAM SHAKESPEARE, Sir Sidney Lee. This is the standard life of Shakespeare, summarizing everything known about Shakespeare and his plays. Incredibly rich in material, broad in coverage, clear and judicious, it has served thousands as the best introduction to Shakespeare. 1931 edition. 9 plates. xxix + 792pp. (USO) 21967-4 Paperbound $3.75

MASTERS OF THE DRAMA, John Gassner. Most comprehensive history of the drama in print, covering every tradition from Greeks to modern Europe and America, including India, Far East, etc. Covers more than 800 dramatists, 2000 plays, with biographical material, plot summaries, theatre history, criticism, etc. "Best of its kind in English," New Republic. 77 illustrations. xxii + 890pp. 20100-7 Clothbound $8.50

THE EVOLUTION OF THE ENGLISH LANGUAGE, George McKnight. The growth of English, from the 14th century to the present. Unusual, non-technical account presents basic information in very interesting form: sound shifts, change in grammar and syntax, vocabulary growth, similar topics. Abundantly illustrated with quotations. Formerly Modern English in the Making. xii + 590pp. 21932-1 Paperbound $3.50

AN ETYMOLOGICAL DICTIONARY OF MODERN ENGLISH, Ernest Weekley. Fullest, richest work of its sort, by foremost British lexicographer. Detailed word histories, including many colloquial and archaic words; extensive quotations. Do not confuse this with the Concise Etymological Dictionary, which is much abridged. Total of xxvii + 830pp. 6½ x 9¼. 21873-2, 21874-0 Two volumes, Paperbound $6.00

FLATLAND: A ROMANCE OF MANY DIMENSIONS, E. A. Abbott. Classic of science-fiction explores ramifications of life in a two-dimensional world, and what happens when a three-dimensional being intrudes. Amusing reading, but also useful as introduction to thought about hyperspace. Introduction by Banesh Hoffmann. 16 illustrations. xx + 103pp. 20001-9 Paperbound $1.00

DESIGN BY ACCIDENT; A BOOK OF "ACCIDENTAL EFFECTS" FOR ARTISTS AND DESIGNERS, James F. O'Brien. Create your own unique, striking, imaginative effects by "controlled accident" interaction of materials: paints and lacquers, oil and water based paints, splatter, crackling materials, shatter, similar items. Everything you do will be different; first book on this limitless art, so useful to both fine artist and commercial artist. Full instructions. 192 plates showing "accidents," 8 in color. viii + 215pp. 8⅜ x 11¼.   21942-9 Paperbound $3.50

THE BOOK OF SIGNS, Rudolf Koch. Famed German type designer draws 493 beautiful symbols: religious, mystical, alchemical, imperial, property marks, runes, etc. Remarkable fusion of traditional and modern. Good for suggestions of timelessness, smartness, modernity. Text. vi + 104pp. 6⅛ x 9¼.
20162-7 Paperbound $1.25

HISTORY OF INDIAN AND INDONESIAN ART, Ananda K. Coomaraswamy. An unabridged republication of one of the finest books by a great scholar in Eastern art. Rich in descriptive material, history, social backgrounds; Sunga reliefs, Rajput paintings, Gupta temples, Burmese frescoes, textiles, jewelry, sculpture, etc. 400 photos. viii + 423pp. 6⅜ x 9¾.   21436-2 Paperbound $4.00

PRIMITIVE ART, Franz Boas. America's foremost anthropologist surveys textiles, ceramics, woodcarving, basketry, metalwork, etc.; patterns, technology, creation of symbols, style origins. All areas of world, but very full on Northwest Coast Indians. More than 350 illustrations of baskets, boxes, totem poles, weapons, etc. 378 pp.
20025-6 Paperbound $3.00

THE GENTLEMAN AND CABINET MAKER'S DIRECTOR, Thomas Chippendale. Full reprint (third edition, 1762) of most influential furniture book of all time, by master cabinetmaker. 200 plates, illustrating chairs, sofas, mirrors, tables, cabinets, plus 24 photographs of surviving pieces. Biographical introduction by N. Bienenstock. vi + 249pp. 9⅞ x 12¾.   21601-2 Paperbound $4.00

AMERICAN ANTIQUE FURNITURE, Edgar G. Miller, Jr. The basic coverage of all American furniture before 1840. Individual chapters cover type of furniture—clocks, tables, sideboards, etc.—chronologically, with inexhaustible wealth of data. More than 2100 photographs, all identified, commented on. Essential to all early American collectors. Introduction by H. E. Keyes. vi + 1106pp. 7⅞ x 10¾.
21599-7, 21600-4 Two volumes, Paperbound $11.00

PENNSYLVANIA DUTCH AMERICAN FOLK ART, Henry J. Kauffman. 279 photos, 28 drawings of tulipware, Fraktur script, painted tinware, toys, flowered furniture, quilts, samplers, hex signs, house interiors, etc. Full descriptive text. Excellent for tourist, rewarding for designer, collector. Map. 146pp. 7⅞ x 10¾.
21205-X Paperbound $2.50

EARLY NEW ENGLAND GRAVESTONE RUBBINGS, Edmund V. Gillon, Jr. 43 photographs, 226 carefully reproduced rubbings show heavily symbolic, sometimes macabre early gravestones, up to early 19th century. Remarkable early American primitive art, occasionally strikingly beautiful; always powerful. Text. xxvi + 207pp. 8⅜ x 11¼.   21380-3 Paperbound $3.50

HOW TO KNOW THE WILD FLOWERS, Mrs. William Starr Dana. This is the classical book of American wildflowers (of the Eastern and Central United States), used by hundreds of thousands. Covers over 500 species, arranged in extremely easy to use color and season groups. Full descriptions, much plant lore. This Dover edition is the fullest ever compiled, with tables of nomenclature changes. 174 full-page plates by M. Satterlee. xii + 418pp. 20332-8 Paperbound $2.75

OUR PLANT FRIENDS AND FOES, William Atherton DuPuy. History, economic importance, essential botanical information and peculiarities of 25 common forms of plant life are provided in this book in an entertaining and charming style. Covers food plants (potatoes, apples, beans, wheat, almonds, bananas, etc.), flowers (lily, tulip, etc.), trees (pine, oak, elm, etc.), weeds, poisonous mushrooms and vines, gourds, citrus fruits, cotton, the cactus family, and much more. 108 illustrations. xiv + 290pp. 22272-1 Paperbound $2.50

HOW TO KNOW THE FERNS, Frances T. Parsons. Classic survey of Eastern and Central ferns, arranged according to clear, simple identification key. Excellent introduction to greatly neglected nature area. 57 illustrations and 42 plates. xvi + 215pp. 20740-4 Paperbound $2.00

MANUAL OF THE TREES OF NORTH AMERICA, Charles S. Sargent. America's foremost dendrologist provides the definitive coverage of North American trees and tree-like shrubs. 717 species fully described and illustrated: exact distribution, down to township; full botanical description; economic importance; description of subspecies and races; habitat, growth data; similar material. Necessary to every serious student of tree-life. Nomenclature revised to present. Over 100 locating keys. 783 illustrations. lii + 934pp. 20277-1, 20278-X Two volumes, Paperbound $6.00

OUR NORTHERN SHRUBS, Harriet L. Keeler. Fine non-technical reference work identifying more than 225 important shrubs of Eastern and Central United States and Canada. Full text covering botanical description, habitat, plant lore, is paralleled with 205 full-page photographs of flowering or fruiting plants. Nomenclature revised by Edward G. Voss. One of few works concerned with shrubs. 205 plates, 35 drawings. xxviii + 521pp. 21989-5 Paperbound $3.75

THE MUSHROOM HANDBOOK, Louis C. C. Krieger. Still the best popular handbook: full descriptions of 259 species, cross references to another 200. Extremely thorough text enables you to identify, know all about any mushroom you are likely to meet in eastern and central U. S. A.: habitat, luminescence, poisonous qualities, use, folklore, etc. 32 color plates show over 50 mushrooms, also 126 other illustrations. Finding keys. vii + 560pp. 21861-9 Paperbound $3.95

HANDBOOK OF BIRDS OF EASTERN NORTH AMERICA, Frank M. Chapman. Still much the best single-volume guide to the birds of Eastern and Central United States. Very full coverage of 675 species, with descriptions, life habits, distribution, similar data. All descriptions keyed to two-page color chart. With this single volume the average birdwatcher needs no other books. 1931 revised edition. 195 illustrations. xxxvi + 581pp. 21489-3 Paperbound $4.50

INCIDENTS OF TRAVEL IN YUCATAN, John L. Stephens. Classic (1843) exploration of jungles of Yucatan, looking for evidences of Maya civilization. Stephens found many ruins; comments on travel adventures, Mexican and Indian culture. 127 striking illustrations by F. Catherwood. Total of 669 pp.
20926-1, 20927-X Two volumes, Paperbound $5.00

INCIDENTS OF TRAVEL IN CENTRAL AMERICA, CHIAPAS, AND YUCATAN, John L. Stephens. An exciting travel journal and an important classic of archeology. Narrative relates his almost single-handed discovery of the Mayan culture, and exploration of the ruined cities of Copan, Palenque, Utatlan and others; the monuments they dug from the earth, the temples buried in the jungle, the customs of poverty-stricken Indians living a stone's throw from the ruined palaces. 115 drawings by F. Catherwood. Portrait of Stephens. xii + 812pp.
22404-X, 22405-8 Two volumes, Paperbound $6.00

A NEW VOYAGE ROUND THE WORLD, William Dampier. Late 17-century naturalist joined the pirates of the Spanish Main to gather information; remarkably vivid account of buccaneers, pirates; detailed, accurate account of botany, zoology, ethnography of lands visited. Probably the most important early English voyage, enormous implications for British exploration, trade, colonial policy. Also most interesting reading. Argonaut edition, introduction by Sir Albert Gray. New introduction by Percy Adams. 6 plates, 7 illustrations. xlvii + 376pp. 6½ x 9¼.
21900-3 Paperbound $3.00

INTERNATIONAL AIRLINE PHRASE BOOK IN SIX LANGUAGES, Joseph W. Bátor. Important phrases and sentences in English paralleled with French, German, Portuguese, Italian, Spanish equivalents, covering all possible airport-travel situations; created for airline personnel as well as tourist by Language Chief, Pan American Airlines. xiv + 204pp.
22017-6 Paperbound $2.00

STAGE COACH AND TAVERN DAYS, Alice Morse Earle. Detailed, lively account of the early days of taverns; their uses and importance in the social, political and military life; furnishings and decorations; locations; food and drink; tavern signs, etc. Second half covers every aspect of early travel; the roads, coaches, drivers, etc. Nostalgic, charming, packed with fascinating material. 157 illustrations, mostly photographs. xiv + 449pp.
22518-6 Paperbound $4.00

NORSE DISCOVERIES AND EXPLORATIONS IN NORTH AMERICA, Hjalmar R. Holand. The perplexing Kensington Stone, found in Minnesota at the end of the 19th century. Is it a record of a Scandinavian expedition to North America in the 14th century? Or is it one of the most successful hoaxes in history. A scientific detective investigation. Formerly *Westward from Vinland*. 31 photographs, 17 figures. x + 354pp.
22014-1 Paperbound $2.75

A BOOK OF OLD MAPS, compiled and edited by Emerson D. Fite and Archibald Freeman. 74 old maps offer an unusual survey of the discovery, settlement and growth of America down to the close of the Revolutionary war: maps showing Norse settlements in Greenland, the explorations of Columbus, Verrazano, Cabot, Champlain, Joliet, Drake, Hudson, etc., campaigns of Revolutionary war battles, and much more. Each map is accompanied by a brief historical essay. xvi + 299pp. 11 x 13¾.
22084-2 Paperbound $6.00

JIM WHITEWOLF: THE LIFE OF A KIOWA APACHE INDIAN, Charles S. Brant, editor. Spans transition between native life and acculturation period, 1880 on. Kiowa culture, personal life pattern, religion and the supernatural, the Ghost Dance, breakdown in the White Man's world, similar material. 1 map. xii + 144pp.
22015-X Paperbound $1.75

THE NATIVE TRIBES OF CENTRAL AUSTRALIA, Baldwin Spencer and F. J. Gillen. Basic book in anthropology, devoted to full coverage of the Arunta and Warramunga tribes; the source for knowledge about kinship systems, material and social culture, religion, etc. Still unsurpassed. 121 photographs, 89 drawings. xviii + 669pp.
21775-2 Paperbound $5.00

MALAY MAGIC, Walter W. Skeat. Classic (1900); still the definitive work on the folklore and popular religion of the Malay peninsula. Describes marriage rites, birth spirits and ceremonies, medicine, dances, games, war and weapons, etc. Extensive quotes from original sources, many magic charms translated into English. 35 illustrations. Preface by Charles Otto Blagden. xxiv + 685pp.
21760-4 Paperbound $4.00

HEAVENS ON EARTH: UTOPIAN COMMUNITIES IN AMERICA, 1680-1880, Mark Holloway. The finest nontechnical account of American utopias, from the early Woman in the Wilderness, Ephrata, Rappites to the enormous mid 19th-century efflorescence; Shakers, New Harmony, Equity Stores, Fourier's Phalanxes, Oneida, Amana, Fruitlands, etc. "Entertaining and very instructive." Times Literary Supplement. 15 illustrations. 246pp.
21593-8 Paperbound $2.00

LONDON LABOUR AND THE LONDON POOR, Henry Mayhew. Earliest (c. 1850) sociological study in English, describing myriad subcultures of London poor. Particularly remarkable for the thousands of pages of direct testimony taken from the lips of London prostitutes, thieves, beggars, street sellers, chimney-sweepers, street-musicians, "mudlarks," "pure-finders," rag-gatherers, "running-patterers," dock laborers, cab-men, and hundreds of others, quoted directly in this massive work. An extraordinarily vital picture of London emerges. 110 illustrations. Total of lxxvi + 1951pp. 6⅝ x 10.
21934-8, 21935-6, 21936-4, 21937-2 Four volumes, Paperbound $14.00

HISTORY OF THE LATER ROMAN EMPIRE, J. B. Bury. Eloquent, detailed reconstruction of Western and Byzantine Roman Empire by a major historian, from the death of Theodosius I (395 A.D.) to the death of Justinian (565). Extensive quotations from contemporary sources; full coverage of important Roman and foreign figures of the time. xxxiv + 965pp. 21829-5 Record, book, album. Monaural. $3.50

AN INTELLECTUAL AND CULTURAL HISTORY OF THE WESTERN WORLD, Harry Elmer Barnes. Monumental study, tracing the development of the accomplishments that make up human culture. Every aspect of man's achievement surveyed from its origins in the Paleolithic to the present day (1964); social structures, ideas, economic systems, art, literature, technology, mathematics, the sciences, medicine, religion, jurisprudence, etc. Evaluations of the contributions of scores of great men. 1964 edition, revised and edited by scholars in the many fields represented. Total of xxix + 1381pp. 21275-0, 21276-9, 21277-7 Three volumes, Paperbound $7.75

LAST AND FIRST MEN AND STAR MAKER, TWO SCIENCE FICTION NOVELS, Olaf Stapledon. Greatest future histories in science fiction. In the first, human intelligence is the "hero," through strange paths of evolution, interplanetary invasions, incredible technologies, near extinctions and reemergences. Star Maker describes the quest of a band of star rovers for intelligence itself, through time and space: weird inhuman civilizations, crustacean minds, symbiotic worlds, etc. Complete, unabridged. v + 438pp. 21962-3 Paperbound $2.50

THREE PROPHETIC NOVELS, H. G. WELLS. Stages of a consistently planned future for mankind. When the Sleeper Wakes, and A Story of the Days to Come, anticipate Brave New World and 1984, in the 21st Century; The Time Machine, only complete version in print, shows farther future and the end of mankind. All show Wells's greatest gifts as storyteller and novelist. Edited by E. F. Bleiler. x + 335pp. (USO) 20605-X Paperbound $2.50

THE DEVIL'S DICTIONARY, Ambrose Bierce. America's own Oscar Wilde—Ambrose Bierce—offers his barbed iconoclastic wisdom in over 1,000 definitions hailed by H. L. Mencken as "some of the most gorgeous witticisms in the English language." 145pp. 20487-1 Paperbound $1.25

MAX AND MORITZ, Wilhelm Busch. Great children's classic, father of comic strip, of two bad boys, Max and Moritz. Also Ker and Plunk (Plisch und Plumm), Cat and Mouse, Deceitful Henry, Ice-Peter, The Boy and the Pipe, and five other pieces. Original German, with English translation. Edited by H. Arthur Klein; translations by various hands and H. Arthur Klein. vi + 216pp.
20181-3 Paperbound $2.00

PIGS IS PIGS AND OTHER FAVORITES, Ellis Parker Butler. The title story is one of the best humor short stories, as Mike Flannery obfuscates biology and English. Also included, That Pup of Murchison's, The Great American Pie Company, and Perkins of Portland. 14 illustrations. v + 109pp. 21532-6 Paperbound $1.25

THE PETERKIN PAPERS, Lucretia P. Hale. It takes genius to be as stupidly mad as the Peterkins, as they decide to become wise, celebrate the "Fourth," keep a cow, and otherwise strain the resources of the Lady from Philadelphia. Basic book of American humor. 153 illustrations. 219pp. 20794-3 Paperbound $1.50

PERRAULT'S FAIRY TALES, translated by A. E. Johnson and S. R. Littlewood, with 34 full-page illustrations by Gustave Doré. All the original Perrault stories—Cinderella, Sleeping Beauty, Bluebeard, Little Red Riding Hood, Puss in Boots, Tom Thumb, etc.—with their witty verse morals and the magnificent illustrations of Doré. One of the five or six great books of European fairy tales. viii + 117pp. 8⅛ x 11. 22311-6 Paperbound $2.00

OLD HUNGARIAN FAIRY TALES, Baroness Orczy. Favorites translated and adapted by author of the Scarlet Pimpernel. Eight fairy tales include "The Suitors of Princess Fire-Fly," "The Twin Hunchbacks," "Mr. Cuttlefish's Love Story," and "The Enchanted Cat." This little volume of magic and adventure will captivate children as it has for generations. 90 drawings by Montagu Barstow. 96pp.
(USO) 22293-4 Paperbound $1.95

CATALOGUE OF DOVER BOOKS

MATHEMATICAL PUZZLES FOR BEGINNERS AND ENTHUSIASTS, Geoffrey Mott-Smith. 189 puzzles from easy to difficult—involving arithmetic, logic, algebra, properties of digits, probability, etc.—for enjoyment and mental stimulus. Explanation of mathematical principles behind the puzzles. 135 illustrations. viii + 248pp.
20198-8 Paperbound $1.75

PAPER FOLDING FOR BEGINNERS, William D. Murray and Francis J. Rigney. Easiest book on the market, clearest instructions on making interesting, beautiful origami. Sail boats, cups, roosters, frogs that move legs, bonbon boxes, standing birds, etc. 40 projects; more than 275 diagrams and photographs. 94pp.
20713-7 Paperbound $1.00

TRICKS AND GAMES ON THE POOL TABLE, Fred Herrmann. 79 tricks and games—some solitaires, some for two or more players, some competitive games—to entertain you between formal games. Mystifying shots and throws, unusual caroms, tricks involving such props as cork, coins, a hat, etc. Formerly *Fun on the Pool Table*. 77 figures. 95pp.
21814-7 Paperbound $1.00

HAND SHADOWS TO BE THROWN UPON THE WALL: A SERIES OF NOVEL AND AMUSING FIGURES FORMED BY THE HAND, Henry Bursill. Delightful picturebook from great-grandfather's day shows how to make 18 different hand shadows: a bird that flies, duck that quacks, dog that wags his tail, camel, goose, deer, boy, turtle, etc. Only book of its sort. vi + 33pp. 6½ x 9¼. 21779-5 Paperbound $1.00

WHITTLING AND WOODCARVING, E. J. Tangerman. 18th printing of best book on market. "If you can cut a potato you can carve" toys and puzzles, chains, chessmen, caricatures, masks, frames, woodcut blocks, surface patterns, much more. Information on tools, woods, techniques. Also goes into serious wood sculpture from Middle Ages to present, East and West. 464 photos, figures. x + 293pp.
20965-2 Paperbound $2.00

HISTORY OF PHILOSOPHY, Julián Marias. Possibly the clearest, most easily followed, best planned, most useful one-volume history of philosophy on the market; neither skimpy nor overfull. Full details on system of every major philosopher and dozens of less important thinkers from pre-Socratics up to Existentialism and later. Strong on many European figures usually omitted. Has gone through dozens of editions in Europe. 1966 edition, translated by Stanley Appelbaum and Clarence Strowbridge. xviii + 505pp. 21739-6 Paperbound $3.00

YOGA: A SCIENTIFIC EVALUATION, Kovoor T. Behanan. Scientific but non-technical study of physiological results of yoga exercises; done under auspices of Yale U. Relations to Indian thought, to psychoanalysis, etc. 16 photos. xxiii + 270pp.
20505-3 Paperbound $2.50

Prices subject to change without notice.
Available at your book dealer or write for free catalogue to Dept. GI, Dover Publications, Inc., 180 Varick St., N. Y., N. Y. 10014. Dover publishes more than 150 books each year on science, elementary and advanced mathematics, biology, music, art, literary history, social sciences and other areas.

THE ELEMENTS OF NON-EUCLIDEAN GEOMETRY, Duncan M. Y. Sommerville. Presentation of the development of non-Euclidean geometry in logical order, from a fundamental analysis of the concept of parallelism to such advanced topics as inversion, transformations, pseudosphere, geodesic representation, relation between parataxy and parallelism, etc. Knowledge of only high-school algebra and geometry is presupposed. 126 problems, 129 figures. xvi + 274pp.
60460-8 Paperbound $2.50

NON-EUCLIDEAN GEOMETRY: A CRITICAL AND HISTORICAL STUDY OF ITS DEVELOPMENT, Roberto Bonola. Standard survey, clear, penetrating, discussing many systems not usually represented in general studies. Easily followed by non-specialist. Translated by H. Carslaw. Bound in are two most important texts: Bolyai's "The Science of Absolute Space" and Lobachevski's "The Theory of Parallels," translated by G. B. Halsted. Introduction by F. Enriques. 181 diagrams. Total of 431pp.
60027-0 Paperbound $3.00

ELEMENTS OF NUMBER THEORY, Ivan M. Vinogradov. By stressing demonstrations and problems, this modern text can be understood by students without advanced math backgrounds. "A very welcome addition," *Bulletin, American Mathematical Society.* Translated by Saul Kravetz. Over 200 fully-worked problems. 100 numerical exercises. viii + 227pp.
60259-1 Paperbound $2.50

THEORY OF SETS, E. Kamke. Lucid introduction to theory of sets, surveying discoveries of Cantor, Russell, Weierstrass, Zermelo, Bernstein, Dedekind, etc. Knowledge of college algebra is sufficient background. "Exceptionally well written," *School Science and Mathematics.* Translated by Frederick Bagemihl. vii + 144pp.
60141-2 Paperbound $1.75

A TREATISE ON THE DIFFERENTIAL GEOMETRY OF CURVES AND SURFACES, Luther P. Eisenhart. Detailed, concrete introductory treatise on differential geometry, developed from author's graduate courses at Princeton University. Thorough explanation of the geometry of curves and surfaces, concentrating on problems most helpful to students. 683 problems, 30 diagrams. xiv + 474pp.
60667-8 Paperbound $3.50

AN ESSAY ON THE FOUNDATIONS OF GEOMETRY, Bertrand Russell. A mathematical and physical analysis of the place of the a priori in geometric knowledge. Includes critical review of 19th-century work in non-Euclidean geometry as well as illuminating insights of one of the great minds of our time. New foreword by Morris Kline. xx + 201pp.
60233-8 Paperbound $2.50

INTRODUCTION TO THE THEORY OF NUMBERS, Leonard E. Dickson. Thorough, comprehensive approach with adequate coverage of classical literature, yet simple enough for beginners. Divisibility, congruences, quadratic residues, binary quadratic forms, primes, least residues, Fermat's theorem, Gauss's lemma, and other important topics. 249 problems, 1 figure. viii + 183pp.
60342-3 Paperbound $2.00

THE PHILOSOPHY OF THE UPANISHADS, Paul Deussen. Clear, detailed statement of upanishadic system of thought, generally considered among best available. History of these works, full exposition of system emergent from them, parallel concepts in the West. Translated by A. S. Geden. xiv + 429pp.
21616-0 Paperbound $3.00

LANGUAGE, TRUTH AND LOGIC, Alfred J. Ayer. Famous, remarkably clear introduction to the Vienna and Cambridge schools of Logical Positivism; function of philosophy, elimination of metaphysical thought, nature of analysis, similar topics. "Wish I had written it myself," Bertrand Russell. 2nd, 1946 edition. 160pp.
20010-8 Paperbound $1.35

THE GUIDE FOR THE PERPLEXED, Moses Maimonides. Great classic of medieval Judaism, major attempt to reconcile revealed religion (Pentateuch, commentaries) and Aristotelian philosophy. Enormously important in all Western thought. Unabridged Friedländer translation. 50-page introduction. lix + 414pp.
(USO) 20351-4 Paperbound $2.50

OCCULT AND SUPERNATURAL PHENOMENA, D. H. Rawcliffe. Full, serious study of the most persistent delusions of mankind: crystal gazing, mediumistic trance, stigmata, lycanthropy, fire walking, dowsing, telepathy, ghosts, ESP, etc., and their relation to common forms of abnormal psychology. Formerly *Illusions and Delusions of the Supernatural and the Occult.* iii + 551pp. 20503-7 Paperbound $3.50

THE EGYPTIAN BOOK OF THE DEAD: THE PAPYRUS OF ANI, E. A. Wallis Budge. Full hieroglyphic text, interlinear transliteration of sounds, word for word translation, then smooth, connected translation; Theban recension. Basic work in Ancient Egyptian civilization; now even more significant than ever for historical importance, dilation of consciousness, etc. clvi + 377pp. 6½ x 9¼.
21866-X Paperbound $3.95

PSYCHOLOGY OF MUSIC, Carl E. Seashore. Basic, thorough survey of everything known about psychology of music up to 1940's; essential reading for psychologists, musicologists. Physical acoustics; auditory apparatus; relationship of physical sound to perceived sound; role of the mind in sorting, altering, suppressing, creating sound sensations; musical learning, testing for ability, absolute pitch, other topics. Records of Caruso, Menuhin analyzed. 88 figures. xix + 408pp.
21851-1 Paperbound $2.75

THE I CHING (THE BOOK OF CHANGES), translated by James Legge. Complete translated text plus appendices by Confucius, of perhaps the most penetrating divination book ever compiled. Indispensable to all study of early Oriental civilizations. 3 plates. xxiii + 448pp. 21062-6 Paperbound $3.00

THE UPANISHADS, translated by Max Müller. Twelve classical upanishads: Chandogya, Kena, Aitareya, Kaushitaki, Isa, Katha, Mundaka, Taittiriyaka, Brhadaranyaka, Svetasvatara, Prasna, Maitriyana. 160-page introduction, analysis by Prof. Müller. Total of 826pp. 20398-0, 20399-9 Two volumes, Paperbound $5.00

CATALOGUE OF DOVER BOOKS

THE PRINCIPLES OF PSYCHOLOGY, William James. The famous long course, complete and unabridged. Stream of thought, time perception, memory, experimental methods—these are only some of the concerns of a work that was years ahead of its time and still valid, interesting, useful. 94 figures. Total of xviii + 1391pp.
20381-6, 20382-4 Two volumes, Paperbound $8.00

THE STRANGE STORY OF THE QUANTUM, Banesh Hoffmann. Non-mathematical but thorough explanation of work of Planck, Einstein, Bohr, Pauli, de Broglie, Schrödinger, Heisenberg, Dirac, Feynman, etc. No technical background needed. "Of books attempting such an account, this is the best," Henry Margenau, Yale. 40-page "Postscript 1959." xii + 285pp.
20518-5 Paperbound $2.00

THE RISE OF THE NEW PHYSICS, A. d'Abro. Most thorough explanation in print of central core of mathematical physics, both classical and modern; from Newton to Dirac and Heisenberg. Both history and exposition; philosophy of science, causality, explanations of higher mathematics, analytical mechanics, electromagnetism, thermodynamics, phase rule, special and general relativity, matrices. No higher mathematics needed to follow exposition, though treatment is elementary to intermediate in level. Recommended to serious student who wishes verbal understanding. 97 illustrations. xvii + 982pp.
20003-5, 20004-3 Two volumes, Paperbound $6.00

GREAT IDEAS OF OPERATIONS RESEARCH, Jagjit Singh. Easily followed non-technical explanation of mathematical tools, aims, results: statistics, linear programming, game theory, queueing theory, Monte Carlo simulation, etc. Uses only elementary mathematics. Many case studies, several analyzed in detail. Clarity, breadth make this excellent for specialist in another field who wishes background. 41 figures. x + 228pp.
21886-4 Paperbound $2.50

GREAT IDEAS OF MODERN MATHEMATICS: THEIR NATURE AND USE, Jagjit Singh. Internationally famous expositor, winner of Unesco's Kalinga Award for science popularization explains verbally such topics as differential equations, matrices, groups, sets, transformations, mathematical logic and other important modern mathematics, as well as use in physics, astrophysics, and similar fields. Superb exposition for layman, scientist in other areas. viii + 312pp.
20587-8 Paperbound $2.50

GREAT IDEAS IN INFORMATION THEORY, LANGUAGE AND CYBERNETICS, Jagjit Singh. The analog and digital computers, how they work, how they are like and unlike the human brain, the men who developed them, their future applications, computer terminology. An essential book for today, even for readers with little math. Some mathematical demonstrations included for more advanced readers. 118 figures. Tables. ix + 338pp.
21694-2 Paperbound $2.50

CHANCE, LUCK AND STATISTICS, Horace C. Levinson. Non-mathematical presentation of fundamentals of probability theory and science of statistics and their applications. Games of chance, betting odds, misuse of statistics, normal and skew distributions, birth rates, stock speculation, insurance. Enlarged edition. Formerly "The Science of Chance." xiii + 357pp.
21007-3 Paperbound $2.50

THE RED FAIRY BOOK, Andrew Lang. Lang's color fairy books have long been children's favorites. This volume includes Rapunzel, Jack and the Bean-stalk and 35 other stories, familiar and unfamiliar. 4 plates, 93 illustrations x + 367pp.
21673-X Paperbound $2.50

THE BLUE FAIRY BOOK, Andrew Lang. Lang's tales come from all countries and all times. Here are 37 tales from Grimm, the Arabian Nights, Greek Mythology, and other fascinating sources. 8 plates, 130 illustrations. xi + 390pp.
21437-0 Paperbound $2.50

HOUSEHOLD STORIES BY THE BROTHERS GRIMM. Classic English-language edition of the well-known tales — Rumpelstiltskin, Snow White, Hansel and Gretel, The Twelve Brothers, Faithful John, Rapunzel, Tom Thumb (52 stories in all). Translated into simple, straightforward English by Lucy Crane. Ornamented with head-pieces, vignettes, elaborate decorative initials and a dozen full-page illustrations by Walter Crane. x + 269pp.
21080-4 Paperbound $2.50

THE MERRY ADVENTURES OF ROBIN HOOD, Howard Pyle. The finest modern versions of the traditional ballads and tales about the great English outlaw. Howard Pyle's complete prose version, with every word, every illustration of the first edition. Do not confuse this facsimile of the original (1883) with modern editions that change text or illustrations. 23 plates plus many page decorations. xxii + 296pp.
22043-5 Paperbound $2.50

THE STORY OF KING ARTHUR AND HIS KNIGHTS, Howard Pyle. The finest children's version of the life of King Arthur; brilliantly retold by Pyle, with 48 of his most imaginative illustrations. xviii + 313pp. 6⅛ x 9¼.
21445-1 Paperbound $2.50

THE WONDERFUL WIZARD OF OZ, L. Frank Baum. America's finest children's book in facsimile of first edition with all Denslow illustrations in full color. The edition a child should have. Introduction by Martin Gardner. 23 color plates, scores of drawings. iv + 267pp.
20691-2 Paperbound $2.50

THE MARVELOUS LAND OF OZ, L. Frank Baum. The second Oz book, every bit as imaginative as the Wizard. The hero is a boy named Tip, but the Scarecrow and the Tin Woodman are back, as is the Oz magic. 16 color plates, 120 drawings by John R. Neill. 287pp.
20692-0 Paperbound $2.50

THE MAGICAL MONARCH OF MO, L. Frank Baum. Remarkable adventures in a land even stranger than Oz. The best of Baum's books not in the Oz series. 15 color plates and dozens of drawings by Frank Verbeck. xviii + 237pp.
21892-9 Paperbound $2.25

THE BAD CHILD'S BOOK OF BEASTS, MORE BEASTS FOR WORSE CHILDREN, A MORAL ALPHABET, Hilaire Belloc. Three complete humor classics in one volume. Be kind to the frog, and do not call him names . . . and 28 other whimsical animals. Familiar favorites and some not so well known. Illustrated by Basil Blackwell. 156pp.
(USO) 20749-8 Paperbound $1.50